13.00

THE DEMON
AND THE DOVE

personality growth
through literature

Books by Adrian van Kaam

A Light to the Gentiles
Religion and Personality
Personality Fulfillment in the Spiritual Life
Existential Foundations of Psychology
The Art of Existential Counseling
The Demon and The Dove
(Co-author Kathleen Healy)

THE DEMON AND THE DOVE

Personality Growth Through Literature

Adrian van Kaam
Kathleen Healy

UNIVERSITY
PRESS OF
AMERICA

Copyright © 1967 by Duquesne University Press

Copyright © 1983 by

University Press of America, Inc.™

P.O. Box 19101, Washington, DC 20036

ISBN (Perfect): 0-8191-2897-X

Reprinted by arrangement with The Institute of Formative Spirituality

UNIVERSITY
PRESS OF
AMERICA

CONTENTS

FOREWORD

PSYCHOLOGY and literature enlighten and complement each other. Both reveal the depths of human experience. It is not by accident that the great modern fiction writers—Dostoyevsky, Tolstoy, Camus, Faulkner—have been, wittingly or unwittingly, existential psychologists. Their novels are, in a sense, textbooks of human psychology. It is one of the tasks of the psychologist and the literary critic to build a bridge between the science of human behavior and the artistic expression of human experience in poetry, fiction, and drama.

The present work is a modest attempt to span these two countries of self-understanding. The first six chapters of the study are written from the point of view of a psychologist in dialogue with the criticism of literature which follows. The five critical analyses, in turn, are composed in dialogue with the earlier chapters on human psychology. It is our hope that some integration of existential psychology and literature is achieved in these essays. More importantly, we hope that the potentialities for self-understanding through existential psychological analysis of literature are clearly demonstrated.

Adrian van Kaam
Kathleen Healy

PART ONE

PERSONALITY IN TRANSFORMATION

LITERATURE AND PSYCHOLOGY

BOTH literature and psychology reveal the meaning of human existence. Both begin with human experience. While literature describes this experience in an immediate and moving way, psychology expresses its underlying structures conceptually. When we speak about our experience of human life, we refer to our awareness of a wide variety of human feelings, attitudes, intentions, and defenses which we perceive in ourselves and others. However, our experience of man also implies a deeper kind of understanding which flows from our grasp of the unity of personality. The diverse phenomena of human existence make sense to us only when we discover their coherence within the dynamic totality of a plan of life characteristic of a personality. Once we understand this unconscious underlying project of existence, all appearances of behavior begin to have meaning for us.

The great novelist or playwright is a master in the gradual unveiling of this structure of human

personality. He possesses a powerful ability to confront the reader with the unique plan of existence
lived by a character in his novel or drama. He may
reveal how this character himself chooses to be what
he is and how this fundamental choice determines the
tragic or happy life he lives. The author may lead his
reader through a variety of critical situations to which
the protagonist responds by self-orientation of his
life. The fascination of the novel or play may not be
in these situations in themselves, however, but in
their revelation of the life of the character. Sitting
quietly in his chair at home or concealed in the darkness of the theater, man as audience can live many
lives motivated in diverse ways. He participates in
the unfolding of these lives, and he does so not from
the outside as a neutral observer, but as one invited
to enter the very core of a human existence, so that he
understands a personality from its most intimate
roots. Instead of being merely told about a life, he is
drawn into a life.

Something similar happens to the psychologist
who engages in counseling and psychotherapy. The
good therapist is not interested primarily in the
variety of daily incidents described to him by his
client. What concerns the therapist is the manner in
which his patient relates to these events, lives them,
and expresses himself in response to them. The therapist thus attempts to read the unique personality of
his client, to understand the unique structure of motivations that directs this life for which he cares. Therapists and novelists are both fascinated by the story of
motivation that underlies the succession of incidents
and situations in a human life. Both are successful in

their art to the degree that they are able to grasp the underlying motivational unity of personality. The psychologist must communicate his understanding to his client. But a further demand is made on the creative writer: he must be able to share his unique understanding with innumerable readers.

A play or novel is usually a success only when the audience cannot escape the impression of an inevitable unity in the characters portrayed. Psychologically, this quality of inevitability can be explained by the fact that the creator of a fictitious character can contemplate and communicate its unfolding from the point of view of its completion. The author can show, for example, how a certain fundamental choice of his character leads to other possible choices, and how any one of these new decisions necessarily initiates a certain development which again opens up further ranges of possible choices. What is inevitable and determined is the limited horizon of possibilities revealed by every new path which the character himself has chosen. Within the range of decisions, however, there is always a freedom to choose one or another possibility. But no matter which of these possibilities is selected, it can be shown *in retrospect* that there is some kind of continuation between this choice and the former one insofar as the limited range of available choices was conditioned by the former option. This situation, understood in its totality by the creator of a given drama or play, helps to create the impression of inevitability or even fatality so striking in the lives of great fictional characters. On the other hand, the good novelist or dramatist also gives reality to the immediate crisis with which the hero is confronted when he faces the necessity of decision within the limits of his situation.

For example, once Shakespeare's Macbeth has made the fatal decision to murder Duncan, he initiates a chain of events which presents him with a series of new choices arising from the murder. These new possibilities for decision are situated in a more limited range of freedom than his original choice: it is inevitable that he either reveal his first crime and accept its punishment or commit further crime. Yet he is still able to choose. After he has decided to murder Banquo, Macbeth again restricts his range of freedom: he must inevitably pay the price for his previous murders or sink even more deeply into new crime. Each new offense thus circumscribes his horizon of freedom. Yet he maintains freedom of decision within the limitations he himself has created until the final tragic choice which precipitates his inevitable death. Macbeth's total situation, because it is comprehended completely at every point of its development by Shakespeare, creates a psychological tone of fatality at the very core of the tragedy.

The psychologist or psychotherapist in real life cannot, like the creative writer, contemplate the life of his client from the point of view of completion. Like the author absorbed in his character, the therapist may observe his client in the crisis of decision, a decision which will significantly determine his future life. But he cannot determine his client's future. The novelist, however, is the creator of a fictional life. He knows what this life will be according to his own inspiration. Consequently, he knows in advance what path his protagonist will choose in the situation he creates. The psychotherapist, on the other hand, confronts an actual person on the boundary line of a crucial decision. But he is not the creator of person-ality. On the contrary, he fosters the self-creation of the other. He may help his client to clarify the limited range of existential choices open to him, but he may never make the decision for him as the creator of the fictional character does. Nor can he predict this decision infallibly.

Yet the writer as well as the psychotherapist serves the self-creation of man. The therapist does so by reflecting the choices that are available to his client and by making him aware of the dark inner forces which inhibit him from experiencing his authentic possibilities. The novelist or dramatist performs a similar service to mankind, but in a different way. He makes man aware of the decisions he may be faced with in the course of his existence by confronting him with dynamic narrations of existential choice situations in fictional lives. More than this, the writer dramatizes the lived consequences of the decisions made by his protagonist. Plays and novels confront us again and again with the concrete impact of a fundamental self-choice upon the character's own life and the lives of others. In Shakespeare's *Antony and Cleopatra*, for example, Antony's decision to follow Cleopatra at the battle of Actium has reverberations in the lives of the citizens of the entire Roman world. On a much smaller scale, Quentin's decision to reject Maggie in Arthur Miller's *After the Fall* seems to change only his own life and hers. But in each play, the consequences of the decision affect human lives radically.

Because literature reveals so much of the underground currents of the human adventure, many counselors and therapists are not satisfied with studying books on psychology, but immerse themselves in creative literature as well. Psychotherapists are the experts of the crisis of existential decision. Novelists and dramatists are the experts in the description of this crisis, of its resolution, and of the lived consequences of the solution or non-solution chosen. Modern man is well aware that Shakespeare and Eugene O'Neill, Dostoyevsky and Camus, are literary geniuses of the first magnitude. But man is only beginning to be aware that their novels and dramas are, in a sense, "textbooks" of human psychology. Creative genius has an infinitude of truth to teach us concerning existential crisis and choice and the art of healing the human psyche.

Thus there seems to exist something like a common ground of experience where psychology and literature meet, a ground in which both are rooted. To be sure, not all psychology and literature relate to this fertile soil of human experience. Certain types of novels, plays, and poems and certain psychological studies seem to be nearer than others to this source of creation in depth. Nearest to this deepest experience of human life is the literature which has been acclaimed as great by the sensitive literary minds of generation after generation. Why is it that certain books which enthrall one age are forgotten by later ages? Why are other books rediscovered as treasures of the past that may still enlighten us about human life even though we live in a culture quite different from that in which the creative work originated? Why is it that certain stories and dramas of foreign and long past cultures may touch us profoundly with a truth of human existence in spite of the barriers of time and space, the unfamiliar situations, and the strangeness of language? Why do certain classics capture the heart of man perennially? From a psychological point of view, the great masterpieces of literature may be said to penetrate beyond the limited concrete experience of human life lived in a tiny segment of time and space. Unlike ephemeral literature or period pieces which reveal only the peripheral aspects of life in a particular era, they transcend the "local habitation and name" and plunge into the fundamental possibilities of human existence itself. They pierce through the personality of a particular character in a particular situation, as it were, to discover what is true of all men. They express the experience of man as man. Thus Aristophanes' *The Birds* is a political satire on life in ancient Athens which has delighted educated minds for hundreds of years, while Maxwell Anderson's *Both Your Houses* was a charming period piece on political life in Washington of the 1930's, but few men read it thirty years later.

To be sure, the experience of any author concerning fundamental human life is necessarily bound to his limited encounter with the men of his own time, place, and culture. The great writer confronts human existence in its concrete appearances in a limited here and now, but his creative sensitivity enables him to participate in the essence of human life which manifests itself in these time-bound phenomena. He possesses a kind of psychological antennae by which he penetrates the core of the life of his contemporaries, to experience at its deepest source their mode of existence. Then, in a mysterious process of both presence and detachment, the creative writer distances himself somehow from the concrete individuality of the people present to him and envisions the fundamental humanness of their lives. This profound vision, incarnated in the images created by genius, exercises imperishable power over generations of spellbound readers and listeners. The great author possesses a mysterious power to make transparent for us what we ourselves could become, what we potentially are. He knows the psychological secret of confronting us with reality. His power to do so makes him and his work immortal.

What makes a work of literature a classic, therefore, is not only or primarily its language, plot, tone, atmosphere, or setting. All of these contribute to its greatness, but they alone cannot elevate the work of art to an organic whole which is an "indefinable but unmistakable" source of light for mankind. The final touchstone of greatness for a drama or novel is the immediate, intimate experience of man. It is as if we have deep within us some lived experience of the fundamental themes of human existence. This potential experience is, in a sense, a predisposition for encounter with great literature. The evocative power of certain themes and images created by the masters makes us aware of what we have already experienced somehow in our encounter with our fellowmen. We have been unable of ourselves to bring this dimension of our existence to full awareness or dynamic expression. We must be confronted with an artistic image of what we have once experienced, as it were, in order to be moved emotionally by our own latent understanding of humanity. And this image must be presented to us in an atmosphere, a setting, a world which is not the world of our everyday existence.

In a sense, it is almost impossible for us to experience the fundamental truths of human existence in pure form in the encounters of our everyday lives. Too many accidental occurrences and personal involvements conspire to obscure in daily life the purity of basic experience. For example, when someone dear to us suffers a sudden malignant illness, we are overwhelmed not only by the deeply human aspect of his situation but also by a host of peripheral practical details. We must make appointments with the doctor, procure medicine, prepare special food, provide for duties that can no longer be fulfilled by the sick person, and even concern ourselves about the insensitivity of visitors or the irritation of the sick person himself. This avalanche of impressions makes it almost impossible for us to be fully and purely present to the tragic experience of a human being who suddenly finds himself in the pain and isolation of fatal illness. It is not true that this calamity escapes us wholly, that it does not move us somewhere in the depths of our being, that it does not confront us with the tragic dimension of human existence which we dimly experience as our own dimension too. This incipient experience remains in us as a seed which has not reached its flowering. It has not been able to grow because of the weeds of daily concern.

The creative novelist, poet, or playwright takes just such a fundamental human experience and lifts it from its setting of practical entanglements. He creates a new setting for it, a new world in which it can come to its full flowering. Tolstoy did precisely this in his world-famous novella, *The Death of Ivan Ilyitch*, a shatteringly realistic dramatization of the theme of fatal illness. This story demonstrates why great literature, by its essence, is never *factually* true to life. If it portrayed precisely the seemingly prosaic details of our everyday experiences, it could not foster in us the growth of our profoundest experiences—those experiences which reveal to us the fundamental possibilities of all human existence. The fact that great literature always refers ultimately to these basic dimensions of human life explains why certain images, themes, and conflicts recur in an infinitude of forms in many poems, plays, and novels. The theme of tragic love, for example, repeats itself again and again in the great stories of the world: Dido and Aeneas, Paolo and Francesca, Troilus and Criseyde, Tristan and Isolde, Heloise and Abelard, Romeo and Juliet, Antony and Cleopatra, Faust and Marguerite. Their names are legion and their sorrows are universal sorrows.

This recurrence of themes seems to indicate fundamental human structures and potentialities somehow familiar to all of us in the depths of our pre-reflective experience. These basic possibilities of human existence have been analyzed by philosophical anthropologists. But they were actually experienced by men and given artistic expression in the images and themes of the literary masters long before the philosopher and the psychologist reflected on them.

In psychological terms, great plays and novels

stir within the reader a conscious response to unconscious experience present within him but never
fully expressed and unfolded. The forms and patterns
of literature give to the reader or listener that clarification or objectification required to awaken the
awareness of his latent experience of human life. Confronted with certain literary themes, we may say
immediately that they are not familiar to us. Yet we
may experience within us a vibration of emotional
recognition which tells us that we have somehow
known them always. They seem to appeal to an
undercurrent of our slumbering experiences and most
intimate emotions.

To be sure, psychological experience teaches
us that a profound response to existential themes in
literature cannot be commanded at will. Sometimes
the reader must live with these themes for a long
time, and particularly at those moments when he is
psychologically disposed for a presence to them which
is unencumbered by practical cares. Also, the help of
literary analysis may be most fruitful as an introduction to the experience of response to literature in
depth. Such analysis is especially helpful when it is a
record of the critic's own experience as he immersed
himself in the existential themes expressed in the
work of art. The experience of the critic is not meant,
however, to be a substitute for our own experience.
On the contrary, he aims at the stimulation of our
personal presence to the work of art by letting us first
participate in his own mode of presence.

Aside from the unquestionable value of the
aesthetic response itself, we may raise the question
of why we should read literature—or literary analysis

—to evoke in us a lived experience of the human situation. Can we not arouse an equally valuable response by reading philosophy and psychology, especially in those areas which deal with man and his experience? While it is true that certain philosophies and psychologies refer more or less directly to human experience, they do so in a fundamentally different manner than literature does, and effect quite different responses. Philosophy and psychology examine human experience conceptually. Both disciplines provide a knowledge of human experience which is largely theoretical and analytical. Ordinarily, they break down our experiential life into elements and integrate them within more or less well-structured philosophical or psychological systems. Such an approach to experience has its own values. It satisfies our need for a conceptual grasp of reality, and it provides the student of philosophy or psychology with a frame of reference which helps him to study and understand man in an ordered way. It does not acquaint us, however, with the lived experience to which such intellectual systems point and in which they are rooted. Lived experience cannot be evoked by concepts alone. We need to appeal to the creative imagination which can represent concrete life situations that evoke emotional patterns.

Lived experience can come to awareness if it is linked with actions and objects that affect us as persons, and if creative language is used to stimulate our imaginations to evoke those situations which can awaken in us corresponding experiences. When existential themes are embodied in concrete life stories, they appeal not only to the mind but also to the heart, to man as man. The great writer possesses not only a rare sensitivity to the human situation, but also to the words, metaphors, and images which are eminently fit to express universal themes. Moreover, he is able to order and structure them so as to evoke their full power. When the reader is capable of responding adequately to the work of art, he will experience the dimension of human life which was experienced by the creative artist himself. Therefore, when we read great literature the question for us is not so much what was in the mind of the author, but what is the experience communicated to us as we are actually present to the poem, novel, or drama. The psychologist sees the task of the literary analyst as not merely to make us aware of the intention of the author but, more importantly, to help us to be present to the experience evoked in us by our immediate involvement in the literary work itself.

The experience communicated by a great novel or drama is embodied in the total unity of the literary work. Obviously, it is impossible for the literary analyst to interpret the entire work in every detail, a task which might be equivalent to a paraphrase expanded by a running commentary. Rather, the critic ordinarily chooses certain key passages on which to concentrate his interpretation. Psychological reflection reveals that certain crucial passages in a narrative or play are so central and rich in meaning that they are clues to a deeper understanding of the human meaning of the whole. It is interesting to note that a psychotherapist in confronting his client experiences something analogous to the response of the critic to a character in literature. The life story of his patient finally becomes meaningful to the therapist when he begins to understand certain crucial experiences that throw light on all the other events in the life of his client. Such understanding of the central passages of the story does not mean that the therapist disregards the remainder of the narrative of his patient's life. The more secondary events give actuality and life to that which is revealed in the key experiences. A significant point for our analogy, however, is that the therapist is able to introduce another person—for example, a second therapist who adopts the client—to an understanding of the life of the patient by communicating to him the meaning of the central experiences of the life story which the patient has told. Indeed, if the communication is successful, the new therapist can enter the situation immediately and understand with comparative ease the less central aspects of the life of the client. He does not need to expend the time and effort required of the original therapist before he came to grasp the fundamental situation.

The analogy between the experience of the therapist and that of the literary analyst is obvious. Intimately present to the work of art, the critic is finally able to select the crucial scenes which condense within themselves the main themes of the story and therefore illuminate its more peripheral aspects. Such key passages unify the play or novel as a whole. If the literary analyst is able both to select the crucial situations of the story and to guide the reader to a personal experience of their meaning, then he has given the reader the best possible preparation for a rich encounter with the work as a whole.

From here on, the reader may be able not only to live intimately with the existential revelations of the work, but also to relate them in an immediate way with the experiences of his own life. Thus it seems crucial for the literary critic to offer analysis of central passages in which the existential meaning of the entire play or novel is concentrated.

Much controversy has arisen in past years, for example, over the interpretation of the character of Shakespeare's Hamlet. To be sure, such controversy is inevitable when we consider the complexities and subtleties of Hamlet's character. Yet the psychologist might point out that at least certain over-simplifications of judgment may be avoided if the critic concentrates on the full meaning of all of Hamlet's key speeches. One-sided interpretations of the character have sometimes developed from almost exclusive attention to the meaning of one or two of Hamlet's soliloquies. Thus Hamlet emerges as only the hesitating hero "sicklied o'er with the pale cast of thought," or only the fearful hero, or only the vengeful hero. An existential psychological interpretation would undoubtedly point to a Hamlet who is all of these and much more—a Hamlet revealed in not one but six crucial soliloquies (and throughout the entire drama as well).

Psychology provides an answer to the question of how the literary commentator discovers the crucial passages in the literary work he is analyzing. A play or novel is a fictional embodiment of the motivational life of man, of its crises and its development. The critic who attempts to uncover the fundamental meaning of a novel or drama therefore traces carefully the motivational development of its characters. He does so not merely by cool intellectual reflection or by functional application of psychological categories. He keeps such fruitful concepts continually in "the back of his mind," ready to be evoked when they are relevant to the experience that emerges in himself while he is present to the literary work with the deepest possible human involvement. His reading is not, therefore, a matter of detached observation, but a constant attempt to participate in the motivational movement of the characters. He is faithful to the emotional experience which he himself undergoes in living through their conflicts. If he is sensitive in his responses, he develops a feeling awareness of various levels of incentive and emotion operating within the fictional personalities who reflect in some way the life of motivation which is possible for every human being. This intense experiential participation enables the critic to know which moments are crucial in the development of the characters. These decisive moments usually reflect the basis of the whole meaning of the work of art. Because a literary work is not a philosophical treatise but rather an artistic expression of the motivational development of human life, these moments cannot be discovered by mere intellectual scrutiny. They demand the wholly human involvement of the critic.

When the reader, enlightened by the good critic, is able in turn to participate in the lived emotional history of the fictional character, he experiences not only the expression of his own perhaps confused feelings and motivations, but also a release or catharsis. The inner forces of emotions that ordinarily seem

to escape our grasp are made palpable and understandable through shapes and forms created by the
author and offered to our imagination. Sometimes the
different characters in a work symbolize various aspects of our emotional and motivational life. Our
entangled and complicated motivations are split up,
as it were, and given separate embodiment in individual characters. Thus we are enabled to face our deepest drives, our conscious and unconscious motivations,
our open and hidden feelings and phantasies, which
otherwise might never appear to us so clearly in their
interactions (except perhaps in psychotherapy). It is
a real release to become clearly aware of hidden
forces that move us. When we experience emotional
tendencies of opposite natures, for example, they are
apt to produce inner tension as long as we are unable
to live in relative harmony with them. The embodiment of such opposed tendencies in the characters of
a drama or novel, together with the portrayal of encounter between these fictional characters, awakens
in us a feeling of relief insofar as it helps us to face—
at least unconsciously—similar interactions between
opposing aspects of our own personalities. Certain
literary critics who have never found a satisfactory
answer to the powerful appeal of Milton's Lucifer in
Paradise Lost might consider the unconscious potentialities in all of us for the motivations of this
villain-hero, and the catharsis evoked by his conflict
with Michael and the good angels, who symbolize
motivations which we affirm much more readily on a
conscious level.

Because they are rooted in human existence
itself, the deepest personality conflicts are basically

the same for all men. Therefore, novels and dramas which have deeply moved men of past generations and cultures repay our special attention. Their universal and timeless appeal implies that they express inner conflicts which are familiar to all of us in the depths of our existence. The chief value of such literary works is never the enlightenment they may offer concerning any particular milieu, but the artistic expression of the emotional and motivational meaning of man's existence. Consequently, the reader should relate to the literary masterpiece with his whole personality, summoning all his resources in order to grow to a genuine encounter with the work and discover what it can mean to him existentially. He must surrender to it and contemplate it at moments when he feels that his whole personality is disposed to respond to its truth.

Great novels and dramas familiarize us not only with the fundamental structure of human motivation and its inherent conflicts, but also with the rich motivational superstructure which has been developed during our own cultural history, which is the history of the Western world. Our emotional responses are not always so natural and spontaneous as they may seem to be. Our motivational life has grown from a matrix of values which we have in common with mankind as it has developed within the Western tradition. In other words, our personal existence is embedded in a larger existence which is that of Western man. The values and motivations common to the Western world are realized, to be sure, in different degrees in various personalities. The manner in which our common heritage grows and expands without losing its fundamental unity is largely a mystery of communication. In the sharing of value, meaning, and motivation, literature is a principal instrument. Therefore, our involvement in the experience evoked by great literature is also a communion in the values discovered by the minds and hearts that have created our culture.

Scientific disciplines may make us aware of this cultural heritage in an intellectual frame of reference. Their primary objective is not to move us but to enlighten our minds. One of the aims of great literature, however, is to evoke attitudes, emotions, and motivations which enable us to participate deeply in the life of our civilization. To be sure, the experience of our Western world which is aroused by literature is different from our everyday perception of the world in which we live. Our Western culture has placed at our disposal, for example, a tremendous range of practical insights on how to use many natural forces in utilitarian ways. We know the practical qualities and uses of wood, rock, water, fire, steel, and coal. Literature does not speak to us about this type of knowledge of our world. Literature leads us to look at our world from a quite different viewpoint, to see the objects named above as symbols which express deep emotional attitudes common to the people of our culture. Water may be a symbol of cleansing from guilt, fire of dynamic force, rock of faith. Such symbols evoke responses which lift us for the moment above personal needs and pragmatic concerns. They raise us temporarily into a universe which is suprapersonal and sublime. Literature thus liberates us from the particularities of our daily situations and enables us to live in communion with the values that have appealed to Western man above and beyond all pragmatic goals. These values are not mere phantasies; they are realities which are and have been actual and effective in the history of the West. By our response to the literature of our culture, we expose ourselves to the reality of the values on which our society was built. As a result of this involvement, we experience a higher degree of unity between our own life of values and that of the whole of Western humanity.

This conclusion does not mean that literature preaches values to be realized. Literature presents man with a whole range of value motivations and with the consequences in life of the decisions for or against these values. The reader is confronted, moreover, with the crises that may emerge at crucial moments of human existence as lived in his own culture. All that is asked of him is to be open to the work of art without prejudice and without repression of any of the responses awakened in him. This openness, which implies a courageous sincerity, will increase his appreciation of the possibilities of life in his own milieu and help him to motivate himself in the light of true insight. At the same time, he will participate in that part of his cultural tradition which through art and literature orders the emotional dimensions of his own life.

The great writer possesses the mysterious power of words through which he embodies the values of his culture in language which evokes an emotional experience similar to his own. This genius for communicating the cultural treasure does not mean, to be sure, that the same response is evoked in every reader. The level of response will vary with each person, depending upon the degree of complex understanding which he is able to bring to the work of art. If the reader is open to his own feelings, however, he will discern spontaneously the images and symbols which call forth in him a response to both the intimate experiences of his own life and the common experiences of his culture.

The literature of the Western tradition embodies, then, a collective background of emotion and motivation. And the individual reader participates in this suprapersonal life according to his personal ability to involve himself in the collective experience. This living through of the motivations of his culture brings him increased awareness of his own life in its creative obedience to the rhythm of the human evolution. Therefore it cannot be said that a great literary artist communicates only his own individual thoughts, sentiments, and motivations. He shares his truly personal expression with an entire tradition and contributes an important link to the culture of the future.

The involvement of the artist in the motivational development of his culture is closely related to language because the connotations of the words and metaphors he uses are also common to his fellowmen who live the same modes of existence. His expression through his art of the experiences lived by his contemporaries helps the reader to become conscious of the common issues involved in existential decision. This discovery is a means of coming to terms with these crucial issues. The literary artist in any society is one of the first to be instinctively aware of a breakthrough in human understanding. He communicates his new insight to the reader who has eyes to see and ears to hear. At times this existential insight may suddenly leap forth and kindle the light of understanding only after the reader has been absorbed in the literary work over and over again. In one moment he may experience the flash of experiential sympathy with its inmost meaning. At this moment he becomes one with the truth of the work of art.

One of the great resources of literature for achieving this effect is the use of symbols. A symbol in literature appeals to our empathic imagination. To take a simple example, when an author uses an arrow in flight as a symbol of the speed of thought, we feel what he means at once even though we were never an arrow in flight. We experience the meaning of the symbol through empathic imagination. We conceive of an arrow flying off toward its target and embody ourselves somehow within its movement so that we feel the speed suggested. Certain basic cultural symbols assimilate strength and intensity in the course of literary history. Striking symbols have been chosen by the most perceptive minds of the race and have been perpetuated in great literary works and sometimes even in daily parlance. For this reason, we are familiar with certain types of symbols which open up to us a whole horizon of experience. The sea of Homer's *Odyssey*, the West Wind of Shelley's famous ode, the fire of Dante's *Inferno*, the armor of Cervantes' Don Quixote are not merely water, wind, fire, and iron. They are the journey of everyman through life, the prophetic trumpet of freedom, the anguish of

personal guilt, and the eternal conflict of human
ideals.

As we have stated earlier in a different context, certain themes of novels and dramas also carry
with them a symbolic quality. We all know that age-
old themes of love stories, for example, are repeated
over the centuries in a wide variety of forms. It is
clear that the creative writer is not presenting such a
theme to us as unknown experience. He uses the
perennial theme, perhaps unconsciously, as a symbol
for crucial recurrent life situations in which we all
may find ourselves. The concrete content of our individual situation may be different, but the fundamental structure of our experience may be very much
like that of the characters of whom we read. For
example, everyone finds himself at some time in his
life confronted with a situation in which two persons
dear to him each demand an exclusive attention which
would offend the other. Such a painful "triangle" can
lead to a variety of complications in the relationships
among the three persons involved. Sooner or later,
it forces each person to an existential decision which
leads to a solution of the ambiguous relationship.
Many love stories are a symbolic expression of just
such a predicament. The clandestine romance of the
brave knight Lancelot and the beautiful Queen Guine-
vere, rooted in their sad unfaithfulness to the noble
King Arthur, is the prototype of hundreds of stories
in world literature. It is not difficult for the reader to
identify with such characters and to become involved
in their experience. In short, one of the unconscious
criteria of the reader in judging a novel is, "Do I find

in the themes and symbols of this story a satisfying expression of some actual experience of my life?"

The representations of crucial human experiences in good literature thus help us to grow to an understanding of our own lives insofar as we respond to literature with full presence and involvement. When we do so, we participate at the same time in the experience of life itself. In the concrete representation of fictional art, we experience not merely the incidental source of inspiration of the author but a manifestation of the mystery of all being. Independent of the satisfaction of our own needs through the work of art, we enjoy the values of life in themselves. In our real presence to great literature, we discover ourselves in an attitude in which our small ambitions and petty desires are silenced. The beauty communicated to us by the novel or drama is not adapted to a pragmatic purpose; it is affirmed and enjoyed in and for itself. The work of art is experienced as having a fullness within itself which enables us to communicate with it again and again, absorbing new insight with every encounter.

Our literary experience may seem passive at first in the sense that aesthetic illumination is experienced as a gift which is given to us rather than a goal to be achieved. We can only accept it in humility and gratitude. We undergo the magic of beauty rather than subjecting it forcefully to the power of our analytic intelligence. At the moment of surrender to aesthetic experience, we do not grapple with questions of language or historical background, with the private ideology or the psychological problems of the author. While we are assimilating the deepest meaning of the work of art, we contemplate rather than reason. When Shakespeare's Othello discovers too late that he has unwittingly destroyed the faithful Desdemona who to him is the dearest woman in all the world, we do not reason. We respond with un-bounded pity. When the once proud King Lear hum-bly discovers himself as he really is, we do not reason. We surrender to the heartbreak of our common hu-manity.

Paradoxically, however, our deepest experi-ence of literature also has an element of personal activity. Outwardly we may seem passive, but in-wardly we are absorbed by an intense dynamic move-ment which orients us at the moment of full presence. Our whole being reaches out toward the work of art. Such concentration implies a conscious suspension of every action incompatible with the anticipation of actual encounter with poetic meaning. When the mo-ment arrives, we experience the beauty of the work of art in wonder and awe. We feel ourselves opening up to new insights as a flower opens to the light. The really great play or novel lifts us far beyond its dra-matic statement to horizons of meaning which escape full definition. Ineffability is characteristic of every experience of the plenitude of the mystery of being. At such moments we are lost to the limited horizons of our daily world. We experience ourselves as one with a reality which unutterably transcends our ordi-nary life. We are no longer motivated by common-place needs and concerns. We no longer strive to control ourselves and our environment in order to im-plement our pragmatic projects. Our response to great literature occurs on a far deeper level of our personalities. It is the level where we are most truly ourselves, where we are most fully present to the authentic values of life, where we really transcend ourselves.

Such transcendence occurs, to be sure, not only in authentic response to literature but in all experiences of ecstasy, whether of human love or religious response. In such privileged moments we find ourselves at one with what we behold, whether it be a work of art, a concept of genius, our beloved, or our God. We feel ourselves united to what we experience as a mysterious whole. In such moments of unity we may lose our functional identity, only to find it again, renewed and refreshed by our experience of transcendence. Conflict, anxiety, and fear give way to fulfillment, serenity, and wonder. We experience ourselves as whole, harmonious, and integrated with the stream of life.

Thus we may transcend through literature the temporality and spatiality of our concrete situation. Absorbed in literature, we may break the confines of our moment-to-moment existence and live in the infinity of values which the world of art presents to us. An hour of reading may indeed be a short moment in which we become suddenly and experientially aware of ultimate meaning. Such poetic experiences are not only valuable in themselves; they transform our daily lives. Once we have reached intimacy with great literature, we no longer consider it an interesting relaxation, but a sacrament of encounter with the meaning of human existence. Instead of a diversion from life, it becomes a source without which life would be less livable in the deepest sense. In literary

experience we discover values more lasting than the
fulfillment of all our ambitions. In a sense, it directs
us toward that which remains when accidents dis-
appear, toward the absolute and eternal. The more
deeply we penetrate the mystery of the great literary
masterpieces, the closer we come to really knowing
and being ourselves.

Our experience of literature may be rich and
intense, or poor and shallow, depending on our culti-
vated sensitivity to art, our openness, and our previous life experience. When we say that our whole
personality opens up to literature, we mean that all
our powers to receive the impression of the artistic
work are actualized. In considering this experience
of openness to literature, we may distinguish various
psychological dimensions of presence to reality. First
of all, the psychobiotic dimension is our involvement
in the world primarily in and through our senses and
sensations. A second dimension is the functional one,
in which we are present to the world through a practical attitude which reveals reality to us as something
to be ordered, controlled, and organized. A more
profound dimension of our human presence reveals to
us values which are deeper than the sensuous and the
pragmatic: love, truth, beauty, religion, and authentic joy.

We are never present to reality exclusively in
any one of these dimensions. At different moments in
our lives, one dimension may color and attune our
presence more than others; nevertheless, all the dimensions of our human presence permeate one another. In the finest moments of our experience, our
presence to reality is a harmonious unity of the vari-

ous dimensions of response which are simultaneously active. Such moments always bring with them a feeling of wholeness and integrity. When we receive the gift of authentic presence to literature, we feel totally absorbed in all the dimensions of our personality. Our sensuous presence is involved insofar as we experience the imagery, sound, and rhythm of the work. The dimension of our ordering presence is actualized in our awareness of its symmetry, harmony, proportion, and artistic structure. Our deepest presence is involved in our experiential awareness of the existential meanings and values expressed in the poem, play, or novel. When our response to meaning in its profoundest sense is actualized, our other modes of presence are relevant insofar as they expand our possibilities of entering in depth into the world of meaning. A keen perception of the images and symbols created by the artist and a response to the artistic texture of the work are necessary for our empathic understanding of the imaginative world of the author. Every sensuous image created, every word and metaphor chosen, the rhythm and tone of every passage, and the total structure of the work of art are meant to dispose us for the human meaning which the writer desires to share with us. He wrote in his unique fashion and ordered his imaginative world in its unique structure because he hoped thus to involve us in the experience of his own response to reality. The meanings of great literary works are thus never experienced as ideas *about* something; they are always incarnated in the artistic creation itself.

When we read a great novel or play for the first time, we may grasp little more than the literal

meaning of the story. Only in contemplative reread-
ing may we become aware of the comprehensive
meaning which it symbolizes. The peripheral meaning of the story points to the comprehensive one
which is suggested and at the same time hidden in the
literal meaning. Every great work of literature,
therefore, is in part a concealment and in part an illumination of its own meaning. It is one of the func-
tions of the literary critic to help to unveil its symbolic
meaning.

When we say that the drama or novel has a
latent symbolic as well as a manifest meaning, we do
not imply that the author begins with a well deline-
ated concept which he then symbolizes through image
and metaphor. The literary creator is primarily present to man and the human condition. In his deep and
sensitive presence he is able to experience the human
predicament in an unique way. In and through the
embodiment of his experience in writing, he himself
becomes aware of insight gained at a deeper level of
his existence. Within the artistic work itself the
writer grows to an awareness of his own intuition.
In making his insight available to others, he makes it
available to himself. He communicates his unique
response to life in the harmonious structure of a work
of art impregnated with the symbolic meaning of his
own experience.

As a mode of finding meaning in human life,
literature is distinct from all other ways of knowing.
Our mode of understanding man through literature is
the poetic mode of existence which differs radically
from all analytical and deductive approaches to
knowledge. When we respond to literature, we are

present to man in an immediate and pre-reflective, experiential and intuitive manner. While it is true that interpretation, reflection, and historical consideration may prepare us for the moment of understanding, this moment itself is a gift of illumination which cannot be guaranteed by intellectual readiness. On the other hand, once we enjoy this more or less gratuitous experience, it may become the starting point for all manner of historical, philosophical, and psychological reflection.

Because literature communicates meanings and values to us which we can know in no other way, the role of literature in the evolution of mankind is incontestable and irreplaceable. Literature enables man to motivate himself in continually new ways in the realm of ultimate values which give light to his existence. Science and its beneficial uses provide one aspect of the drama of human evolution, an aspect which is overstressed by man in our century. The fundamental orientation of the total adventure of humanity is dependent largely on the dialogue between man in any given era and the ultimate values of mankind. This lived dialogue finds one of its most vital expressions in great literature which helps man to grow to awareness of his own motivational struggles.

A final consideration of the experience offered to us by literature is the question of the aesthetic component of our full response to the work of literary art. As we have already pointed out, in the contemplative surrender to great literature we experience a deep revelation of the very core of reality which may be called the aesthetic experience. The term *aesthetic* thus refers to transcendence, a quality which goes

beyond the particular meaning of the individual work
of art and participates in the existential theme of universal values. Consequently, our aesthetic experience is related to union with mankind, with ultimate
values, with the cosmos. We lose our functional
identity as a pragmatic center by which we order our
daily lives, but we discover our deepest identity
which is a personal openness for the values which give
meaning to human existence. This aspect of integration with the supra-personal is the fundamental center
of the aesthetic response. We experience a truth so
profound that it cannot be understood completely; we
know ecstasy in surrender to its mystery. We transcend time and space. But just how is this gift of
beauty given to us?

A completely satisfactory answer is impossible. We know, however, that the beauty experienced in the aesthetic response is not found in
ourselves. Neither is the experienced beauty present
in the literary creation independent of ourselves.
Beauty is found in our existential *relationship* to the
work of art. Only in this encounter can the aesthetic
experience emerge. This is one reason why the experience is personal for each reader and also different
from the personal experience of the writer. The
aesthetic response of certain readers may be even
more profound than that of the creator of the work of
art. This phenomenon is not so surprising when we
realize that literature is the living embodiment of an
existential relationship between a human being and
supra-personal reality. Real participation in this living embodiment will therefore evoke an original
dynamic openness for supra-personal meaning ac-

cording to the aesthetic sensitivity of the reader. Just as the response of the reader is different from that of the author and that of other readers, it will also differ for the same reader at different moments of his life. Thus it may be said, from an aesthetic point of view, that a work of literature exists in limitless degrees.

The present chapter has developed, from the point of view of an existential psychologist, the common ground on which literature and psychology meet. The phenomena of the experience of the literary creator, of the literary critic, and of the reader who responds to the great novel, drama, or poem have been explored psychologically. The aesthetic experience itself has been defined existentially. Central to the entire discussion has been the unique value of the literary experience in opening man, especially modern man, to the meaning of reality. In the power to unveil ultimate values of existence, the literary experience is incomparable.

THE DEMON AND THE DOVE

LITERATURE is the artistic expression of man's deep-est experience. I recognize myself in the creations of the masters of poetry, fiction, and drama. They tell my story. They reveal what I am in the depths of my being. The conflicts of the protagonists of great nov-els are multi-dimensional portrayals of the victories and defeats which may be mine in some measure if I grow to the fullness of life. Great fiction will fascinate mankind as long as there are men who choose not to hide from experience but to live real lives. Literature is timeless because it is more universally true, as Aristotle said long ago, than historical reports of hu-man events. The artistic imagination is a magnifying mirror in which I may recognize myself if I only dare to look. I have to be brave to do so, for what I see is not always pleasing; at times it may evoke dread and terror. Unconsciously, I may be so fearful of self-discovery and its concomitant agony that I remain complacently unaware of the theme of a novel or drama in spite of my conscious desire to discover it. I may need to be prepared for the pain and splendor of my baptism of self-discovery.

Psychology and literature may be partners in this revelation. Psychology tells the same story of man as literature does, but in a different manner. What fiction communicates in moving characterization and description is revealed by psychology in concept and explication. While the novel is close to lived experience, the science of psychology is further removed from actual life. By means of both literature and psychology, I may enter into the gray area of my hidden motives and desires. I may transport myself from the light of my conscious motivation in which my choices are etched against the clear sky of apparent reason, into the dusk of pre-reflective desires and inclinations where springs of action are twisted and ambiguous. Psychology leads me into this obscure region in a more scientific, literature in a more experiential way. Together they may illuminate my existence. Psychological understanding alone may remain lifeless and even artificial, too much a matter of mind, too little of the human heart. Insight into experience through literature, on the other hand, may sometimes be too emotional and fragmented—too much of the heart, too little of the mind. I need a frame of reference in which I can understand my experience conceptually, and I need a vital insight into experience to keep this structure alive. Psychology provides structure, literature insight.

The great psychologists and the great literary masters have both unveiled the depths of human existence. They have discovered to us unthought of potentialities for goodness and depravity, for beauty and squalor in every man. The denizens of the unconscious discovered by Freud are no more fearsome than the mythic monsters of *Beowulf* and *The Nibelungenlied*, to say nothing of Dante's *Inferno*, Milton's hell, and Goethe's Walpurgis Night. On the other hand, symbolic figures of the ideal, from Sophocles' Antigone to Dante's Beatrice to Claudel's Prouheze, emerge in every era of our cultural history. Images of darkness and images of light reveal the fundamental strife of universal man.

As man, I too am darkness and light, demon and dove. The struggle between the two is the conflict which I share with all men. Demon and dove are symbols of the utter realities of my existence. Such symbols are apt to haunt my dreams at moments of crisis in which I experience the climax of tension between the opposite poles of my personality.

The demon signifies my dark side—my potentialities for boundless self-centeredness, for hatred and hostility, pride and conceit, ruthless ambition, dishonesty and deceit, exploitation of my fellowman, brute or seductive abuse of the other. The demonic in me can hide itself in an infinite variety of seemingly virtuous behaviors; it may be dormant but it is never absent; it may be tamed but never annihilated; it dominates me precisely to the degree that I am unaware of its sly and everlasting presence. The confrontation of man with his demon is a primary source of inspiration for dramatist and novelist. The artistic climax of this conflict—whether it is resolved in catastrophe or happy denouement—has always been the core of the powerful appeal of great literary masterpieces. For the clinical psychologist, the uncovering of the demonic often provides the drama of psychotherapy in which awareness must replace repression of insight. The crucial self-recognition scene in Shakespeare's *King Lear*, for example, is analogous to the critical moment of self-discovery in the therapeutic situation. Lear's tragic self-revelation terminates in death. The confrontation of the demonic in successful psychotherapy, however, may lead to a new mode of existence.

The dove, on the other hand, symbolizes my longing for innocence, simplicity, candor, generosity, and love. It is my homesickness for paradise lost in myself and others. It is my openness to goodness, truth, and beauty. The dove may be bound and imprisoned, but it will not be slain so long as I live. I can never silence its voice. When the demon dominates my life, this voice penetrates the barriers of repression and makes itself heard—particularly at crucial moments of encounter with others in whom the dove is stronger than the demon.

As man, I shall never be demon or dove alone. I shall always be both. To transcend the demonic in myself is my never-ending struggle. This hope for transcendence necessarily implies a growing recognition of the power of the demonic in my life. Dramatists and novelists have captured man's groping toward the light over "acres of darkness" in the greatest stories of world literature. Prometheus and Hamlet, Job and Ahab, Adam and Faust are mythic symbols of the dark journey of every man which is the price and seal of his humanity.

Self-centeredness, the refusal to be man and

not God, is the core of the demonic in human nature. The present chapter will present a psychological skeleton, as it were, of the demon in man. The literary explications of the later chapters will fill this skeleton with muscle, flesh, and sinew.

While the basic polarity of my being is perhaps best expressed in metaphor, it is a reality. If self-centeredness, self-concentration, self-enhancement dominate my existence, then I am demonic in my behavior toward others. If self-transcendence is the center of my life, then I reach out toward the goodness and truth in others, in nature, in the world. I do not always find these values at hand for my striving. But I can always discover them in their potential strength and radiance. When I do so, I experience love. My love liberates the potentiality for love in the other; even more, it frees me from the prison of self-centeredness. In the gift of myself, I grow to liberty; in the withholding of myself, I remain a captive.

Man is called to go beyond himself to the other, and thus to penetrate the mystery of reality that surrounds him. His deepest existential movement is toward all goodness, truth, and beauty. To be sure, these words represent abstractions. In reality, I find goodness only in its concrete, limited realization in objects, events, and people—in a snowfall, a painting, a symphony, a loved person, even in myself. But the limited splendor revealed in these manifestations points to a deeper splendor in which they participate and which excels them all. They are as so many figures which can be seen only against a deeper background. Therefore, like Goethe's Faust, I am never satisfied completely. I say to myself, as it were, "not enough," "this is not all." I am always striving to transcend myself, always in search of the infinite which I cannot embrace. This movement of becoming, of self-transcendence, is the most basic motivation of my life. It is the movement which is my very existence. And herein lies the greatest threat to my richest involvement in reality: my striving for existential meaning can lose its course and run afoul.

Precisely because I can experience the good only in its concrete manifestations—in myself, my talents, my success, in others, in the world around me, it can happen that I direct my existential movement toward the good in myself alone, or in one person or object alone. I identify this movement with the whole of my existential striving. When this happens, I limit my life itself to one fanatic movement toward one goal or person. I am incapable of any other vision, though I am usually unaware of my blindness. I transfer all my possible motivation to one isolated objective. This experience is called existential transference. The consequences of such a limitation of my life of motivation are most disastrous of all when my fixation is on myself. Such a narcissistic transference means that I unconsciously imagine that I shall find light and love in myself alone, that I concentrate all the energy of my life in my own self-enhancement, self-protection, and self-defense, that I use others for myself. To be sure, in order to maintain such an attitude I have to become blind to reality insofar as it tells me that I am not alone in the world, that I cannot find satisfaction in fantastic isolation, that values continually reveal themselves all around me, that I can fulfill myself only by surrendering myself.

The consequences of such an existential transference to my own ego are, when candidly considered, alarming. First of all, I have to become god-like in my own imagination, for as long as I am aware that I am not god I am compelled to realize that there are values outside myself which I should respect, cultivate, and foster. An actual existential transference to myself leads, therefore, to a basic delusion, to a deification of myself. This delusion implies, to be sure, that I repress or negate all experiences which prove my limitations, my imperfections, my dependence on others. I can do so only by developing a fantasy life which protects me against reality, which distorts daily events, cushions the impact of truth, and sustains me in a make-believe world of my own creation. Dwelling in a twilight of fantasy and dream, I live a counterfeit life. Authentic existence develops only through a candid openness for the reality in myself, in others, and in the world. But my self-idolization closes my eyes to any reality that would compel me to doubt my distorted world. I live, therefore, a twisted life in an unauthentic universe.

Great literature reveals innumerable instances of lives warped through self-idolization. In the tragicomedy, *Measure for Measure*, Shakespeare created, for example, the character of Angelo, whose life was unauthentic because of existential transference to his own ego. Angelo fondly imagined that he was not susceptible to the evil he condemned in others. Unconscious of his own demon, he conceived of himself as a "saint," and therefore lived in a false world in which he became his own god. Angelo's self-deception was so profound that he came to self-knowledge only through a sudden and cataclysmic encounter with Isabella, a character who was simple, candid, and good, but aware of the potentialities for evil in herself and all men. Unlike Angelo, she lived in the real world.

People who live a life of neurotic fantasy often reveal that they cherish dreams of momentous events which are to happen to them. These expectations help them to rationalize the fact that they do not achieve in daily life the marvelous feats which they should accomplish according to their exalted self-image. They naively await the moment of truth in which they will reveal to the world what they really are. Sometimes their very existence degenerates into a life of mere empty anticipation. To be sure, the moment of greatness never arrives, for even the potentially great must prepare for eminence by performance. Death may be the tragic revelation in which the veil of self-deception is suddenly dropped, and the life-long dreamer discovers himself in the shocking nudity of a failed existence.

The character of John Marcher in Henry James' *nouvelle*, *The Beast in the Jungle*, provides a model of the man whose narcissistic transference is so extreme that he devotes his entire life to empty expectation of unique experience which is to single him out from all mankind. Though his self-revelation at the moment of death is merely pathetic to the observer, Marcher's late discovery of the simple truth that he is like other men—neither god nor devil—

affects him like a bolt of lightning. The shock which annihilates his world of fantasy and uncovers reality to him actually precipitates his death. His life has been a complete failure.

If I am guilty of existential transference to myself, I cannot completely hide my failure from myself and others. I know somehow deep within my being, pre-reflectively, that I am failing, that I am in essence a betrayal of human dignity and therefore of all men. This repressed awareness of universal betrayal of myself, mankind, and the world leads to the experience of existential guilt. Because of my repression, I do not know the source of my overwhelming feeling of guilt. It frightens me, crushes me with anxiety, and threatens to paralyze my already warped life. Existential guilt terrifies me because it is a constant threat to my repression of the demonic in my existence. Every person has his shadow, his weakness, his demon. But only the person who represses his awareness of his own potentiality for vice is its defenseless victim. His so-called virtues smell of malignancy. There is no more demonic self-centeredness than that of the "pious" person who fancies himself a saint and plays skillfully at being one without realizing that his life is a clever game of pretense.

The most ludicrous character in Graham Greene's satiric novel, *A Burnt-Out Case*, is Father Thomas, an absurdly conceited missionary who lives his religious "vocation" on a completely superficial level and imagines that he is undergoing a dark night of the soul on a highly supernatural plane. With sharp insight, Greene reveals that, despite Father Thomas' conscious self-admiration, he is terrorized on a deep unconscious level by spiritual inadequacy. His comic pursuit of "soul-to-soul" talks with characters whom he canonizes as "saints" is, to the detached observer, the perfect reflector of his masochistic religiosity. The pathetic fellow is overburdened all unknowingly with existential guilt.

Once the feeling of existential guilt seizes a person, it becomes increasingly painful to bear. If I am the victim of such suffering, I suspect that others around me sense my anguish. I feel certain that they must know my guilt and condemn me. I begin to look anxiously for tell-tale indications of censure in their words, expressions, and gestures. The faintest sign of disapproval causes me to feel like a leper expelled from the human community. I read contempt in all eyes, I imagine that every man is pointing an accusing finger at me. I do not know the reason for my rejection and isolation; so I feel hateful and hostile to all who condemn me. I, the innocent one, am good and generous, but I am disliked, envied, and vilified.

For some victims, this feeling of existential guilt becomes so unbearable that they escape only through drugs which dull the agony of guilt and provide a false euphoria in the sweet paradise of fantasy. Others respond with senseless self-torture. Such a masochistic reaction is a blind attempt to kill the pain of guilt through self-destructive expiation.

In Tolstoy's great masterpiece, *Anna Karenina*, the beautiful heroine is overwhelmed by guilt because of her abandonment of her husband and child. Her existential transference is to her lover, Count Vronsky. On a deeper level of her personality, however, her transference is to her own ego because, as she ultimately discovers, she does not really love Vronsky. She desires him passionately for herself alone, and her desire eventually erupts in hate. At times Anna's crushing guilt is conscious; at other times, she represses her shame so that her unconscious guilt becomes even more unbearable. At one point in her life, Anna punishes herself by seeking public humiliation without even knowing the source of her masochism. As her guilt becomes more and more unendurable, she resorts to morphine and opium to deaden her anguish, and finally to complete self-destruction through suicide. At the moment of death she tears away the veil which imprisons her from reality and sees herself as she actually is.

Unlike Anna Karenina, some men attempt to escape self-condemnation by projecting their guilt to all mankind. They make themselves the judges of all; they become sniffling experts in unearthing the demonic in the lives of others. They can endure existential guilt only by censuring all men. As judges of others, they maintain themselves as idols, for only a god can sit in judgment on mankind. The judge of all does not seek a standard of judgment. Subscribing to a sanction would diminish his god-likeness, for it would imply dependence on someone outside himself. He himself becomes the criterion of goodness. To be sure, all these defenses only intensify the frightful isolation of the person who experiences the hell of extreme existential guilt. If he becomes aware of his real situation at some unguarded moment, the terror of his loneliness may overpower him with utter despair.

The great existential novelist, Albert Camus,

has created a merciless portrait of such a man in Jean-Baptiste Clamence, the "judge-penitent" of his satiric masterpiece, *The Fall*. This repulsive anti-hero wears the mask of penitent only to dominate others by forcing them to confess their guilt. He can endure his own guilt only by sitting in god-like judgment of others, projecting his own gross culpability to them. But beneath his conscious and insolent tyranny over others is a hell of self-condemnation and despair.

The characters created by literary genius often reveal to us the demonic qualities we ourselves possess on a more mediocre scale. When I become my own idol, I live an existence of inflated fantasy as well as guilt and isolation. My deluded self-image constantly affects my attitude toward other people. Unconsciously, I expect others to adopt my exalted self-conception. Consequently, I can never reveal myself as I really am. I must always wear a mask of unauthenticity. I am a pale reproduction of the dynamic frauds of literature. The lustful Angelo of Shakespeare's *Measure for Measure* wears a mask of rigid virtue; selfish John Marcher in *The Beast in the Jungle* assumes a social disguise of generosity; the conceited Father Thomas of *A Burnt-Out Case* masquerades as a humble man; Anna Karenina pretends to a life of happiness and fulfilled love; and Jean-Baptiste Clamence conceals his despair beneath the mask of "judge-penitent." With the exception of Clamence, not one of these characters is aware that his life is a counterfeit. Each must assume an imposture to maintain either his self-idolization or his divinization of another human being.

The deception of the person who is plagued

with existential guilt is not to be confused with the
adoption of the normal social "mask." To be sure, everyone wears a mask at times. I do not reveal to
everyone my most intimate feelings, hopes, and
dreams. I assume in society a manner which is acceptable and expected. Society itself could not exist
without an implicit code of civility. If everyone, always and everywhere, insisted on expressing his innermost self, chaos and anarchy would prevail. I need
a mask to shield my personal existence from society,
to safeguard my privacy, and at the same time to protect others against my own imposition or intrusion.
This preservation of privacy is achieved through a
flexible social mask which becomes increasingly per-
sonalized so that it tends to destroy itself as mask. In
other words, when I am not over-anxious and rigid,
when I do not live a neurotic fantasy life, my social
mask gradually assumes the features of my own personality. I become identified by the individual way in
which I adopt the customs of my community. My
mask is really a mask no longer. It is a gracious way
of being personally present to others in an acceptable
common style. Moreover, my behavior is not a mask
in the strict sense because I do not adopt manners
which mislead others concerning my real responses.
I do not distort my deepest feelings: I am simply
present in a different mode of existence, in a social
dimension in which more peripheral aspects of my
personality are lived and communicated in a style
which is both mine and that of my community. To be
able to assume this type of "mask" presupposes maturity and inner security. At times it demands a subtle
pervasion of both restraint and veiled revelation of

the inexpressible which safeguards the personal without betraying true presence to others.

The mask of unauthenticity, on the other hand, is quite different. When I wear it, I do not merely withhold myself; I positively express what I am not. Consciously or unconsciously, I impose a falsehood on others. When I am unaware of the mask I wear, I am an impostor, an impersonator, a masquerader not only for others but also for myself. I am caught in my own game, trapped in my own deception.

Literature sometimes has the power to expose my guile to me precisely because literature is an unmasking. It is a mirror of life, both its truth and its fraud. Paradoxically, a good novel can reveal the beauty of life to me by laying bare the deformation of imagination which permeates the iron curtain of my repression. Literature thus becomes a cry of freedom beaming its truth beyond the border of my daily defenses. A novel or drama may indirectly evoke my response to the splendor of life by unmasking its sad disguises.

Literature uncovers reality for me through a variety of means ranging from the tragic to the comic. Tragedy can represent, for example, the anguish which would be mine if my self-deception caused my downfall. Comedy can reveal to me how ridiculous I am in my self-centered fantasy. It is difficult to resist a smile when my vanity is ludicrously exposed in the mirror of a realistic comedy. Suddenly and unexpectedly, the comic can break through my pretentious deceit. I am caught off guard because my fraud is exaggeratedly portrayed by characters sufficiently distant from me to circumvent my defenses. The drama becomes a fascinating Trojan horse enthusiastically welcomed to the walled city of my unconscious existence. Before I realize it, I am aware of the absurdity of human life, of my own life.

When literature presents tragic truth without brutality or sentimentality, comic truth without merciless mockery, my unconscious defenses are more easily attacked. The pity and fear aroused in me through involvement with the agony of a great tragic hero like Oedipus or Lear impel me to recognize something of myself in the unmasked hero. The horror or revulsion aroused by extreme violence or mawkishness, however, leads me to divorce my own existence from that of the unmasked protagonist. It is not easy for me to identify with Shakespeare's melodramatic Richard III or the somewhat emasculated Edward II of Marlowe. Similarly, my smile of self-recognition is best achieved in comedy not through derisive ridicule, but through a liberating humor which punctures the balloon of my vanity, my laughable tendency to mask my faults or even to idealize my perversities. Falstaff's vanity is a delightful and lively mirror of everyman's conceit, but what man could be persuaded to view himself in the character of Moliere's Tartuffe without protest? Again, Cervantes' great knight, Don Quixote, lives in a world of fantastic self-exaltation; yet the author inspires the universal involvement of readers through not only wit but mercy and understanding. But whether painfully or painlessly, great literature always has the power to unmask. And by breaking down man's unconscious defenses, it also has the power to free him for true encounter with his fellow men.

The lonely person whose life is poisoned by the image of his own importance, whose unconscious is flooded by guilt, is incapable of existential encounter. He must wear his mask of unauthenticity always. Even his legitimate social mask is worn in spurious fashion, for he cannot personalize social conventions. His true individuality is buried under a fake character which substitutes for his real self and permeates his social communications. Therefore, he is unable to encounter others in love and respect, which can exist only between two real persons. Even ordinary neighborliness can subsist only between persons who somehow reveal themselves through social conventions. To be sure, they may communicate to each other only the most peripheral aspect of their personalities. But this particular profile of their lives is truly theirs and not a falsification. The man who has deified himself, however, can never truly encounter others, even on a peripheral level. He is condemned to play his role always and everywhere. He is forced to elaborate a net of deceptive performances which grows daily more intricate. Consciously or unconsciously, the truth haunts him and compels him to escape into ever new fantasies in the frantic pursuit of make-believe excellence.

If I cannot be myself in relationship with others, I cannot find comradeship, friendship, or love. All of these are authentic relationships. In and through them I am rooted in the community of men. If I do not develop any of them in the true sense, I shall be tortured by my basic need for human encounter which remains unfulfilled. The unauthentic man may repress the awareness of his intense need for others, because it threatens his image of god-like self-sufficiency. But however he deceives himself, his repressed need grows stronger and wilder in the hot-house of his unconscious existence where the coolness of reality cannot check its development. Because his need for others cannot be sublimated to respect, friendship, or love, the victim of an existential trans-ference to his own limited ego necessarily falsifies his human relationships. They become dehumanized, based on desperate want rather than respect.

Human relationships rooted in respect are constructive; rooted in need, they are destructive. My raw, unsublimated need for the other can lead to a form of gross or subtle enslavement of him. I do not respect him as an independent existence; I use him for my own satisfaction. I manipulate him as an object; I force or seduce him to minister to my de-sires. I may even call this perversion love or friend-ship and believe it to be so.

In Henry James' story, *The Beast in the Jun-gle*, the protagonist John Marcher accepts the devo-tion of May Bartram during the richest years of her life, using her only to serve his egoistic needs. He calls this perversion friendship. Again, Anna Kare-nina in Tolstoy's great novel compels her lover Vron-sky to obey her least whim until he becomes her abject slave. She, in turn, becomes subhuman in her subservience to Vronsky in order to bind him to her. Anna Karenina calls her perversion love.

Paradoxically, the person who can relate to others only by enslaving them is always in danger of being enslaved himself. If I am unable to encounter people on the personal level and am at the same time overwhelmed by my need for human relationship, I may become the slave of another in order to buy his presence to me. My loneliness and despair may drive me to a subhuman relationship. This slavish subservience may unconsciously deteriorate into a form of masochistic self-torture. Existential guilt over my betrayal of my own humanity and of life itself may break through my inner defenses, flood my consciousness, and overwhelm me with anxiety without my knowing its real source which remains hidden by my repression. I may unconsciously aggravate my slavish dependence in order to find relief from nagging guilt through self-destructive expiation. But this weird feeling of guilt without a cause, instead of being relieved, will be merely intensified. For blind servility is only a further betrayal of my own humanity. It is precisely this treason which is the source of my unbearable experience of guilt in the face of life. I now become the victim of a vicious dilemma. Increased guilt feeling leads to intensified slavish subservience, which in turn leads to exaggerated feelings of existential guilt. It is clear that so desperate a situation can precipitate all types of sexual promiscuity, aberration, masochism, and sadism.

To treat another person as an object in order to satisfy my own desires is immoral. I should not confuse such manipulation, however, with an honest appeal to another to serve my needs. So long as I do not claim that this need is the essence of love or friendship, so long as I leave the other free to fulfill or not to fulfill my appeals, or to make counter requests, my relationship is wholesome. The fullness of human existence demands affiliations based on the mutual fulfillment of needs. Many professional, political, and commercial partnerships embody this type of human interaction. Such a relationship should not be devoid of respect, for it is human, but I should not pretend that its primary purpose is to foster the other as other. Here there is no question of enslavement. My partner is free to end his service without feeling guilty of betrayal. For example, I may spend years in the service of a creative writer, painter, or composer without being enslaved by him. My reward may be that my need to serve humanity is fulfilled through him, that I learn much from my association with him, that I am introduced into an aesthetic world which I would never enter otherwise. He too realizes that he cannot demand slavish devotion as a person, that my service is more to his creative work than to himself. To be sure, if the gifted person becomes self-centered, he will attempt to impose his own ego on his followers and use them for his own gratification rather than for his creative task.

A Burnt-Out Case, by Graham Greene, provides an excellent example of such a perversion. Querry, the main character of the novel, is a creative personality and a famous architect. Because of his charm and achievement, he has many devotees eager to serve him. Only after he has unmasked his hidden self-divinization does he discover that he has used his admirers to minister to his vanity and lust. In total self-revulsion, he demonizes himself and vows never again to involve another human being in his lack of love.

The demon in man has many faces, but no face so frightening as that which is masked by repression. Man conquers and transcends his demon best through open confrontation. The conflict of Shakespeare's Macbeth is terrible and tragic, but he knows the measure of the evil which is the object of his deliberate choice. The struggle of Job, on the other hand, is with an unknown demon in dark, twisted, and awesome regions of the soul. The greatest literature man has created records his struggle toward the light through the subterranean darkness of his existence.

Literature records not only man's experience of the demonic, however, but also the existential crisis which he undergoes when the protest of the dove becomes too agonizing to bear, when the demon in himself and others horrifies him, when the nothingness of his life appalls him. The following chapters, therefore, will offer a psychological account of the existential crisis which literature reveals experientially.

DEATH, DECISION, AND
REBIRTH OF PERSONALITY

LITERATURE invites me to communicate with my own existence. It helps me to break through the boundaries of my existence, to transcend myself. The main themes of great dramas and novels are symbols of the changes, conflicts, and crises of my own life. In a sense, one basic symbolic meaning underlies the literature of the world: the recurring death and rebirth of personality, a death which prophesies resurrection on a higher level of existence. This need for psychological death recurs again and again in the development of my personality. Not every psychological death, to be sure, leads to existential rebirth. There are ways of dying which do not lead to a renewal of life; rather, they impede the further growth of personality. At certain moments of my life I am faced with a crisis which I can solve only by dying to a former mode of existence. I have no choice: I must decide either to die authentically to my past or to die unauthentically in a fixation on a past mode of life which will fossilize my existence. The death wish when permeated by the desire for restoration of my personality is crucial in my life. It expresses the fundamental structure of all human growth.

Before considering the symbolic expression of this human situation in literature, I may observe the phenomenon of death and rebirth in myself. As man, I am both "potentiality" and "actualization"; these are the two poles between which my life develops. Human potentiality is not something inert. On the contrary, I experience my potentiality as a dynamic tendency toward self-actualization which permeates my whole personality. I am not only what I actually am; I am also a constant movement toward self-realization. As soon as a new human potentiality announces itself in my life, I experience a powerful motive to actualize it. For example, if my association with my fellowmen has been one of mere pragmatic interaction, I may feel a strong incentive at a certain moment in my life to die to my functional existence and to live as a generous person. Up until now, my world has been structured as a field of realization of utilitarian goals. But the emergence of this new possibility of living may change my world into a field of conflict between the old familiar way of life and the invitation to actualize an unknown mode of presence to men which will radically change my life. Such situations of crisis are often created by dynamic encounters with other human beings. Fortunate encounters may lead me to an awareness of myself and my world which compels the realization of a challenging mode of being. When I affirm and actualize a new potentiality, my world becomes restructured in terms of the new life to which I am born.

My unique personality cannot be regarded, therefore, as an object that is completed. I am "becoming"; I am potentiality for dying to my life at any moment and for being born to what I am not yet. It is my essence not to be closed in upon myself like chairs, tables, or rocks that do not live. I am a restless, spontaneous movement toward new modes of self-realization. I experience myself as incomplete, unfinished, as longing to be. In short, the fact that I am a man implies that I can be reborn.

But I am not potentiality only. Every time that I advance to a new mode of existence I am, in a sense, partially determined by this rebirth. For example, I may be born to leadership after dying to a child-like dependency. Leadership is now a factual determination of my life which can be described and analyzed. This new determination of my personality carries with it, however, new possibilities for death and rebirth. Because of my new life situation, I may now become a leader in a variety of ways formerly closed to me. But if I feel called to a new type of leadership which implies the death of an old, I may experience a psychological crisis. I am again confronted by choice. Thus, even when I am partially determined by rebirth, essentially I am always non-determined. I always remain able to die and to be reborn within the limits of my earlier determinations. Even the actual "birthmarks" of my personality are not *real* determinants of my life except within the context of possible rebirth. For example, I may have become a hero in the eyes of myself and of others, but if my actual manner of living does not imply the possibility of heroic achievement, then I never *really* grew to heroism. Whether I am child or adult, simple man or hero, prisoner or free citizen, I am always potentiality for rebirth in manifold ways. If I were to "freeze" myself into becoming a "thing" by repression of my lasting desire to transcend what I am, I should die to authentic life.

The deepest revolt of many heroic figures of great literature is against the impossibility of actualizing themselves in a new way. The tragic hero often chooses destruction in preference to the abdication of his desire for rebirth—even if this denial of selfhood would enable him to live splendidly in a "vegetable state." He prefers annihilation to a fixation of life which robs him of the one possibility which makes life worth living. The most sordid crime against man is to destroy that which man basically is: self-transcendence.

Sophocles' Antigone prefers death rather than failure to bury her brother according to the ritual of the Greek religion; the medieval hero, Roland, elects to be slaughtered in battle rather than surrender to the enemy of his king; Hamlet chooses death rather than failure to right his father's wrongs; Shaw's St. Joan (like the historical Joan of Arc) prefers to be burned at the stake rather than deny her transcendent visions. All of these characters are offered attractive alternatives of "comfortable" living. It should be emphasized that self-transcendence is not at all incompatible with actual physical death, as these heroic figures demonstrate. On the other hand, certain tragic heroes with deeper human flaws, perhaps, such as

Lear and Othello, achieve transcendence in the very act of self-discovery, with its concomitant affirmation of higher values. Though actual death is inevitable for both Lear and Othello, it is comparatively inconsequential to them in the glory of their ascent to a higher level of existence. Their very deaths affirm the values they freely choose.

The happy romances and great adventure stories of world literature also tell of man's need for self-realization. The delightful medieval lovers, Aucassin and Nicolete, would freely die rather than forfeit their love, even though ultimately they are not called to do so. Sir Galahad and all the great knights of legend triumph in contests of unbelievable valor in search of the Holy Grail or its equivalent, symbol of the quest for transcendence. Shakespeare's joyful heroines, Rosalind and Viola and Beatrice, and their happy lovers all accept the challenge of self-fulfillment in existential crises of varying levels of depth. Transcendence to new life in literature is not limited to either tragedy or comedy. It is at the core of all great literature, whether the resolution of the story brings physical death or joyful life.

And what of dramas and stories in which the characters freely choose not to be reborn? What of Macbeth, who deliberately perpetrates actions which cause the disintegration of his own personality? What of Aeschylus' Clytemnestra, who exults in the murder of Agamemnon and draws down the anger of the gods upon herself and her children? Some of the greatest literary figures of the past have pursued the death wish without the desire for existential rebirth. They have sought self-destruction rather than self-transcendence. Innumerable protagonists of contemporary literature, too, have negated their own existence. Ionesco's *The Chairs* offers a typical example. Here a distinction must be made between the explicit and the implicit themes of literature. Three hundred years of Shakespearean criticism, for example, have reinforced the interpretation of Macbeth's life experience as tragic waste, or the implicit theme that only self-transcendence makes the life of man desirable. Macbeth's negation of life is an implicit plea for the existential values he denies in action. Many contemporary literary works whose protagonists choose self-destruction, on the other hand, reveal no implicit denial of the code of values embraced by their characters. The pervasive philosophical tone of these books is nihilistic. Significantly, critics frequently refer to the protagonists of these novels and dramas as anti-heroes or non-heroes. This very nomenclature points to the fact that these characters are not symbolic of the profoundest values of mankind.

Great dramas and novels which symbolize the theme of death and rebirth move man deeply because they arouse the strongest emotional patterns of his life. He can identify with protagonists who fulfill their personalities freely in the very teeth of danger. Man feels the innermost movement of his existence symbolized in the great imaginative figures of literature, just as he feels it in nature itself. The setting of the sun at evening and its morning rising, the colorful death of nature in the fall and its resurrection in spring have profound emotional significance, intensified through centuries of cumulative literary tradition which has used these symbols to celebrate the existential death and rebirth of man. Even before the emergence of literature, prehistoric man expressed this fundamental movement of existence in ritual and dance, symbolizing the renewal of the life of the tribe in the flowering of nature under the divine influence of the new-born sun.

When I observe closely my own experience of psychological death and rebirth, I become aware of dramatic and dynamic changes in my life. I experience the emergence of a potentiality for a more meaningful life, first of all, as dissatisfaction with my past. Meanwhile, a restless anticipation of a new life springs up within me. Such emotional discontent may invade me over and over again during my life, for my fullness is at the same time emptiness; my satisfaction is clouded by displeasure; my security is encumbered by uncertainty. No matter what success I experience, my contentment is never final; I carry with me always a secret desire to die to the old man and rise to the new. Paradoxically, my existential death wish will never die, for hidden like a worm in the delicious apple of my life is the certainty that no mode of existence can ever fulfill me completely. Whether I fulfill myself as thinker, artist, scientist, or lover, I am never complete; I am always on the frontier of dissatisfaction with my past; my "yes" to life is never ultimate.

My need to negate my life in order to transcend it may lead to self-depreciation. I may become bitter, bored, or rebellious. I may desire new life without knowing to what I should be reborn. My negation of my past may lead me to self-destructive hatred of myself and my world. Only when my death to my former mode of life has been accomplished, and a period of mourning has fulfilled its purifying and liberating purpose, will my rebirth take place. Then I may accept my past again in the radiance of the present. Instead of rejecting my former life, which was part of my process of dying, I can now, in a relative sense, affirm it. I can now realize that my past life was not worthless, but relatively valuable and meaningful in the light of my new mode of existence. Thus I can integrate my past and present life and safeguard the continuation of my unique personal existence.

Existential death and rebirth is thus a vital process. First of all, the rich outward flow of my existence becomes stagnant. Enthusiasm is gone: I feel bored, disinterested, frustrated, not at home in my world. Gradually, the outward movement of my life is replaced by inward movement, by recollection and self-presence. In my absence from external involvement, I become aware of new possibilities of existence. My emotional distance enables me to see life in new perspectives. This new vision is the condition for my transcendence. In the days of stillness, of meditating on my own potentialities, my energies gather strength for rebirth. This period of death and isolation is in effect a preparation for new life. I am suspended between the two poles of return into myself and progress to new self-orientation. Existential renewal is thus a psychological sequence of frustration, retirement, new self-orientation, and finally rebirth to new motivation and behavior. If I did not die repeatedly, I should become capsulated in past forms of life which I have already realized.

If death and resurrection are my only means of keeping alive the spontaneity which I am always in danger of losing, the same is true for my community as for myself. My community embodies its self-orientation in systems which are necessary for the implementation of common motivations, but which alienate the members of the community if they preclude the possibility of renewal. Social customs, economic structures, programs of education perpetuate motivations that were once born from new insights. These functional endeavors protect the achievements of the past and the continuation of the human evolution. But they may also alienate man from the sources of his own inspiration. Thus man may be destroyed by his own past.

My recognition of the need for renewal does not mean, however, that I should strive for the destruction of traditions of civilized life. It means that I should grow to a free and humane assimilation of vital traditions, but that I should die increasingly to a blind, automatic conformity to any tradition. Thus I may personally affirm certain traditions precisely because I discover their value and wisdom. Like every man, I am called to self-realization not in isolation but in encounter with the great traditions of mankind.

In every age man must bring to rebirth the traditions which he has inherited from his fathers. Only when he has brought the treasure of the past to life again is he able to harmonize it with the demands of his own age. Among the disciplines which keep the heritage of civilization alive, literature is central. The renewal of the vigor of tradition through literature safeguards the continual death and rebirth of mankind as self-transcendence without loss of self-identity.

Whether ancient or modern, literary master-pieces are always marked by existential conflict and crisis. They symbolize the turning points of decisive change in the life of every man. A great drama or novel captures me, as reader, suspended between alternatives. I share the tension of characters confronted with the necessity for decisions which will orient their lives, to some degree, in irreversible directions. Freedom and choice are at the core of these existential crises. Stories and plays of less universal interest may arouse suspense through external calamity, but the catharsis of great literature always springs from the inner torment of death and possible rebirth. Sometimes internal is united with external crisis to form a harmonious whole. In many popular detective tales, so little of inner crisis is present that one could readily switch characters from story to story without altering the desired effect, which is precisely suspense. On the other hand, Flannery O'Connor's superb short story, "A Good Man Is Hard to Find," develops powerful inner crisis against the background of an external atmosphere which is completely matter-of-fact in its simplicity. Again, dramas like Chekhov's *The Cherry Orchard* and Eugene O'Neill's *Long Day's Journey into Night* blend internal and external crisis so harmoniously that the two become one in the response of the reader.

Though the death and resurrection crisis of literary characters is often larger than life, its tensions and conflicts are somehow familiar to me as reader.

I can identify with the crucial situations in which some men fail while others are reborn. The crisis of the literary character always presents a struggle between a positive and a negative pole. He must work through the conflict if he is to advance to the next stage of his life. He is offered a choice between love and isolation, courage and cowardice, creativity and conformity. Innumerable sets of alternatives are possible. But in each case it is clear to the reader that the subsequent life of the hero will be definitely changed by his option. One choice leads to growth, the other to decay; one fosters ascent, the other decline. In the falling action of the literary work, the author frequently pictures the concrete results of the decision of the protagonist.

Thus literature, as well as psychology, teaches me that life is marked by crises which all men experience to a greater or lesser degree. They may be sudden or gradual, depending on the temperament and life history of the person involved. Whether the experience is cataclysmic or slow-moving, there is always a critical period in which the ultimate decision to hold back or go forward must be made. Every important decision of my life implies a birth trauma of cutting myself free from a past in which I felt safely embedded like a foetus in the womb. Existential rebirth is exposure to the threats of the unknown. But the separation of rebirth is not passive. I must separate myself by a decision to accept my new mode of existence as a daring thrust into life. I must take the risk.

When I am present to moments of crisis in literature, I become aware that they often emerge when the meaning of a particular way of life has collapsed. The character experiences that he must retreat and begin again in a new direction; he must make way for a newly discovered dimension of his existence. The crisis is evoked by a demand for commitment, whether in love or in battle, and from it is born personal responsibility. The character may find himself in a period of unbearable stress. If he risks the unknown, he may discover a stability and serenity in which his world is transfigured in the light of his new commitment. To be sure, literature (like psychotherapy) also reveals the character who refuses the pain of transformation and clings to the false security of his past. Terrified by the uncertainty of new life, fearful of the collapse of his former self, he holds fast to old patterns of existence. Such a character suffers defeat because he will not risk exposure to death and rebirth. At best, his refusal of renewal can result only in compromise. At worst, he will experience existential guilt, for the invitation to self-transcendence can be repressed but not obliterated. Cardinal Wolsey, in Shakespeare's *Henry VIII*, is an excellent example of a character who clings to false security rather than risk transcendence. His famous soliloquy is the measure of his existential guilt:

> O, how wretched
> Is that poor man that hangs on princes' favours!
> There is, betwixt that smile we would aspire to,
> That sweet aspect of princes, and their ruin,
> More pangs and fears than wars or women have;
> And when he falls, he falls like Lucifer,
> Never to rise again.

On the other hand, the Archbishop of Canterbury, Thomas Becket, facing a similar situation in T. S. Eliot's *Murder in the Cathedral*, accepts the pain of personality transformation and dies in transcendent glory.

In great literature, powerfully demanding life situations precipitate the inner crisis which forces the protagonist to come to terms with his personal destiny. Existential crisis threatens his life itself, places at stake the very meaning which he gives to his existence. Such total threat lifts him from the routine of daily life to face in loneliness the unique decision which only he can make. Cut off from his former foundations, he confronts his future in creative freedom. His situation implies both the possibility of failure and the potentiality for rebirth through a bold decision to transform himself in response to the demands of reality.

The descriptions of personal crisis found in literature always highlight the conflict between two poles or centers of energy within the personality. Like psychology, literature points to this dual aspect of every human being. It is as if two incompatible forces are simultaneously active in the fictional character, each with its own perceptions, desires, and purposes. The protagonist seems to be a dialectic of opposites, a living polarity between freedom and determination, potency and actualization, emptiness and fulfillment. He is stretched between what he is and what he ought to be. Existential crisis emerges when a demanding new life situation actualizes this latent polarity which is rooted in the very structure of man's existence. In self-encounter, the character becomes aware of what reality demands of him. Precisely at this crucial point, he can either freely surrender or hold on to his past. Humility and renunciation are therefore necessary for effective resolution of the existential crisis. While the protagonist may perceive clearly the old way of life which he should abandon, he cannot be certain about the opposite pole of his conflict—the new life calling to him as a vague ideal shrouded by the unknown. Often the commitment which resolves the crisis, therefore, is not so much a stern willfulness as a gentle yielding to new life with its subtle revelation of inspiration for the future. Thus the character experiences a crisis of self-surrender which is the vital turning point in the process of death and rebirth, the either/or of his decision.

The fundamental polarity of human existence between what is and what ought to be, between lack and fulfillment, between determination and freedom, is not abnormal but rather the norm. Literature illuminates this normal experience to which every man is exposed because of his inescapable human structure. If indeed human existence itself is a crisis, and literature a re-creation of existence, then all great literature is an impressive expression of the crisis that life is. Literature takes us by the hand, as it were, and helps us to experience the darkness of descent into crisis followed by either fixation on darkness or the light of ascent to new life.

Explicitly or implicitly, great literature reveals that the only desirable resolution for the character in existential conflict is to detach himself from his past and transcend to a higher unity of personality. When the character succeeds in this solution, his restlessness is transformed into serene certitude, and he experiences new strength. Literature seldom dwells, however, on the period of regained equanimity and joyful fidelity to life. It centers on the conflict and crisis through which man becomes what he is. "And they lived happily ever after" is the capsule expression of joy after rebirth.

We may conclude that the most profound existential crises in literature have three phases: death, decision, rebirth. The death phase is one of frustration, anxiety, conflict. The phase of decision binds death to rebirth in the turning point of choice which is the transition to new life. The final phase of resurrection is one of transcendence, transformation, and reintegration. These three aspects, which may be found in either tragedy or comedy in the broadest meaning of these terms, are so profoundly intertwined that it is often difficult to perceive them as distinct in the actual situation presented by the novelist or playwright.

Literature reminds me that the life of every man is a concatenation of turning points in which he is faced with the question of the meaning of his existence and called upon to decide. When I am really present to literature, therefore, I turn from the distractions of my daily life to contemplate the meaning of my existence. Presence to literature is a recollection of myself in unifying inwardness; it is a transcendence of my daily life of sometimes chaotic multiplicity. I can perceive how even despair may be a gift which poses for a fictional character the choice between disintegration and integration of personality in the light of values to which he is called to commit himself. I also become aware that I myself am destined always to move toward new integration. If I accept myself as I truly am, my life becomes a permanent possibility of new crises and decisions. Characters in literature remind me that the development of my personality is not a performance to be achieved once and for all, but a project to be courageously reaffirmed in every new moment of choice. In my presence to literature, I may experience a movement from the superficiality of functional life to the depth of personal existence. Like the fictional character in crisis, I ask myself the fundamental question, "Who am I?" Doing so, I experience the call to transcendence that is at the core of my own being. At this moment of grace, I know that literature has granted me its most precious gift.

This gift is perhaps more to be prized in the contemporary world than ever before. I am in danger of losing spontaneity of life in the technological surroundings of my world. The functional society in which I live creates institutional organizations which protect me but which also tend to alienate me from my deepest inspirations. I need traditional systems to safeguard me, but I also need to revitalize them and to integrate them within my own personal life. Authentic life is a personalization of the wisdom of the past, a continual adaptation to both the old and the new treasures of human learning. As man in a functional society, however, I tend to experience this process of free, personal assimilation as slow, impractical, and ineffective. I am inclined to categorize living traditions in streamlined theoretical systems. Then I tend to adopt these systems as life guides. If I lack a living dialogue with the wisdom of the past, my life may become fragmented, estranged, alienated.

Consequently, if my life does not unfold in openness to living tradition, I am in greater need of the experience of personal death and rebirth. The inescapable demands of functional existence in my society may tend to paralyze the spontaneity of my personality. Temporary self-alienation may lead to a hardening of experience until finally I am separated from my deeper self. Herein is the essence of personal tragedy. I may even internalize functional systems in the form of a rigid superego which takes the place of my living existential conscience. Empty structure may thus replace living thought. If I desire to escape the benumbing systems which destroy my spontaneous experience, I must sacrifice functional security and accept the pain of death and rebirth. If I refuse to accept the invitation to transcendence, I am in danger of becoming a meaningless cipher in a lifeless structure. Without transformation of personality, I may suffer annihilation in the sense that I am emptied of my essential human qualities.

Many contemporary sociologists have written of the "mechanical man" whose functional life is that of an automaton. Books like David Riesman's *The Lonely Crowd* and Herbert Marshall McLuhan's *The Mechanical Bride* have lamented the alienation of man in our society. Moreover, modern plays like Elmer Rice's *The Adding Machine* and Karel Capek's *R.U.R.* have dramatized the plight of the "manufactured person," who is unbelievably efficient but devoid of sensibility and therefore easily seduced to brutality and violence. Indeed, the estrangement of contemporary man pervades the literature of two continents.

The pursuit of everyday occupations in contemporary society illustrates well the danger of functional existence without rebirth. My labor may either humanize or dehumanize my life. I may become a tool, a commodity, an instrument of impersonal production. A rebirth to a new meaning of my labor may not change the task I perform, but it can deeply change the meaning of labor in my life. Instead of a means of economic production, labor may become for me a means of growth, sacrifice, atonement, service to humanity, and creative expression of my unity with mankind. When my main concern is the product of my labor, it alienates me; when I care for the meaning of my work, it heals me and makes me whole.

Normally I become aware of the possible deadness of my life only when I am faced with a situation for which my functional systems provide no answer. Suffering introduces me to myself, to encounter with reality, and perhaps even to dialogue with the voices of human beings who existed before me. Here is the old story, the recurrent ritual of death and rebirth. If I desire to live and grow, I must suffer, I must renew my vitality in an act of sacrifice. I may have to renounce primitive impulses, status seeking, egocentrism. My offering symbolizes my willingness to renounce my past identity as a condition for my resurrection as a new person.

In Katherine Anne Porter's novel, *Ship of Fools*, a heterogeneous group of people who ordinarily live according to functional patterns are thrown together in the isolated closeness of life aboard ship. When their functional systems suddenly break down, they fall into an orgy of violence. They are quite incapable of transcendence. The situation in this novel may be contrasted to that of Guy Crouchback in Evelyn Waugh's novel, *The End of the Battle*. Crouchback discovers himself to be a part of a brutal, soulless society living by meaningless patterns of action. He redeems himself by a single act of complete unselfishness: he remarries his selfish former wife (whom he no longer loves) simply because she needs him. His sacrifice is a deed of pure self-transcendence.

The resurrection theme in literature mirrors what may happen over and over again in my own life. To be sure, my involvement in the crisis of a literary protagonist can only create in me an aesthetic, emotional purification, not an actual rebirth. I am able to bear and even to respond with aesthetic pleasure to the death and resurrection of the fictional hero because his crisis is transformed into art. The emotional experience of involvement in the conflicts of literary characters has a healing power, however, insofar as it helps me to involve myself positively in the painful change and transcendence to which all men are heir. Response to the work of art prepares me for the onset of existential crisis in my own life.

EXISTENTIAL CRISIS: NEGATIVE PHASE

EXISTENTIAL crisis, when it leads to personal fulfillment, is a sequence of psychological death, decision, and rebirth. But man may remain fixated in the negative stage of existential crisis. In this case, he fails to experience the positive phase of crisis, or rebirth. The negative stage often reveals itself in a total revulsion against the past. If the victim is weak in existential will, this revulsion may lead him to utter despair, suicide, or self-destruction through alcohol or drugs. Many persons undergo such a crisis without even being aware of the unconscious source of their agony. If the person is open to reality, he may gain a dynamic insight into his negation of life which opens up for him a totally new perspective for the future. Whether the crisis ends in hope or despair, his response to the negative phase of this decisive stage of his life determines the direction of his existential choice.

The term "existential crisis" as used here refers not to the ordinary crises of life but to those significant crucial situations which involve the very meaning of one's existence. Faced with personal tragedy or with a life-or-death situation, man may respond with either hope or despair. Despair refuses to affirm the possibility of transcendence in seemingly impossible situations. Hope, on the other hand, affirms the possibility of self-realization against tremendous odds. On the last frontier of the possible, it answers "yes" to life. The person who refuses to hope, who chooses despair, may regard his situation as absurd. He may choose either to reject life or to face, in estrangement and alienation, a reality which for him is meaningless. It should be noted that the man who freely decides for hope and the man who decides for despair both confront reality: neither one denies, represses, or attempts to escape the tragic reality of his situation. The person who chooses hope may transcend his tragic past and experience joyful rebirth, while the person who opts for despair either dies or remains fixated in a kind of death-in-life.

Both of these men are closer to authentic existence, however, than the person who rejects decision. The man who becomes fixated in negative existential crisis because he has not the courage to choose either hope or despair refuses to be present to himself in the profoundest depths of his being. He prefers complacency and security to confrontation with reality. Such a person will inevitably attempt to still his awareness of his fundamental restlessness and anxiety. Normally, however, his destiny is unbearable guilt. His rejection of his humanity demands its price.

Though the negative phase of existential crisis has certain common characteristics, the experience of it varies with each individual. The person suffering it may experience a painful "dark night" preliminary to decision and joyful transcendence; he may be caught up in terminal despair; or he may be fixated in negativism which rejects change. In ordinary life, moreover, the existential phases of death, decision, and rebirth are often so interlocked as to resist neat description. The same is true of the presentation of existential conflict in the characters of great novels and dramas.

In his novelette, *Heart of Darkness*, Joseph Conrad portrays the disintegration of the character of the famous Mr. Kurtz under the impact of his desire for power in a savage setting in darkest Africa in the mid-nineteenth century. At no stage in the story can the reader point out precisely the beginning of Kurtz's existential crisis nor the crucial moment of decision beyond which there is no possible return. His complete subjection to the demon in himself, however, is horribly present to the reader at the conclusion of the story.

Again, in Henry James' novel, *Portrait of a Lady*, Isabel Archer faces existential crisis, makes a false choice in real freedom, and then confronts herself in self-dialogue in which the necessity for repentance and suffering emerges. The exact point at which Isabel decides to accept reality as it presents itself to her is not clarified, but as the novel ends she is well on her way to redemption.

Whether or not the stages of personal struggle are clearly demarcated, however, the negative phase of existential crisis always has as its basis, in one form or another, a dissatisfaction with reality which finds its terminus in hopeful decision and transcendence, in desperate decision and failure, or in rejection of decision and fixation in negativity.

The crisis may be precipitated by a long-standing mode of life which is fundamentally a negation of reality. In terms of existential psychology, "negation of reality" has a special meaning. Obviously, it does not refer to reality in a superficial sense as related to the practical demands of everyday life or to the pragmatic pursuit of conformity to social patterns. What is expressed in the cliché, "hard cold reality," is merely one aspect of reality as conceived in a far deeper sense. Existential reality as used here is the revelation in a person's life situation of that which he is called to be according to his highest potentialities. In other words, being open to reality is being open to the richest possibilities within himself. To be realistic is to transcend the practical and pragmatic in order to respond to that which on the one hand surpasses the pragmatic and on the other justifies practical involvement in the world. For example, when a person is open to the challenge of love for others, he may be inspired by this inner appeal to embody his love in activities such as slum clearance, antipoverty projects, or civil rights movements. In the harmonious personality there is a profound consonance between faithfulness to the deeper meaning of reality and to its more practical, secondary aspects.

Indeed, much of the perennial appeal of a great characterization like Rostand's romantic Cyrano de Bergerac lies in the perfect consistency between his high ideals and his actual deeds of valor. Cyrano is the hero many men would like to be. On the other hand, in Willa Cather's complex character study, *A Lost Lady*, Mrs. Forrester is a finely sensitive woman, the vulgarity of whose external actions seems to contradict her inward response to reality. This very dichotomy in her character is perhaps the chief source of fascination to the reader.

Unfortunately, man is capable of splitting off his practical pursuits from his openness to the deeper ground of all his actions. Thus he may build for himself a career tremendously impressive to his fellow men while he actually becomes increasingly alien to reality in its profoundest sense. As a result, his life is impoverished; it becomes superficial, boring, and meaningless. However, his continual preoccupation with innumerable pragmatic tasks, plus the intoxicating wine of acclaim by those who admire his brilliant performance, may make it difficult for him to be even aware of his inward emptiness. The horrifying abyss of loneliness which faces him is so hard to bear, moreover, that the functional man unconsciously escapes every possible insight into his real situation. In terms of existential psychology, he incessantly represses the awareness of his own emptiness. His response to reality on a deeper level becomes increasingly negative. He *must* negate meaningful reality more and more because every acknowledgment of the actual meaning of his life threatens his repression, confronting him with the nothingness in which he lingers. Thus his life becomes a frantic pursuit of the superficial.

To be sure, it is impossible to make superficial activity itself a final goal in life. Consequently, the functional man sooner or later makes *himself* the ultimate purpose of his existence. All the love which he should have given to persons around him and to the mystery of being behind all things now reverts back to himself. He attempts to find meaning not only in the satisfaction of receiving homage from others, but in the feeling of dominance he experiences in manipulating others in such a way that they cannot appeal to him from the depth of their own reality. Encounter becomes impossible for him. Perhaps the most morbid manifestation of existential sickness is his so-called love-life, for his abortive attempts to love reveal only his impotence to love. His conquests are merely superficial assays at pleasure. For pleasure reaches only the surface of the other; love fathoms the mystery of the other. Perhaps this is why the Don Juan type of character is one of the most superficial in world literature.

Many people who lead empty lives die without ever knowing the depth of the meaninglessness of their pragmatic existence. Some, however, are impelled by the grace of a traumatic experience or a sudden flash of blinding insight to confront the failure of their lives. Such an existential crisis erupts most often in middle age. It is at once the heaviest blow and the most precious gift which the person has ever received. It shocks him into experiencing on a conscious level the incredible vacuum which his existence has been until this dramatic moment. As an initial result of this discovery, he no longer feels able to maintain his usual feverish activity which now seems devoid of meaning. The clamor of his admirers now sounds hollow. He feels repelled, moreover, by the cheap manifestations of erotic or sentimental love which formerly fascinated him. He may suffer a complete emotional let-down which causes paralysis of all his desires, energies, and ambitions. Revulsion against the past becomes total. He cannot even tolerate his own existence. In one word, he feels really burnt-out. Indeed, the best phrase that the psychotherapist can use to describe him when he comes for counsel during this negative phase of his existential crisis is Graham Greene's epigrammatic "burnt-out case."

When a person experiences this type of negative crisis, he usually reverses his existential transference of the past. If he formerly divinized himself, he now undergoes a demonizing transference in which he views himself not as a god but as the essence of evil. When one is in the stage of deifying transference, he makes gods of limited people and objects; when he is in the demonizing phase, he makes devils of those whom he previously idolized. Both forms of transference, to be sure, are based on fantasy. They do not reveal reality as it is, namely, as a limited but true manifestation of the goodness, truth, and beauty of Being. A person in the negative stage of crisis may perceive only the defects of others without even a glimmer of awareness of the limited or at least potential goodness present in every human being. His style of life, in short, does not comprehend the tempered wisdom and mellow judgment of a mind that has transcended both deifying and demonizing.

John Steinbeck's beautiful little exemplum, *The Pearl*, tells the story of the Mexican fisherman, Kino, who one day dives into the sea and finds an oyster which contains a priceless pearl. Kino immediately divinizes his possession, transferring all his hope for a full and happy life to his precious jewel. When he discovers that his pearl brings him only anguish and despair, he demonizes his former treasure and casts it back into the sea. Kino symbolizes all men who, in existential crisis, demonize what they once deified.

The immediate symptom of the most bitter negative crises is often an existential boredom so profound that the unauthentic person feels himself sinking into blank despair. He has actually come to the end of everything which up to the present moment has given meaning to his life. He has tasted to the full the nauseating emptiness of his own existence. His new insight changes, in turn, his evaluation of the lives of others. His judgment develops a quality of merciless "honesty." Psychologically, he is so wounded that he cannot bear even the joy of simple people who, to his way of thinking, are still immersed in the superficialities of existence, not having experienced the sickening triviality of much that is considered of the highest importance by the average bourgeois.

Undoubtedly, the number of burnt-out cases is bound to be high in a society which in fact prepares people for dominantly pragmatic lives. Contemporary society is, in a sense, one-dimensional. It concentrates on the functional dimension of reality and tends to neglect the implications of the mystery of life. As a result, many modern men, particularly those in the second half of their lives, become victims of the existential neurosis just described. Not many of

them go into psychotherapy. Most of them live out
the last half of their lives in "quiet desperation" or
unconscious self-torture; a certain number surrender
to despair and destroy themselves through direct or
indirect suicide; not many achieve a satisfactory solution of their crisis by working it through in their own
way.

These typical responses of "burnt-out cases"
to the existential crisis highlight the novels and
dramas of the mid-twentieth century. Jean-Baptiste
Clamence, of Camus' dramatic monologue, *The Fall*,
presumes at the end of the novel to live out his life in
the insolent despair of the "judge-penitent." Eugene
O'Neill's Tyrone family in *Long Day's Journey into
Night* choose slow suicide through alcohol and drugs.
In Arthur Miller's *After the Fall*, the tragic Maggie
ends her existential struggle by destroying her own
life. Old Mr. and Mrs. Rooney in Samuel Beckett's
All That Fall drag out a macabre existence which
exudes the decay of death-in-life. And Graham
Greene's burnt-out case, Querry, is on the road to
repentance and redemption when an ironic fate
harshly cuts off his new mode of life. All of these
characters live or die in a wasteland of despair which
reflects—at least for their creators—a strong segment of the contemporary human situation.

From a psychological point of view, all the
bitter and condemnatory responses of a person experiencing the negative period of existential crisis
cannot be accepted as objectively valid. They may be
considered as vivid expressions of the emptiness and
nothingness which the unfortunate person endures.
When the meaningfulness of life as a whole is no

longer experienced, all the real—though limited—
goodness of people, events, and objects in life loses
its luster. It is as if the central lighting system of a
city is struck by a tornado and all the lamps go out.
But if the central system recovers its power, all the
lamps light up again and radiate their limited, but
real brilliance. They break through the darkness of
the city like innumerable small gems. Something
analogous to this situation is observed when the
existential crisis is worked through successfully in
psychotherapy. The life of the client gains depth and
meaning. In the light of this meaning, he is now able
to see the relative significance and even beauty of
many people, events, and objects against the appalling
darkness of his former life.

Much contemporary literature, however, restricts itself to the experience of existential suffering
or the painful process of regaining the meaningfulness of life. The novel or drama frequently ends in
negativity or stops short before the protagonist is
able to re-evaluate his past in the light of his newly
achieved attitude toward his existence. In the literary
analyses of the later chapters of this book, for example, none of the modern existential crises discussed
presents the positive phase of resolution. One character closes the negative crisis with suicide, one with
indirect self-destruction, one with sardonic nihilism,
and one with an abortive struggle to find meaning in
life. Significantly, only Shakespeare's Renaissance
creation of the character of Angelo in *Measure for
Measure* works through the complete cycle of existential transference, negative crisis, and positive rebirth
culminating in redemption. But then, the resolution

of *Measure for Measure* seems "unrealistic" to many twentieth century readers! A positive solution of the human struggle does not often provide the matrix for the art of our time.

Innumerable aspects of the negative phase of crisis are found, however, in contemporary literature and psychology. One of the common accompaniments to existential negativity is the ironic attitude toward life. The significance of irony for existential psychology lies in its revelatory power. Irony as a mode of life may be good or bad, helpful or harmful, fostering of growth or inhibiting it. Depending on the existential situation, any of these opposites may be true. For example, the ironical approach to reality may be beneficial as a temporary means of devaluating persons or objects which have been over-valued or even deified in the past. Irony may function as a sledge hammer to destroy the false gods in one's life so that the true god may appear. Again, it may be a sharp instrument to pierce the veil of pretense shrouding unwelcome truth. Irony as a way of life is a means of de-masking reality. Although the breakdown of outward appearances may be revealed in ironical statements, verbal expression is not the essence of the ironic mode of existence. One may pursue an ironic evaluation of life without necessarily communicating to others his inner process of de-masking in order to uncover true values. To the person who lives the ironic style of life, the whole world may appear in the light of mockery. Great novelists and dramatists are masters of the creation not only of the ironical mind, but also of the world as observed by that mind.

Jonathan Swift created the incomparable

Gulliver and set him adrift in an upside-down world
of giants and midgets whose ironic distortions
nakedly revealed the social, political, and personal
repressions of eighteenth century man—and of universal man as well. A hundred candid cameras could
not have exposed so well the vagaries of neuroses.
Again, Moliere in seventeenth century France filled
his comedies with human types of exaggerated
neurotic fantasy. Moliere's audiences recognized
themselves in the mirror of his drama, but his mockery was so merciless that he produced enemies as
well as masterpieces. The great creators of literary
irony perform a curative function for society as a
whole, and particularly for the well-balanced individual. But the victim of negative existential crisis
is often too deeply wounded to benefit psychologically
from irony against himself. He must live through his
own ironic way of life.

In the negative phase of existential crisis,
then, irony may have a special meaning. It may help
the person to destroy the deifications of his past, such
as his existential transferences to himself or others,
and so to be free for authentic commitment to reality.
A danger is that the person may become fixated in
his state. In this case, the ironic way of existence
gradually becomes the center of his life style around
which all other modes of being are centered. His behavior becomes permanently bitter and negative. No
possibility appears for the breakthrough of a joyous
approach to reality. The person has learned to abdi-
cate the superficialities of life, but not to grow to a
daily celebration of the feast of existence in the light
of the truth of Being.

Varied manifestations of irony, both explicit and implicit, may be present throughout the entire negative phase of crisis. At the end of this stage, as the crucial moment of resolution approaches, a complex phenomenon is often observed. An understanding of aspects of reality which never reveal themselves in the life of irony, but only in the life of faith and commitment to the mystery of Being, begins to appear. At this point, irony is a light that illuminates reality insofar as the person who experiences it participates unknowingly and implicitly in commitment to Being, for irony enlightens only when it prepares the way for Being by destroying that which is non-Being. Indeed, all the superficial pursuits of which the "burnt-out case" has been the victim have concealed from him the radiance of Being itself. Therefore, Being reveals itself to him in his negative crisis only by making him aware of what it is not. In the discovery of what Being is not, appears a first glimpse of what it might be. In this sense, the ironic mode of life manifests indirectly—as through a glass darkly—the brilliance of Being. If irony were not a real and all-pervading aspect of the human situation, the ironic mode of existence could not reveal—as it does—so much of the truth of life. Nor would contemporary writers, confronting the complexity of a twentieth century world, use it as extensively as they do.

One becomes intensely aware, in reading representative ironic novels like Camus' *The Fall* and Greene's *A Burnt-Out Case*, that irony is the unique method for communicating the ambiguous and inexplicable attitudes toward the human condition

which their authors wish to project. Both stories close
on enigmatic situations couched in cryptic statements. Psychologically, the existential crises of
Jean-Baptiste Clamence and Querry in these two
novels are far from simple. Obscurity, their creators
imply, is at the core of the human struggle today.
And irony is its proper mode of expression. Such an
artistic approach often centers in negative crisis.

When we probe more deeply the psychological
phenomenon of the negative phase of existential
crisis, and attempt to understand why its victim is
often unable to transcend his despair, we inevitably
come to the history of his intersubjectivity. It is possible to transcend a meaningless existence only in
real encounter with others. Authentic love in all its
forms always means an opening up to the infinite, a
going beyond the changing appearances of the external world. Man becomes himself only through encounter, which is a transcendence of himself. No
wonder, then, that the problems of human love and
friendship play so important a role in existential
crisis. The core of the struggle is often revealed in
symbolic dreams, particularly at the beginning of the
working through of the existential neurosis. It is impossible to overcome the attitude that life is meaningless if one does not discover the mystery of the infinite in encounter with others. The frustration and
futility of such an attitude is like a night without
stars. Some are caught in this darkness permanently.
Their existence deteriorates into a sad sequence of
disappointment and bitterness: life is insipid, the
power for growth is paralyzed, nothing has meaning.
Others move toward the slow dawn of self-recogni-

tion, the hesitant passage through the maze of self-deception, the final acceptance of the real self in confrontation with reality.

When a person whose negative crisis is rooted in transference to his own ego begins the long journey out of the darkness of self-centeredness, his first glimpse of light is in incipient encounter with others. As he begins at last to doubt himself, to be aware of the irony of his self-idolization, he is ready to see others in a new perspective. To be sure, his painful awareness of his existential emptiness still implies a self-absorption which makes it almost impossible to encounter others in the fullness of their individuality. He sees them, not in themselves, but in relation to his own self-discovery. His new perception of others differs radically, however, from that of the past. In his phase of conceited self-sufficiency, he was able to approach others only insofar as they enhanced his pride. Now he sees their personalities as mirrors of both his own deficiencies and his true potentialities. Encounter with others now offers a possibility for confrontation with both the false and the true aspects of self.

The person who is moving toward authenticity has need of encounter, however, not only as an opportunity for self-dialogue. Even more, he needs to experience the other as one who grants him acceptance, respect, and understanding without demanding anything in return. If he is fortunate enough to find such generosity in a fellow human being at this particular moment in his existential crisis, he may be saved. He may be able to discover his self-identity which is weakly developed, covered over by thick layers of self-exalting fantasy, rigid defenses, and repressed feelings of guilt for his betrayal of life. In his former unauthentic existence, he was unable to actualize himself in response to reality. Instead, he substituted the approval of others for reality itself. It became crucial for him to appear good, important, or powerful in the eyes of others. While he may have been a "star" according to vulgar standards of success, he was a misfit in the realm of real values. Then he received the grace to distance himself, perhaps through ironic insight, from the counterfeit values which made him over-dependent on others. Now he needs the grace of encountering a loving person who will accept him unconditionally when he reveals his true self.

Literature, as well as clinical psychology, reveals over and over again the power for redemption which lies in the unrestricted acceptance of the other in loving encounter. Dostoyevsky's classic *Crime and Punishment* offers a superb example of a character who is healed through such encounter at the very moment that existential crisis has brought him to the boundary of utter despair. Raskolnikov, the murderer, has the rare good fortune to meet the girl Sonia, a loving person who accepts him unconditionally. After this encounter, his rebirth is secure. In Maxwell Anderson's romantic tragedy, *Winterset*, the young Mio Romagna is intent upon revenging his father's unjust execution. Mio's encounter with the young girl Miriamne, who falls in love with him, convinces him that his father would have forgiven his killers. But Mio is still determined to reveal the truth and thus precipitates his own death despite Miriamne's efforts to redeem him.

In loving encounter, the person advancing toward rebirth may dare to be himself for the first time—no matter how feeble and crippled this self may be. Only then he experiences himself, his true self, as openness to life itself. For the first time, he is able to make free decisions in confrontation with reality. He may be so overwhelmed by this new experience of freedom that he makes the wrong decision. He may temporarily decide for what is false. But what is important at this moment of his life is that the decision is actually his own. His openness to reality implies acceptance of the consequences of his false decisions. He will discover their undesirability in their real effects. With such awareness, he may experience existential remorse and the decision for change, when he realizes that he has betrayed the truth revealed to him in the openness of his existence. Thus he will accept responsibility toward reality. Responsibility means literally his *ability* to *respond* to what reveals itself in reality perception. Before his existential crisis, he was not capable of such response, for reality was veiled by his self-idolizing fantasy.

A person who divinizes himself cannot experience the core of existential regeneration which is true repentance. Self-deification implies the fantasy of creating reality rather than respectful response to reality, which is a gift and not a product. If a person attempts to create reality, he is his own standard. He need not repent his mistreatment of others, for they are simply objects in a world of his own making. But true openness to what is, including the realistic consequences of behavior, leads to the repentance and responsibility which are sources of authentic existence. Only in gradually expanding openness does the once unauthentic person discover redemption from his prison of isolated self-centeredness. He is at home at last in a world he never made. He is a gift and the world itself is a gift. From now on, he will experience life not as a problem to be solved but as a mystery to be lived in openness and love.

The final chapters of the present study analyze fictional characters who undergo existential crisis. Angelo in *Measure for Measure*, Querry in *A Burnt-Out Case*, Anna in *Anna Karenina*, John Marcher in *A Beast in the Jungle*, and Jean Baptiste in *The Fall*—all are seen first in the darkness of existential transference and then in the negative phase of existential crisis. All of these characters are prototypes of real human beings. Each of them reflects an aspect of human nature in conflict with reality. In all five cases except that of Anna Karenina, the existential transference is to the individual's own ego. Each character is strongly self-centered, thus precipitating a negative crisis. Anna's transference is to her lover, Vronsky, but even in her case—as she herself recognizes in the final hours of her life—the source of her transference is self-regarding passion. Self-centeredness is the core, in the ultimate analysis, of all destructive types of transference. Therefore the discussion of the present chapter has been concentrated on existential transference to the ego and the negative crisis it initiates.

If man's response to reality in the five literary works to be discussed is dark, the darkness is that of irony for the percipient reader. The truth of the human condition is often best revealed through the ironic penetration of darkness. The beauty of reality, of that which man is called to be, is commonly perceived only through a comprehension of what Being is not. The authentic man's entire life on earth is a slow process of becoming, of self-transcendence through regions of greater or lesser darkness. Being is revealed to man only through a glass darkly. But the light obscurely seen is the core of human joy. As reality is slowly revealed, the light of Being becomes more radiant.

EXISTENTIAL CRISIS:
POSITIVE PHASE

AT THE precise moment when despair seems unconquerable and life itself seems to be a monstrous absurdity, a person may experience a positive phase of
existential crisis which saves him from unbearable
emptiness and isolation. His redemption depends on
his positive existential choice of life over death, of
transcendence over stagnation. When we look back on
the negative phase of the crisis which preceded his
option for rebirth, we discover in it a prelude to his
rejection of a past which was no longer a response to
the challenge of his present life. Even the most painful aspects of his negative crisis are somehow different from those of the person whose crisis ends in rejection of transcendence.

The experience of the person who gravitates
toward hope may be compared with that of the protagonist of a great play or novel who moves through
anguished decision toward inevitable fulfillment. The

character experiences extreme anxiety as he feels
compelled by a free choice which will alter his future.
The turmoil of his mood gives form to the agonized
expression which reflects his inner conflict. Precipitated into the climax of existential crisis, he is overcome by hesitation because he feels that the radical
transformation demanded of him is a threat to his
very personality. His life itself seems to disintegrate.
In dialogue with himself, he is aware that his un-
questioned former life was somehow inadequate, an
affront to his authentic possibilities. The crucial situation which he faces now reveals him as aroused from
false slumber and forced to self-discovery. In the detachment of his unusual situation, he experiences
himself and his world as somehow strange, mysterious, and incomplete.

In the third act of Shakespeare's tragic *Richard
II*, when the young king at last becomes pathetically
aware that his enemies are about to depose him, he is
plunged into an anguish of self-discovery which
emerges in a completely new vision of his existence:

> O that I were as great
> As is my grief, or lesser than my name!
> Or that I could forget what I have been!
> Or not remember what I must be now! . . .
> What must the king do now? Must he submit?
> The king shall do it. Must he be depos'd?
> The king shall be contented: Must he lose
> The name of king? In God's name, let it go:
> I'll give my jewels, for a set of beads;
> My gorgeous palace, for a hermitage;
> My gay apparel, for an alms-man's gown;
> My figur'd goblets, for a dish of wood;
> My sceptre, for a palmer's walking staff;

My subjects, for a pair of carved saints;
And my large kingdom, for a little grave,
A little little grave, an obscure grave:—
Or I'll be buried in the king's highway,
Some way of common trade, where subjects' feet
May hourly trample on their sovereign's head:
For on my heart they tread, now whilst I live;
And, buried once, why not upon my head?

The reader who becomes involved in the experience of such a character transcends with him the commonplaces of his own everyday world. He may become suddenly aware of the limits of his own life, and his very awareness implies that he has already transcended those limits. He is one with his authentic self, oriented toward new possibilities in his personal life. To be sure, not all readers are emotionally able to experience such a conversion, even when absorbed in a great classic. They may not yet be sufficiently mature for this type of response. Or they may suffer from repressions and insecurities which render it impossible for them to experience a breakdown of their daily defenses. Again, certain types of people are able to be really present to crises in literature only after they have confronted their own personal demons.

The literary character moving toward transcendence is thus seen to suffer a sharp change from his ordinary life. His very separation from familiar experience demands transcendence. It leads, moreover, to loneliness, for the moment of personal decision is always one of isolation. The dramatic situation which calls for choice not only isolates the character from his former life but places this life—with all its deception and illusions—before his eyes with a strange new objectivity. He is lifted, as it were, to a lonely mountain top where he can observe his own existence from a distance, like a mountain climber who looks down upon his own village in the valley from a new, unfamiliar perspective. This fresh vision clears away the obscurity, pretense, and concealment which formerly made it impossible for him to really observe his own life. He becomes aware of superficialities and limitations; he realizes his potentiality for a different, richer existence.

Maxwell Anderson's historical tragedy, *Mary of Scotland*, presents the agonizing situation of the Scottish queen's choice between her duty to her kingdom and marriage to her lover. Bothwell appeals to her love for him as the glory of her life:

"My lady,
I will speak softly. Have no fear of me
Or what I intend. But there have been days I remember
When you had less care what hostages you gave
The world. I think you showed more royally then
Than now, for you loved then and spoke your love, and I
Moved more than mortal for that while. Oh, girl,
If we would be as the high gods, we must live
From within outward! Let the heavens rain fire
Or the earth mud. This is a muddy race
That breeds round us. Will you walk in fear of mud-slingers,
Or walk proudly, and take my hand?"

But the queen's answer reveals her in the tragic loneliness of her existential decision:

"No, for I think I've been
At the top of what I'll have, and all the rest
Is going down. It's as if a queen should stand
High up, at the head of a stair—I see this now

As in a dream—and she in her dream should step
From level to level downward, all this while knowing
She should mount and not descend—till at last she walks
An outcast in the courtyard—bayed at by dogs
That were her hunters—walks there in harsh morning
And the dream's done."

The reader, too, experiences with the character a disruption of his being-at-home in the everyday world. He becomes aware of the unimportance, irrelevancy, and even meaninglessness of many of his own daily concerns. He may feel real anxiety in the face of this revelation. While such anxiety is only one element in his aesthetic response to the work of art, it can be a terrifying experience if transferred to actual life. On the other hand, the reader senses that the crisis of the literary character is not only crushing but also elevating insofar as he experiences an openness to new possibilities of existence never before suspected. The reader shares the fascination of liberation for a new life.

In the examples of positive existential crisis quoted above, the two characters have reached the turning point of decision. The responses of both Shakespeare's Richard II and Anderson's Queen Mary to their situations free them to realize their potentialities. They are now called to take the leap of transcendence, to be uniquely and authentically themselves. If they do not do so, they will feel guilty not for what they have done but for what they are. Great literature often communicates the feeling that the protagonist feels guilty before life, feels indebted to powers beyond himself. It is as if he is brought to trial, forced to accept or reject the demands of life. He experiences that he must accept responsibility: he must make a response in conscience to what he is called to be. His answer is precisely the turning point from a perhaps unauthentic life of the past to the authentic existence of the unique person he is. His positive decision leads to rebirth or resurrection. The demand made upon Richard II and Mary of Scotland is to die courageously, to remain a king and a queen to the end. Both meet the challenge. Their actual death and their rebirth thus become one.

To be sure, the reborn hero in great literature often experiences resurrection to an actual life on a higher level of meaning. He is in essence the man who has achieved his personal identity. His existential decision has generated the integral unity of his personality. He has found his destiny, affirmed his heritage with all its inherent possibilities. He no longer lives in a multiplicity of fragmented incidents and isolated moments. He recalls the past and anticipates the future in terms of his new project of existence, and thus lives in full presence to each moment that he integrates within his personal destiny. Therefore he achieves a clarity of perception radically opposed to the psychological dispersion of his former unauthentic existence.

Great literature reveals somehow that this openness to reality is not merely an accomplishment of the protagonist; it is a gift to him. The reader feels wonder and awe before the mystery that reveals itself in the character, a mystery that transcends the hero himself, his author, and his audience. The reborn hero achieves joy, peace, and serenity because he has found his own identity. Such confidence differs radically from the complacency of the unauthentic man who has lulled himself into false security as a defense against self-discovery. The self-possession of the re-born character is the precise opposite of the self-satisfaction of the person who avoids confrontation with all that transcends dull conformity. Indeed, the new serenity of the hero is often in direct ratio to his ability to live with anxiety. He has dared to tear himself away from the familiar in order to confront the demands of real life.

The great contemporary French dramatist, Paul Claudel, dramatizes in his masterpiece, *The Satin Slipper*, the peace and serenity achieved by the heroine, Prouheze, who courageously renounces her lover Rodrigo in order to make the leap of transcendence which she believes life demands of her. Indeed, most of Claudel's plays, including the strangely beautiful *Tidings Brought to Mary* and the tragic *Hostages*, involve the reader in a subtle realization that his protagonists somehow receive existential re-birth as a mysterious gift.

After experiencing transcendence of reality as he once knew it, the reborn character may return to his daily surroundings with a new sense of reverence. He knows how to enter into dialogue with his life situation and to answer it constructively. He rejects blind conformity. He has experienced destruction of familiar attitudes during his existential crisis; now he renews his motivations in the light of his radically changed vision. His rebirth is often a transformation from the common viewpoints he shared with "the crowd" to personal attitudes of his own. To be sure, he does not reject the treasure of tradition. But, having found himself, he has found the source of creativity, which is a personal openness to the revelation of life.

The mythical "reborn hero" whom we have been considering has many counterparts in world literature. Goethe's Faust, for example, experiences his whole life as a sequence of death and rebirth, moving always toward higher transcendence. So do Cervantes' Don Quixote and Shakespeare's Henry V. However, the reborn hero is also, in a sense, a prototype of all men who experience rebirth after existential decision. Their number is legion; their experience is universal.

Great literature thus symbolizes the struggle of my own personality toward self-identity through the discovery and release of authentic potentialities which lie hidden within me. The recurrent crisis of death and rebirth in my personal life prevents my falling into a stereotyped pattern of social reactions; moreover, it revitalizes the soil of tradition in which my real identity is rooted. The existential crises about which I read in literature make me aware of my own struggle toward decision when a new way of being myself presents itself to me in my life situation. As a human being, I am an unique power of self-actualization within a structured world of tradition. I face the danger that structure may paralyze my spontaneous creative potentiality. If this happens, structure becomes equated with death, and the re-emergence of creativity with rebirth. I can find true self-fulfillment only through a continued dialogue between the structured world in which I move and my own personal potentiality.

Literature provides an incentive for my maintenance of this dialogue. Symbolizing humanity, the reborn hero of the drama or the novel is a projection of my unconscious desire to transcend and renew my structured world. He symbolizes that aspect of my personality which inspires me to overcome dead conformity; he personalizes my striving to actualize my creativity. I too am heroic insofar as I listen to the call of transcendence. The projection of myself into the hero helps me to realize my own desire for nobility, for somewhere I have an image of myself as hero. To be sure, this image is necessarily one-sided because even if I achieve nobility, I shall always do so within the commonplace setting of a daily life that is partially disintegrating and self-alienating. Pure heroism is impossible. The best I may hope for is that an aspect of nobility will develop in my life which will redeem me from self-estrangement within dead structures. Life always has an element of mediocrity, but the heroism of rebirth can save me from sheer mediocrity. An acceptance of everyday mediocrity is necessary for a normal self; complete mediocrity is incompatible with a free self. I can maintain my freedom by my willingness to undergo death and rebirth.

It would be false for me to identify the source of my possible self-alienation as completely in my environment and not in myself. Like every man, I am to some degree commonplace, selfish, corrupted. The unavoidable need for a structured world is, moreover, an estranging force for all men. The art of living demands that I affirm my need for structure and at the same time enrich it by actualizing new potentialities. When I do not accept this two-pronged challenge, I may either become the hardened victim of lifeless structures or rebel against my human condition in a foolish attempt to overreach myself. In the latter case, I arrogantly overleap the limits of my existence through a pride which strives to burst the bounds of human reality. I attempt to be pure hero; I repudiate the necessity of incarnation of my nobility in limited concrete situations.

Literature, especially classical tragedy, projects this desperate rebellion against the limits of life, which is called *hubris*. It reveals how the violation of the order of existence leads inevitably to destruction as a punishment for immoderation. The conflict of the literary hero who attempts to overreach the bounds of human freedom is, in a sense, a mirror of the existential predicament of mankind. Great drama makes us feel that the anguish of the protagonist in his abortive struggle with reality extends itself to life as a whole. The inevitable downfall of the overreaching hero brings the painful discovery that life itself is limited, that freedom is situated, that growth is bound by dialogue. Thus great drama has cosmic dimensions.

Maxwell Anderson's modern tragedy, *Night Over Taos*, dramatizes the struggle of an old Mexican chieftain, Pablo Montoya, against the democratic principles of the young American republic. In his excessive pride, he kills his own heir, Frederico, only to find his younger son, Felipe, hostile to his deeply rooted belief in monarchical government. When Pablo finally realizes that a new world is being born before his eyes, he destroys his own life. Just before he drinks poison, he speaks:

"Our race is done.
The Spanish blood runs thin. Spain has gone down,
And Taos, a little island of things that were,
Sinks among things that are. The north will win.
Taos is dead; you told me this before,
But I wouldn't believe it. I believe it now.
Yes, and it's right. It's right
Because what wins is right. It won't win forever.
The kings will come back, and they'll be right again
When they win again. Not now. The gods are weary
Of men who give orders, playing at God. And why
Should a man, an old man, looking forward to nothing,
Take pride in breaking men to his will? Meanwhile
The years creeping up at his feet, and all he has
Going down around him? And then to stand there,
alone,
Helpless . . . . an old man, playing at God."

Anderson's tragic hero represents puny man
beating his fists against a world he cannot control,
only to become pathetically aware in the end that he
is a sorry creature "playing at God." Because tragic
drama often presents an excessive heroic dimension
of personality, it necessarily has a certain quality of
unreality for the ordinary reader. I know deep within
myself that I shall never be an Oedipus, a Prometheus, an Ahab—or a Pablo Montoya. Nevertheless,
my identification with these heroes enlarges my
vision of my own possibilities for both transcendence
and immoderation. One of the strongest threats to
rebirth after existential crisis is immoderation.

The hero as rebel against lifeless tradition
suggests another powerful threat to wholesome rebirth. To be sure, the hero as rebel presents a magnifying mirror of my own praiseworthy attempt to
escape absorption in lifeless conformity. He demon-

strates that even actual death is preferable to dead tradition which stifles identity. He proves that to drink from the springs of living tradition, and thus to be reborn, requires an heroic gesture of separation from outworn custom and convention. However, by my very act of heroism, I run the risk of fixation on my gesture of separation. If my repudiation remains merely repudiation, I am condemned to a life of nihilism. To be sure, it may be necessary for me to isolate myself inwardly from conformity in order to protect my human spontaneity. But my rebellion against self-alienation may overreach itself in an exalted vision of an autonomous freedom which fails to recognize the bounds of situation and incarnation. When this happens, I contradict my very nature. I aspire to that imaginary freedom which is the ultimate deception of man. I am seduced to exchange one kind of alienation for a far more terrifying and monstrous kind—alienation from my fellowman, from the world, from life itself. To choose for absolute autonomy and freedom is to choose for a schizoid existence.

This type of schizoid alienation confronts me in the estrangement experienced by the anti-heroes of certain contemporary dramas and novels. The climax of the self-isolation of the protagonist is communicated in strange and erratic behavior. He experiences all authority as a threat to freedom and all fellowmen as possible authority. His striving for unbridled freedom necessarily implies an inability to love, for the self-surrender of love is impossible to the person who attempts to break all ties with others who might possibly limit his freedom. His conflicts present the subtle complication of human relationships that results from neurotic exaltation of the heroic stand. If I desire to avoid this ultimate type of alienation, I must die not only to lifeless convention but also to the exalted desire for a god-like, infinite freedom. Only such a death will prepare me for the resurrection to a life that is human—a life that is transcendent in its openness and spontaneity and at the same time submissive to the unescapable authority of my limited situation.

Dostoyevsky's darkly satiric work, *Notes from the Underground*, is a shattering autobiographical novel of the anti-hero who chooses to live in hostile alienation from his fellow men. The subtle perversities of his necessary human relationships are the background for the mounting horror of his pathological estrangement. Again, Camus' novel, *The Stranger*, presents the coldly erratic behavior of a schizoid character completely incapable of love. Sartre's *No Exit* is an emotionally suffocating dialogue of four characters who use their freedom for sadistic torture of one another. Because of their abuse of freedom, none of these characters is capable of rebirth.

In my rebirth after existential decision, then, I need to experience my self-transcendence freely without falling into a false fixation on unlimited freedom. Once having achieved transcendence, I must also avoid the danger of refusing the heroic dimension of my existence. If I do refuse, I shall experience existential guilt. If I attempt to be absolutely heroic, which is arrogance, I shall feel guilty; if I fail to be heroic in any way, which is cowardice, I shall feel even greater guilt. Once I have accepted my obligation to live an existence which is necessarily part heroism and part mediocrity, I must live out these two dimensions of my reality with some degree of serenity.

Contemporary literature offers innumerable examples of characters who experience existential guilt because they have failed to accept both the nobility and the mediocrity of their lives. Sometimes a massive accumulation of guilt in such characters leads to suicide, which the reader experiences as inevitable. Such self-destruction is a tragic and ill-advised attempt at atonement and sacrifice.

The pathetic Joe Keller in Arthur Miller's *All My Sons* refuses to accept the dimension of ordinary mediocrity in the lives of his sons and himself. He is guilty of gross inhumanity in his attempt to secure status for his family. When he is finally confronted with his crime and offered the possibility of repentance and redemption, he again refuses the dimension of heroism which would save him. Joe Keller ends his life in suicide. On the other hand, Henry James' great novel, *The Wings of the Dove*, offers a classic example of a character who experiences rebirth after surrendering to his worst demon and finally triumphs in accepting both the heroism and the mediocrity which his human situation demands. Merton Densher does not anticipate that his encounter with Milly Theale, "the dove," will redeem him from the awful duplicity of his crime against Milly. But Densher's scheme backfires and Milly becomes the unwitting agent of his rebirth. As the novel ends, Densher accepts the heroism demanded of him by not marrying the woman who has been his accomplice in deceiving Milly. He also accepts the inevitable mediocrity of his future life which is the price of his deceit. Responsibility for his own actions is inherent in his rebirth.

The positive existential crisis and its consequence of rebirth is, then, a call to heroism within human limits. It is possible to all men. It carries with it the built-in dangers of desire for unlimited freedom and refusal to accept the demands of transcendence. It confronts man with a paradoxical life of simultaneous nobility and mediocrity. It makes man aware of the "splendor of our angry dust." From the dust of the earth, man must reach for the stars. This is the truth of his existential situation.

PERSONALITY GROWTH
THROUGH LITERATURE

THE manner in which literature contributes to the transformation of my personality has deep psychological roots which deserve exploration. Literature is, in a sense, the story of the growth and transformation of my personality. It symbolizes in some way that I should die and be reborn continually. It awakens me to the necessity of death and resurrection and prepares me to receive this gift when it is offered to me.

It is obvious that I cannot personally realize the various modes of existence represented by the characters in the plays and novels which I read. In my daily life I cannot possibly be present to reality in all the roles which my literary heroes assume in their dialogue with the world. Yet I undoubtedly experience a feeling of liberation, of expansion, of inner catharsis when I participate vicariously in their lives. This experience of free participation has all the qualities of death and rebirth. When I am really in-

volved in a great drama or novel, I die to my daily
life and I feel temporarily reborn to a new way of life
expressed in the work of art. As I resume my ordinary
life after such an experience, I feel strengthened and
renewed.

Thus I experience in literature not only a
preparation for real rebirth in actual life, but also a
type of temporary aesthetic death and rebirth. In this
latter process, I am reborn not to a life that I shall
live in my daily surroundings, but to a life that might
have been mine if my background were different. My
feeling of expansion in human experience is not surprising, for my horizon widens indeed when I live
vicariously a great number of exciting lives. This experience is also one of liberation because my temporary absorption into a totally different existence
which I experience as my own frees me from the
limitations of my concrete historical and personal
situation.

One of the greatest of American poets, Emily
Dickinson, has captured this psychological truth of
liberation of spirit through literature in a brief poem:

> He ate and drank the precious words,
> His spirit grew robust;
> He knew no more that he was poor,
> Nor that his frame was dust.
>
> He danced along the dingy days,
> And this bequest of wings
> Was but a book. What liberty
> A loosened spirit brings!

In another of her concentrated lyrical expressions,
Dickinson communicates the startling thought that a

slender volume can bear the weight of the profoundest human experience:

> There is no frigate like a book,
>> To take us lands away,
> Nor any coursers like a page
>> Of prancing poetry.
>
> This traverse may the poorest take
>> Without oppress of toll;
> How frugal is the chariot
>> That bears a human soul!

My immersion through literature in possibilities of existence other than my own has a purifying or cathartic value insofar as these potential but unrealizable modes of life may be very much alive in my secret imaginations, desires, and dreams. Many hidden modes of existence may have a vitality all their own in the depths of my being. I may have repressed the awareness of these underground potentialities all my life with the result that they have grown unchecked within my unconscious fantasy life. Their concealment does not mean, however, that they are without influence on my experience and behavior. Such underlying, secret modes of existence have an intimate relationship to the life of which I am aware. I may even say that I live my existence in two dimensions; namely, a fantasy existence that consists of those wishful, possible modes of life which I cannot realize in actuality, and my daily life which comprehends the actual modes of presence to the world which I have accepted and affirmed as mine.

The contrast between the life of actuality and the life of fantasy has always been a rich subject for both humor and pathos in literature. James Thurber's classic short story, *The Secret Life of Walter Mitty*, is a tragic-comic portrait of a henpecked and ineffectual little man who pursues a fantasy life of heroic daring. Shakespeare's Malvolio in *Twelfth Night* is a handsome, dashing lover in his fantasy, but in actuality he is a simpering fool. For the detached observer, fantasy life often evokes laughter because of its incongruity with reality. A fantasy existence seldom seems ludicrous, however, to the person who experiences it.

For example, I may be daring and bold in my fantasy, while at the same time I may experience myself as shy, retiring, and insignificant in my everyday life. The greater the aggressiveness and audacity of my fantasy self, the more I shall feel guilty, depressed, and bitter about my smallness in my daily relationships. If I am not able to acknowledge the existence of my fantasy life, then I shall also be unable to recognize it as the secret source of my exaggerated anxiety and frustration when I experience the prosaic aspects of my real life. This unwholesome guilt feeling may drive me to devour exhortatory books about heroic, saintly, or glamorous personalities. When I read such books in this mood, they merely intensify my secret fantasy and therefore produce in my real life increasingly exaggerated feelings of shame and self-depreciation. Sooner or later, I shall project these unbearable guilt feelings to others in my environment, whom I shall make responsible for the fact that I cannot live out my exciting, wishful modes of life in my daily surroundings.

This example illustrates how my actual daily

life is in continual dialogue with my imaginary existence which affects it intimately. The possibly pernicious impact of my fantasy life would be less powerful and disturbing if I could make myself at home in my secret existence, could live through and explore my wishful potential modes of being without confusing them with my real life. Then I should not be tempted to gratify my fantasy in my actual dealings with my fellow man. I should no longer feel dejected and offended when people refused to treat me as a hero, a prince, or an oracle. I should not feel wounded if the behavior of my neighbor implied that he considered me less than a saint, a genius, or a superman. I cannot deny, of course, that it would be fascinating to live such remarkable lives. Yet I should realize that I cannot do so in reality, but only through a vicarious "as-if" existence.

Literature offers innumerable examples of the ill effects of the confusion of fantasy with reality in actual life. Tennessee Williams' memory play, *The Glass Menagerie*, presents a rich characterization of a woman who creates a fantasy life of rare gentility and then responds with anger and self-pity when the members of her family cannot enter into her unreal existence. Amanda Wingfield lives out her fantasy dominantly on an unconscious level. On the other hand, Sherwood Anderson's short story, *I'm a Fool*, is a delightful account of an adolescent boy who consciously creates his own fantasy world, only to discover that the reality he has attempted to destroy is his dearest desire. On a more serious level, F. Scott Fitzgerald's novel, *The Great Gatsby*, offers a study of a man who pursues a materialistic dream and lives it out on a highly artificial level, unaware of the essential vulgarity of his fantasy.

It is not harmful to live through unrealizable modes of existence on an imaginative level, so long as I experience them as *not* being possible in my actual daily life. Indeed, to divert myself with them fancifully may help me to come to terms with them, to be really conscious that they cannot be mine, granted the concrete limits of my unique personality. When I become deeply aware of the imaginative quality of my fantasies by living them through in my "as-if" existence, then they lose their secret hold and continual operation on my daily behavior. This awareness can lead me to an experience of catharsis, of purification from confused feelings of guilt, ambition, and painful uneasiness which are initiated by unrealizable desires existent only in pre-reflective or unconscious fantasy.

In other words, a wholesome life implies the continual interaction of actual existence, fantasy existence, and "as-if" existence. The latter is a necessary bridge between my daily life and my fantasy life. It purifies my emotions insofar as my life of feeling is disrupted by my secret ambitions and repressed passions. My "as-if" life may liberate me from enslavement to hidden modes of existence by granting me the gift to recognize them for what they truly are when I embody them in imaginative experience which I fully acknowledge as such.

It is precisely in the creation of this "as-if" life of mine that great literature is matchless. My tastes in literature may be richly revealing of my secret fantasies. If I am unconsciously ambitious, I may be strangely fascinated by Shakespeare's *Macbeth* or *Richard III*; if I am secretly proud and vain, by *King Lear* or *Coriolanus*; if I am naively jealous, by *Othello*; if I cherish hidden desires for grandeur and magnificence, by *Henry V*. I may feel a profound intimacy with certain works of literature because they reflect my unconscious demon back to me as through a mirror. When I am not afraid to view myself in this mirror, literature is a precious gift to me. This is not to say that every demonic character in literature whom I appreciate reflects a similar demonic quality in myself. It is merely to say that literary tastes often reveal the self.

Since I am dove as well as demon, however, my strong attraction to particular literary works may also reveal the more desirable fantasies hidden within my deepest self. My reverence for human dignity may be reflected by my involvement in Hawthorne's *The Scarlet Letter*; my unconscious desire for natural benevolence in Fielding's *Tom Jones*; my idealization of love in Bronte's *Wuthering Heights*; my admiration of simple courage in Faulkner's *The Mansion*.

In my "as-if" world of literature a variety of potential selves can come to birth and be lived through vicariously. Literature is truly an "as-if" world, for I experience the imaginative situations evoked by the novel or the drama as real and yet different from daily reality; they are a sublimated reality in which I can live through my hidden, unrealizable modes of existence *as if* they were real, while fully aware at another level of my existence that they are *not* real in the sense of my daily reality, and that I do

not affirm them willingly and consciously as mine in
my project of life. My rebirth to a variety of selves in
my "as-if" existence during my absorption in literature helps to liberate me for actual rebirth and self-
realization in everyday life. Moreover, my real life
will be less poisoned by my hidden wishes and passions that have found clarification in my "as-if"
existence. Paradoxically, the wholesome development of my conscious "as-if" existence leads to
sound realism in my daily life, while its underde-
velopment enslaves my daily life to unconscious
fantasy. This fact may explain why certain rationalistic personalities who have neglected the development of an "as-if" existence sometimes suddenly surprise us with an unreasonable stubbornness or other
behavior which seems totally out of keeping with
their style of life. For example, amazingly precipitate
sexual aberrations in rigidly logical persons may
sometimes be attributed to the absence of a wholesome "as-if" existence.

In the tragic Spanish play, *The House of Bernarda Alba*, Garcia Lorca creates a violent dramatization of the emotional eruption of a family of women
domineered by a rigid, unyielding, resolute matri-
arch. The passionate outbursts of the daughters of
the family, and the ultimate suicide of one of them,
are the inevitable climax of a situation arising from
Bernarda Alba's neurotic tyranny. Suicide is also the
tragic conclusion to an unbearable emotional tension
in the powerful naturalistic drama, *Miss Julie*, by the
Scandinavian playwright, August Strindberg. Miss
Julie's headlong plunge into dissolute passion is also
caused by an inflexible situation created by a neurotic

mother. Again, Edith Wharton's classic American novel, *Ethan Frome*, captures the emotional violence which suddenly explodes in a seemingly quiet atmosphere when there is no normal outlet for strong tensions. In this story, a maimed existence rather than death by self-destruction provides the catastrophe. In all of these dramatizations of powerful human responses to inhuman tensions, the awareness on the part of the characters of their real psychological situations differs greatly. The same may be said of awareness in real life experience.

Certain potential modes of existence are very much alive in the depths of my personality while others are not. To understand this, I need to consider the structure of my personality. It is a more or less integrated whole of various modes of existence which I live and am. These form a unity insofar as they are permeated by my fundamental motivations or lasting value commitments. Such basic motivations manifest themselves in each of my modes of life and render them interdependent and continuous. As already explained, my personality expands and differentiates itself through repeated rebirth to successively new ways of existence. One significant meaning of this continual rebirth is that I grow increasingly toward freedom and insight. Each new rebirth liberates me from my past, from the deterministic influences of my childhood, not by destroying them but by transcending them. Crucial human situations, which may be presented to me in my actual life or vicariously through literature, help me to become aware of infantile and other past modes of existence which interfere with my free personality development here

and now. I may be confronted by both life and literature with challenging new situations which question
me and my former existence. They may awaken me
to the sudden insight that my discarded past still
retains a strong hold on my present. I may be invited
to grapple with unintegrated and fragmented modes
of existence which I lived long ago, and which my
present situation now invites me to transcend.

In other words, my being questioned by life
or literature may be the precious beginning of a
regenerative crisis which enlightens me about my
enslavement to deterministic, quasi-autonomous
modes of life that prevent the full development of my
unique personality in the present. At such moments
I become sensitively aware that certain of my responses to life relate to what I should be, to my
uniqueness, to my personal plan for the future. At the
same time, I experience other more or less concealed
modes of existence as alien to my authentic self;
moreover, I become painfully aware that these foreign
modes within me possess their own dynamic core of
drive and motivation. I realize that they influence
and modify my behavior. I feel somehow responsible
for them because I experience them as mine.

But I experience these alien, discarded modes
of life as mine in a different sense than I experience
my affirmed modes of living as mine. For one thing,
I do not consciously and willingly identify myself
with these alien reactions; I do not ratify them in my
actual daily life. While I cannot avoid acknowledging
them as part of my personal history, I nevertheless
experience them as ways of living which intrude upon
me, which are more the product of my past than of my

freedom. However, I am ashamed of them in a sense, and I feel guilty about their presence. I feel them to be profoundly at odds with my self-project and still somehow mine. This is why I refuse to live them out in my daily life. Their source was in my early years: they embody primitive, pre-reflective attitudes which I once adopted toward reality, toward the people around me, toward my father or mother, brothers or sisters. Perhaps I indulged feelings of omnipotence, of rivalry, of hate, jealousy, slavish dependency, or strong sexual desire. As I grew older, I was reborn again and again to many other attitudes which were more realistic, mature, and harmonious with my authentic development. But somehow those primitive, discarded modes of life survived in the hidden depths of my personality, to live there a life of their own. I am sometimes startled to find that those attitudes which I rejected in former rebirths still permeate in an intimate, subtle manner the new modes of life to which I have been reborn. The new modes together with the old, in constant dialogue with the old, make up the personality which I am at this moment. It is as if my rebirths were unable to relinquish my former personality. The primitive modes seem to have a dynamism and autonomy of their own.

Some of the most powerful stories in world literature are built upon the theme of primitive modes of existence which come to conscious life in the characters and incite unbearable conflict. Jacinto Benavente's great tragedy, *The Passion Flower*, dramatizes the stark pity of a girl's passionate but unconscious love for her stepfather and its primitive childhood sources. On a different level of experience,

Eugene O'Neill's famous psychological drama, *Strange Interlude*, presents Nina Leeds' unresolved primordial relationship with her father, which precipitates conflict in the lives of all those with whom she is intimately concerned. O'Neill's Freudian interpretation of the tragic effects of unconscious primitive motivations also pervades his great trilogy, *Mourning Becomes Electra*. Lavinia Mannon, moved by forces which she only partly comprehends, drives her entire family to headlong destruction in this modern version of the Greek tragedy of Electra and her brother Orestes.

To be sure, I am not likely to find myself in a situation similar to that of Benavente's Acacia or O'Neill's Lavinia. But I carry within me unconscious and discarded modes of life which retain a certain power of their own. In my daily functional life, when I am involved in my duties, I may be unaware of these other selves in me. But when I relax my functional control, as in my free enjoyment of literature, then I feel these repressed modes of life emerging in me, blending themselves with the experiences of the characters in the drama or novel in which I am involved. I do not experience the lives of these characters as strange or alien, but as if they were my own. Absorbed in the literary work, I experience myself as the multiple personality which, in a certain sense, I am. The hidden dynamisms of my repressed or forgotten modes of existence seem to come to life in my vital presence to the imaginary personalities with whom I am confronted. In identifying myself with these characters, I become aware of responses in myself which originated long ago and which have not been evaluated and integrated within the whole of my personality. The creative writer has incarnated these attitudes toward life in his play or novel, enabling me to grasp them, as it were, and to live them through. I become aware of what I might have been; I discover myself in the possibilities of other lives. I recapture what the possible unfolding of my own existence would have been if I had actually affirmed modes of life which I rejected at some point in the development of my personality.

Drama and novel thus reveal to me an elaboration of modes of life which are in some sense really mine. They are not merely fiction; they are also real life, my life. Great literature helps me to live out creatively my own secret modes of existence so that they are raised to a level of awareness where I can feel and understand them. Literature introduces me into that "as-if" world which is so necessary to me if I hope to come to terms with my hidden self. The vicarious living of imaginatively created lives is essential for the integration of my personality. For what else is integration but a living through of all my past and present modes of existence in such depth that I can merge them in an uniquely rich and deep self? In the functional and technical society in which I live, not many approaches remain to assist me in living through these modes of experience. Involvement in literature is one of the few means left to me for this vital adventure. Literature helps me to become aware of and to resolve the conflicts which exist among my various conscious and repressed modes of existence. Because my past modes of life have a constant impact on my life in the present, the dynamic conflicts and tensions represented by literature illuminate both my past and my present problems. Therefore, I may experience the conflict of the literary character as strangely, yet intimately, related to my own conflicts.

Literature enables me to emerge in diverse times, places, and situations in which I live different lives while still remaining myself as reader or spectator. The characters in literature remain mere structures of sentences on paper if I do not live their lives for them. By becoming a plurality of persons, I am able to breathe life into printed chapters in books. Doing so, I become aware of how infinitely rich I am in potential modes of existence. In reading literature, I become soldier, sinner, saint, child, father, mother, hero, and lover. Literary experience is thus a very real part of my most intimate existence.

My involvement in literature, moreover, is not only a confrontation with my past and present modes of life; it is a preparation for my future. It helps me, in a sense, to experiment with future modes of existence which are compatible with my project of life. I enjoy a vicarious experience which emerges in self-exploration that is also exploration of my possible future. When I am immersed in a play or novel, I can live out fantasies about my future possibilities of existence while at the same time I work through, existentially and creatively, past modes of life which I have never confronted before in their dynamic impact on my life. Participation in literature is thus a significant way of learning by experience, by vicarious experience. Therefore it is most important that this confrontation happen through the medium of great literature, which is bound by artistic universals that preclude the wild or neurotic living out of fantasy as a positive theme. Cheap literature never leads to growth and real self-insight; it may provide a fast, painless gratification; it does not require the effort to grow mentally and emotionally demanded by deeply human conflicts and crises.

One may question why it is that certain masterpieces of literature appeal to people universally and help them to work through their repressed modes of existence. Is not the past life of every individual unique? In a sense, the answer is yes; in another sense, no. All human beings are exposed to certain fundamental situations which are given to us with our human nature. For example, one of the ways in which man is different from the animal is that he requires a long period of education within the family before he is able to venture out on his own initiative. Thus every child is faced with the necessity of taking an existential stand toward his parents, two adults who are far more powerful than he and on whom he is fully dependent for bodily and emotional survival. There are only a limited number of attitudes which he can adopt, each one of which will lead to the emergence of certain modes of existence, implying their own possible tensions and problems. Great literature presents in dramatic language these basic human responses, their inherent conflicts, their potential resolutions. While it is true that every individual lives these fundamental modes of life in his own way, it is also true that he somehow shares with all men these basic attitudes on which every child was once obligated to take a stand. Therefore, he is able to identify with the universal conflicts represented in great literature, and yet to do so in his own unique way.

The dynamic theme of a great play or novel mobilizes the repressed dramas of childhood. Long forgotten feelings, perceptions, imaginations, and actions are re-awakened in the reader or spectator. It is as if he recognizes in an obscure way a conflict of his own; he therefore feels deeply involved. He recaptures a vague and forgotten crisis of childhood and later crises which it precipitated. He becomes dimly aware of discarded modes of life in a faraway past that he does not consciously remember. He realizes in a subterranean way the impact of these modes on his present life. In a sense, his varied modes of existence unite in the crucial present moment of his full response to literature. Past modes of life now become open aspects of experience, as represented in the drama or novel, and enable the person to respond again to long-forgotten experience, but now with all the power of his adult insight and freedom.

Psychological analysis of the primordial sources of human conflicts common to all men thus clarifies the perennial appeal of certain great themes in literature to men of all eras. For example, one of the fundamental themes which has always called forth a powerful response from men of all countries is that of the unhappy lovers who, in the consummation of their love, violate their loyalty to a third person. In his fourteenth century epic, *The Divine Comedy*, Dante recorded the sad story of Paolo and Francesca, punished in the *Inferno* for their great but tragic love. The offended third character was Paolo's brother and Francesca's husband, Giancotto. Since the time of Dante, the story has been retold over and over again in world literature. The Belgian dramatist, Maurice Maeterlinck, created a symbolic tragedy in French on Dante's theme. He called it *Pelleas and Melisande*, and it became the source of Claude Debussy's famous opera of the same name. George Henry Boker, nineteenth century American poet, recreated Dante's theme in a romantic tragedy in blank verse which he called *Francesca da Rimini*. Gabriele D'Annunzio, probably the greatest of modern Italian dramatists, used the story of the unhappy lovers for his best-known play, *Francesca da Rimini*. Again, the English playwright, Stephen Phillips, projected his own interpretation of the drama of the sorrowful lovers in his early twentieth century production of *Paolo and Francesca*. This love story, first recorded in great literature by Dante, appeals to all of us because it involves us in a human situation which we understand experientially in the depths of our being.

Great literature thus offers me an "as-if" world within which I may explore and reintegrate the plurality of modes of existence which form me as a personality. I am a plurality in unity. The same may be said of literature. Both the human personality and literature represent the multiplicity of possible modes of human existence. Literature is essential for the discovery of that part of reality which cannot be explored by non-literary or scientific language. Orientation to reality is openness not only to a physical view of the external world, but also to a dramatic view of the world of inner life. Literature helps us to be at home in the humanizing aspect of reality.

PART TWO

PERSONALITY IN LITERATURE

ANGELO IN SHAKESPEARE'S
MEASURE FOR MEASURE

JUST AS literature, perhaps more than any of the arts, has continually thrown new light on the study of psychology, so psychology during the past twenty years has opened up new approaches to the interpretation of literature. To certain literary scholars, some of these approaches have been both unwelcome and highly suspect. For example, E. F. Sharpe's Freudian interpretation of King Lear's madness as a reflection of traumatic experience of Shakespeare himself has been branded by Professor Kenneth Muir as "wildly improbable." [1] Similarly, Professor I. A. Shapiro has cast a cold eye on Harold Grier McCurdy's *The Personality of Shakespeare: A Venture in Psychological*

1. Ella Freeman Sharpe, *Collected Papers on Psycho-Analysis*, 1950. See Kenneth Muir, *Proceedings of the Leeds Philosophical and Literary Society*, 1952. Quoted in Muir, "Madness in King Lear," *Shakespeare Survey*, *13* (Cambridge: The University Press, 1960), p. 30.

Method.[2] On the other hand, Ernest Jones' psycho-analytical study of Hamlet was well received by a number of responsible scholars long ago and stimulated Sir Laurence Olivier's challenging, if controversial, stage production of the great tragedy.[3] Again, Karl Jung's theories of the collective unconscious and of archetypes have been welcomed by many literary critics as opening up new avenues to artistic interpretation,[4] while others have found Jung's theories at best superfluous to an understanding of literature.[5] In spite of all specific objections to psychological interpretations of poetry, fiction, and drama, however, the literary world by and large has accepted the psychologist as a contributor to the explication of literature on the level of understanding personality in depth. It should be noted, however, that many literary scholars welcome psychological interpretation so long as it does not concern the author. Fresh analyses of the character of Hamlet are challenging, but attempts at psychoanalysis of a long-dead Shakespeare are often considered to be taboo!

One avenue of approach to psychological analysis of literature which is comparatively untouched is the utilization of the findings and insights

2. Harold Grier McCurdy, *The Personality of Shakespeare: A Venture in Psychological Method* (New Haven: Yale University Press, 1953). See I. A. Shapiro, "The Year's Contribution to Shakespearean Study," *Shakespeare Survey*, 8 (Cambridge: The University Press, 1955), pp. 148-49.

3. Ernest Jones, *Hamlet and Oedipus* (New York: Doubleday Co., 1949).

4. See, for example, Maud Bodkin, *Archetypal Patterns in Poetry* (London: Oxford University Press, 1934).

5. See Victor Hamm, *Patterns in Literary Criticism* (Milwaukee: Bruce Publishing Company, 1960), pp. 137-140.

of contemporary existential psychology. To be sure, many articles on existential *philosophy* in literature have been published; most of these have tended to emphasize certain aspects of specific existential philosophies.[6] An almost virgin area for literary analysis, however, is awaiting scholars who will use insights developed by existential psychologists. While some of their discoveries have been inspired by concepts of existential philosophers, their meaning has been altered and developed under the impact of psychological experience, analysis, and practice. Contemporary existential psychologists are using such insights currently and testing them in empirical, applied, and clinical psychology. When these theories are confirmed by actual psychological practice, they provide an approach to literature from a new level of understanding which may help to clarify dilemmas of meaning which occur on aesthetic or moral levels. To be sure, such psychological constructs should be discarded by the critic when they throw no new light on the literary work under analysis.

It is the purpose of this chapter to demonstrate how the existential psychological construct of authentic will may provide a basis for a new understanding of the development of character in one of Shakespeare's plays. The character of Angelo in *Measure for Measure* has been chosen for existential psychological analysis. First, we shall comment briefly on the existential psychological approach to

6. See, for example, Gordon E. Bigelow, "A Primer of Existentialism," *College English*, XXIII (1961), 171-78; Alexander Gelley, "Staiger, Heidegger, and the Task of Criticism," *Modern Language Quarterly*, XXIII (1962), 195-216.

literature in general and on the problems of *Measure for Measure* in particular.

EXISTENTIAL PSYCHOLOGICAL APPROACH

The existential vision of reality is a multi-vision. The existential psychologist is strongly aware that it is impossible for man to comprehend at once the whole of reality. He is also aware that it is impossible for man, the subject, to exist as separate from the world: this is the central hypothetical construct of existential psychology. As man exists in the world, therefore, he participates at one time in one part of reality; at another time, in another part. The existentially oriented literary critic, as a subject existing in the world, can never comprehend at once *all* the possible implications of meaning in a literary classic. But he can examine and interpret the root meaning—the irreducible core of meaning—of a poem, a novel, or a drama. In so doing he can throw light on the partial visions of a literary work already revealed by those critics who have approached it from more peripheral angles of vision. The existential critic cannot accept, therefore, the approach of the "one-vision" critic—the one who insists, for example, that there can be no Freudian meaning in Hamlet's character simply because Hamlet is "the hero of a Renaissance revenge tragedy and only that." Provided the two interpretations are not mutually exclusive, the existential critic sees no conflict between two meanings, both of which can be validly explicated. Indeed, many valid meanings may be comprehended at once in the multi-vision of the existential-psychological approach to a literary work. And all of these may be given some unity and clarity by the critic who attempts to uncover the irreducible core of meaning of the work of literary art.

Of all the plays of Shakespeare, perhaps *Measure for Measure*, variously classified as tragedy, tragicomedy, comedy, and "dark comedy," has posed the most complex problems of interpretation for contemporary critics. In some cases, controversy over the play has been based on only apparent contradictions, that is, on two or more angles of vision which can exist side by side as two parts of the multi-vision of the reality that is the play. In other cases, the critical debate is based on actually contradictory ideas.

In those criticisms which hold to what has been called the "Christian interpretation" of *Measure for Measure*, we find approaches to the meaning of the play which, while differing, are not essentially contrary to one another. G. Wilson Knight believes that the central theme of the drama is taken from the Lord's prayer: "Forgive us our debts as we forgive our debtors." [7] To R. W. Chambers, the theme is "Judge not; for what measure ye mete it shall be measured to you again." [8] In the major character of the Duke, Roy Battenhouse sees a Christ figure whom he relates to the Incarnation, the Second Coming, and the Judgment of Our Lord. [9] E. M. Pope believes that

7. G. Wilson Knight, *The Wheel of Fire* (London: Oxford University Press, 1930), pp. 80-106.

8. R. W. Chambers, *Man's Unconquerable Mind* (London: Jonathan Cape, 1939), pp. 277-310.

9. Roy W. Battenhouse, "*Measure for Measure* and the Christian Doctrine of Atonement," *PMLA*, LXI (1946), 1029-1059. A more recent evaluation which reinforces Battenhouse's view is John W. Dickinson's "Renaissance Equity and *Measure for Measure*," *Shakespeare Quarterly*, XIII (1962), 287-297.

Measure for Measure simply reveals the ordinary Christian doctrines of Renaissance England as related to rulership and justice.[10] S. L. Bethell, using a "multi-conscious" approach to the play, states that the reader should be at once aware of the Duke as human on a literal plane and as divine on an anagogical plane.[11] The view of Nevill Coghill is that the drama is religious in basis, belonging to the central medieval convention of comedy.[12] Now, it is clear that these varied viewpoints are not, in essence, mutually exclusive. One may agree in varying measure with all of these interpretations at once and still maintain a unified approach to the drama.

On the other hand, what are we to say of approaches to the play which are in more or less direct contradiction to these so-called "Christian interpretations"? Dover Wilson, advocate of the "dark interpretation" of *Measure for Measure*, sees its theme as the discovery of base, odious, or foolish motives in all the characters, developed in a satirical manner such as that of Huxley's *Point Counter Point*.[13] Cole-

10. E. M. Pope, "The Renaissance Background of *Measure for Measure*," *Shakespeare Survey*, 2 (Cambridge: The University Press, 1949), pp. 66–82. For a more recent evaluation of *Measure for Measure* as related to Renaissance law and equity, see Wilbur Dunkel's "Law and Equity in *Measure for Measure*," *Shakespeare Quarterly*, XIII (1962), 275-285.

11. S. L. Bethell, *Shakespeare and the Popular Dramatic Tradition* (North Carolina: Duke University Press, 1944), *passim*.

12. Nevill Coghill, "Comic Form in *Measure for Measure*," *Shakespeare Survey*, 8 (Cambridge: The University Press, 1955), pp. 14-27. For further discussion of the play as comedy, see C. L. Barber, *Shakespeare's Festive Comedy* (Princeton, 1957); Russell Brown, *Shakespeare and His Comedies* (London, 1957); and Harold S. Wilson, "Action and Symbolism in *Measure for Measure*," *Shakespeare Quarterly*, IV (1953), 375-384.

13. J. Dover Wilson, *The Essential Shakespeare* (Cambridge: The University Press, 1937), p. 117.

ridge considered the play disgusting in its comedy.[14] The great Shakespearean scholar, A. C. Bradley, saw it as scandalous in its moral conclusions.[15] Clifford Leech finds Shakespeare's Duke to be not at all a Christ figure, but rather a character lacking in "common decency and kindness" whose actions affront the reader by their "impertinence." [16] Moreover, he states that the "Christian coloring" of the play is only intermittent, that it "wells up from Shakespeare's unconscious inheritance," and that it does not determine the characteristic tone of the drama. Obviously, the views of Wilson, Coleridge, Bradley, and Leech are not mutually exclusive. They can, to some degree at least, exist side by side with equanimity.

We have here, to be sure, two contradictory multi-visions: a cluster of differing but not contrary approaches which may loosely be called the "Christian interpretation," and a syndrome of various but not mutually exclusive approaches which may be named the "dark interpretation." Scholars have expressed in diverse ways their consternation at what seems to be an immovable block to their mutual understanding of the play. E. M. Pope, for example, has lamented that when critics are not staggered or repelled by the ethical suppositions upon which the characters in *Measure for Measure* act, they attempt to justify and explain the play on the opposing ground

14. T. M. Royson, ed., *Coleridge's Shakespearean Criticism* (New York: Dutton and Co., 1960), I, 102.
15. A. C. Bradley, *Shakespearean Tragedy* (New York: MacMillan Company, 1929), Lecture II.
16. Clifford Leech, "The Meaning of *Measure for Measure*," *Shakespeare Survey*, 3 (Cambridge: The University Press, 1950), pp. 66-73.

that its morality is specifically Christian.[17] Clifford Leech, after examining the seemingly inexplicable contradictions of the critics, declared sensibly that the "meaning" of the play cannot be stated in terms of a simple thesis.[18] "Secondary meanings" are to be taken into account, he said, and these may largely determine the impact of the drama. Finally, the distinguished Shakespearean scholar, L. C. Knights, after pondering the "disturbing effect" of *Measure for Measure*, suggested that the difficulty of interpretation lay in Shakespeare's own moral ambiguity in handling his characters.[19] Knights proposes that Shakespeare's obscurity may have been due to temporary "emotional bias." A more recent response to the problem is a serious examination of Elizabethan marriage-contracts, the intricacy of which is believed to account at least partially for otherwise inexplainable moral attitudes on the part of the characters in *Measure for Measure*.[20]

Even our brief and over-simplified summary of the difficulties involved in literary analysis of *Measure for Measure* points to the fact that the central problem for the majority of critics is one of meaning. The actions of the characters in the play have moral implications colored with profound ambiguity. Existential psychological analysis of the key character of Angelo in *Measure for Measure* may throw new light

17. Pope, *op. cit.*, p. 66.
18. Leech, *op. cit.*, p. 72.
19. L. C. Knights, "The Ambiguity of *Measure for Measure*," *Scrutiny*, X (1942), 225-228.
20. Ernest Schanzer, "The Marriage Contracts in *Measure for Measure*," *Shakespeare Survey*, *13* (Cambridge: The University Press, 1960), pp. 81-89.

on this central problem. Such light may help to provide a satisfactory answer to the question of whether the play should be viewed as a "Christian" comedy with a "felix culpa" theme,[21] as a "dark" comedy which may better be called tragic satire, or as a type of drama perhaps more complex than either of these.

EXISTENTIAL VIEW OF AUTHENTIC WILL

The existential psychologist is always concerned with the observable behavior of people. Existential psychological constructs, when tested and interpreted by clinical and theoretical psychologists, provide frames of reference for the data of human behavior. As suggested above, they may also be used to throw new light on fictional or dramatic characters by critics who have some understanding of existential psychology. A brief explanation of the existential construct of authentic will may clarify the use of the psychological construct as a framework for analysis of the character of Angelo in *Measure for Measure*.[22]

Man discloses his true nature by his participation in reality. From an existential point of view, one may say that man actualizes himself only when he participates spontaneously in reality as it reveals itself in his own personality and in his daily situation. If he attempts to take a vantage point outside of himself from which he strives to control all that happens in his life, he becomes a compulsive and withdrawn "outsider." But by owning his spontaneous "lived"

---

21. Coghill, *op. cit.*, p. 27.
22. See Adrian van Kaam, "Clinical Implications of Heidegger's Concepts of Will, Decision, and Responsibility," *Review of Existential Psychology and Psychiatry*, I (1961), 205-216.

experiences, he becomes aware that human life is necessarily "ex-sistence" and involvement. Then reality posits itself as a challenge to which he can respond in a variety of ways. The basic condition for such a response is an authentic openness to reality which does not repress any awareness which announces itself in his lived experience. The man who refuses to be open to reality is unethical; the man who cannot be open to reality is more or less neurotic or, at worst, psychotic. At times, man may be both unethical and neurotic. One may question, however, whether a violent segregationist, for example, is sufficiently open to the deeper meanings of reality to be aware of the unethical aspects of his prejudice. Is he perhaps so estranged from his authentic self that he *cannot* deviate from the pattern imposed on his functional self by a prejudiced collectivity? Man is authentic to the degree that he opens himself to reality; he is unauthentic to the degree that, consciously or unconsciously, he closes himself to his own lived experiences. Man's fundamental option, then, is to open or to close himself to reality.

The first psychological characteristic of the authentic person is to be open spontaneously to reality. This openness develops man's sensitivity to the differentiated manifestations of reality within himself and his environment. He experiences, for example, particular feelings of joy, anger, sadness, hostility, or enthusiasm which correspond with the aspects of reality in which he is involved. His will leads him to respond to these feelings in a variety of ways. The person of unauthentic will, on the other hand, is not tuned in spontaneously to reality. He represses the awareness of his "lived" experiences. He may feel anger, hostility, or pleasure without being aware of it. His will is for him a "thing" that controls his life without respect to his own immediate reactions and their subtle complexities. This "thing" may even lead him to attempt the impossible: to manipulate his relationship to reality in a quasi-scientific way. Thus his natural energy is drained in compulsive action precluding spontaneous openness. Or, worse yet, he may attempt in a schizoid way to distinguish between his functional self and a "higher" self whose duty it is to force, repress, and manipulate all his bodily space and time relationships with his environment.

The second psychological characteristic of authenticity is insight. The term "insight" as used here does *not* mean a cool, scientific, rationalistic approach to reality. It means a perception of reality evoked by a fundamental openness to what-is, and it includes taking a "stand" toward the uncovered reality. Psychologically, such understanding is fostered only by commitment to reality without repression. It can never be achieved through a reasoning process alone. It can never be imposed on one who is not open to it. The person who achieves such understanding in a thorough-going manner is a responsible, complete individual. He unveils reality without attempting to re-create it in his own image. He continually discovers who he is, and he is fundamentally ready to make decisions which arise from the core of his own being, not so-called "decisions" which are imposed on him from outside.

The third psychological characteristic of the authentic human being is dialogue. On a psychologi-

cal level, the authentic person is engaged in a never-
ending dialogue with the reality which he uncovers.
By means of this dialogue, he listens to the multi-
farious manifestations of reality and is able to respond
in differentiated judgments, choices, and actions. His
functional (or secondary) willing is a natural out-
growth of this dialogue with reality. For the unauthentic person, on the other hand, the functional will
becomes dominant over the primordial will. Such a
person is in danger of a schizoid split in his personality. Less and less able to respond spontaneously and
intuitively to reality, he becomes more and more inclined to conform blindly to whatever collectivity
governs his functional will. In certain cases, this split
may lead to a sudden "explosion" in the unauthentic
functional will. The isolated real self may then reveal
itself indirectly to the bewildered environment in the
"nervous breakdown" of a person who up to now has
"functioned" so marvelously. On the other hand, the
real self may sometimes happily emerge, in such a
crisis, as an authentic personality.

The existential psychological construct of authentic will as openness to reality, with its three
dominant characteristics of spontaniety, insight, and
dialogue, provides a practical framework for close
observation of the character of Angelo in Shakespeare's *Measure for Measure.*

AUTHENTICITY   AND   UNAUTHENTICITY

The very opening scene of *Measure for Measure* presents Angelo the Deputy as a man of outstand-
ing external "virtue," in the words of Duke Vin-
centio:

> Angelo,
> There is a kind of character in thy life
> That to the observer doth thy history
> Fully unfold. . . .

The Duke continues with praise of Angelo's goodness so exalted as to be almost suspect. Two scenes later, the probable irony of the Duke's statement is confirmed when he confides to Friar Thomas his doubts that Angelo is what he *seems* to be:

> Lord Angelo is precise,
> Stands at guard with envy, scarce confesses
> That his blood flows, or that his appetite
> Is more to bread than stone; hence shall we see,
> If power change purpose, what our seemers be.

The word "seemers" is especially to be noted as the basis of the Duke's proposed test of Angelo's virtue. It is a key word to the interpretation of Angelo's character, and its meaning is expanded as the drama unfolds.

In the very next scene, when Lucio pleads with Isabella to beg mercy of Angelo who has condemned her brother Claudio to death, we find another description of Angelo's character which reinforces the reputation already attributed to him by the Duke. Lucio, no doubt, is only echoing the general impression of Angelo's character held by the populace of Vienna:

> . . . . a man whose blood
> Is very snow-broth, one who never feels
> The wanton stings and motions of the sense. . . .

Now, a man who "scarce confesses that his blood
flows" and "whose blood is very snow-broth" is a
man who has repressed his natural human responses
to the point that he is unaware of his own feelings.
The Duke and Lucio thus corroborate each other's
judgment of the Deputy. Shortly thereafter Angelo
himself unwittingly confirms and enlarges upon the
characterization of himself already reported. When
the ancient lord, Escalus, questions him as to whether
he himself has never erred in the sin of the flesh for
which he now condemns Claudio, Angelo responds
with prophetic arrogance:

> 'Tis one thing to be tempted, Escalus,
> Another thing to fall. . . .
> When I, that censure him, do so offend,
> Let mine own judgment pattern out my death,
> And nothing come in partial. Sir, he must die.

It is over-simplification to state that Angelo lacks
self-knowledge. Indeed, he believes that his unauthentic self, which is closed to the reality of his own
propensity to evil, is his true self. With sharp irony,
Shakespeare allows Angelo to declare in the very
same speech, but in a different context:

> . . . . what we do not see
> We tread upon, and never think of it.

Angelo is blind to the reality of his own being, but he
is about to uncover inadvertently a shocking actuality.
For he is just at the threshold of his encounter with
Isabella.

When Isabella comes into Angelo's presence,
she immediately reveals that, unlike Angelo, she is

engaged in an authentic dialogue with reality. She declares with magnificent clarity:

> There is a vice that most I do abhor,
> And most desire should meet the blow of justice;
> For which I would not plead, but that I must;
> For which I must not plead, but that I am
> At war twixt will and will not.

Isabella has a decision to make: she must plead for mercy for the perpetrator of an act which she detests, or condone strict justice for the criminal and thus consent to her brother's death. Her considered (and also intuitive) response is to choose mercy, and she does not hesitate once her choice is made. Feeling that Angelo, who holds the power of judgment, must of necessity engage his will in a similar dialogue with reality, Isabella fails to understand his unwillingness even to consider her plea for mercy. His blunt "I will not do't" puzzles her. And so she approaches him a second time:

> But can you, if you would?

Angelo's reply is purely functional, indicating a refusal to involve himself in actual dialogue or debate:

> Look, what I will not, that I cannot do.

But Isabella refuses to be answered so arbitrarily. Challenging Angelo a third time, she proposes to him an action grounded on more than a purely rational, machine-like decision:

> But might you do't, and do the world no wrong,
> If so your heart were touch'd with that remorse
> As mine is to him.

Isabella is frankly suggesting to Angelo that if he
engage in dialogue with his actual situation, he may
arrive at a justifiable decision that is more than a perfunctory exercise of "law" and "justice." But Angelo's mind remains closed. He replies stubbornly:

> He's sentenc'd; 'tis too late.

Now, urged on by Lucio, Isabella attempts for the
fourth time to break down the barrier Angelo has
placed between himself and reality. She demands:

> How would you be,
> If He, which is the top of judgment, should
> But judge you as you are?

Still Angelo maintains his perfunctory self-righteousness. For him, there is only one rational, "objective"
approach to the situation. He answers:

> It is the law, not I condemn your brother.

Claudio is sentenced, as it were, by a machine-like
law which "judges" all cases according to prescript;
Angelo himself is a thing-like functionary who de-
crees the law.

Isabella now becomes desperate in her frustration. Angelo's very immovability moves her to
passionate eloquence. Caught up in her emotion, her
own intuitive response leads her directly to an unerr-
ing diagnosis of Angelo's unauthenticity. She cries
out:

> . . . . man, proud man,
> Dress'd in a little brief authority,

> Most ignorant of what he's most assur'd,—
> His glassy essence—like an angry ape,
> Plays such fantastic tricks before high heaven
> As makes the angels weep. . . .

Angelo's most profound ignorance, she perceives clearly, is of his own "glassy essence," his unauthentic self, brittle as glass, and apt to crash to bits about him. Isabella is subtly aware that even a tiny opening to reality may break down the facade of Angelo's unauthentic, functional will and expose his real, repressed will to a true understanding of what-is. And her passionate outburst is prefatory to just such a climactic breakdown. For, only a few minutes later, Angelo exhibits the first intimation of openness in his encounter with Isabella. Continuing her impassioned plea, she declares:

> . . . . go to your bosom,
> Knock there, and ask your heart what it doth know
> That's like my brother's fault: if it confess
> A natural guiltiness such as is his,
> Let it not sound a thought upon your tongue
> Against my brother's life.

And Angelo suddenly begins to feel himself drawn physically to Isabella—he of the "snow-broth blood" who has never been lured by woman. He is astounded. "She speaks," he says aside to himself, "and 'tis such sense that my sense breeds with it."

Entering into an experience that he has never known before, a response to reality that shakes him to the core of his being, Angelo quickly dismisses Isabella, telling her to return the next day. Only when she has left him does he face openly the shattering im-

pact of what has just happened to him. With no
warning, the "glassy essence" of his functional, unauthentic self has cracked, leaving him face to face with
his true self. Unlike the Angelo of the interview with
Isabella, who answered in curt, laconic words, he
enters now into authentic understanding expressed in
interior dialogue. Shakespeare allows him twenty-
five superb lines of soliloquy in which the reader
observes the emergence of the true Angelo. He first
declares amazement that modesty in woman can en-
snare man's senses "more than wantonness ever
could." Then he is even more amazed that he, Angelo, should feel sensual desire for her who has only
now come freshly from her convent. From a somewhat detached sense of astonishment, he passes
quickly to complete involvement in his immediate
reality, and his existential dialogue begins. Interestingly enough, Shakespeare overtly indicates this
interior dialogue by letting Angelo address himself
by name. More than this, Angelo asks himself the
very question that existential discovery universally
calls forth in man:

What dost thou, or what art thou, Angelo?

And the new voice of the authentic Angelo now pleads
with his unauthentic self:

O, let her brother live!

Then, in the chaos of his discovery of himself, Angelo
again falls to marveling that he is so enamored of
Isabella. He does not rationalize; he knows his desire
for precisely what it is. But Angelo's authentic will,

like his unauthentic will, is proud. His want of humility exposes him with sharp irony as he addresses
himself to Satan:

> O cunning enemy, that, to catch a saint,
> With saints dost bait thy hook!

If the reader has been doubtful of the outcome of the
dialogue, he now clearly foresees Angelo's imminent
fall in his attribution of sainthood to himself. The
humility briefly born in the phrase, "O, let her
brother live," now dies, and Angelo's commitment
to evil follows inevitably:

> Dost thou desire her foully for those things
> That make her good? . . . Most dangerous
> Is that temptation that doth goad us on
> To sin in loving virtue: never could the strumpet,
> With all her double vigour, art and nature,
> Once stir my temper; but this virtuous maid
> Subdues me quite. Ever till now,
> When men were fond, I smil'd and wonder'd how.

Thus the unauthentic, functional will of Angelo is
broken down by encounter with Isabella, and all the
repressed passion of his nature is brought to the surface to be deliberately pursued.

Two scenes later, Shakespeare allows Angelo
a second revealing soliloquy. His interior dialogue
continues. Discovering his real self for the first time,
and knowing no self-discipline except the former
false discipline of his unauthentic will, Angelo finds
himself seemingly powerless before his uncurbed passion. He attempts to pray, but recognizes that his
prayers are "empty words," mere functional and ster-

eotyped mouthings, while his "invention" or real thought "anchors on Isabella." The "holy" thoughts which he formerly imagined he loved are now grown "sere and tedious." Facing truth with intense clarity, he now declares himself ready to exchange the "gravity" he has cherished for "an idle plume, which the air beats for vain." Caught up at last in spontaneous response, he breaks into a passionate apostrophe:

> O place, O form,
> How often dost thou with thy case, thy habit,
> Wrench awe from fools and tie the wiser souls
> To thy false seeming!

Using the same epithet of "seeming" first attributed to him by the Duke at the beginning of the drama, Angelo is completely aware that his own "false seeming" or unauthentic self has deceived wise and foolish alike, and most of all himself. Casting aside all defense, he now cries out at the climax of his soliloquy:

> Blood, thou art blood!

The simple depth of the statement catches up boldly both the irony of his self-discovery and the unauthenticity of his "snow-broth blood." Angelo now openly accepts the reality of his guilt. And he adds, with pointed self-mockery:

> Let's write 'good angel' on the devil's horn;
> 'Tis not the devil's crest.

His own name was once as fitting an appellation for the false Angelo as "snow-broth blood," but now the awakened man knows that for him, as for all men, "blood is blood." No man is an angel; propensity to sin is common to all.

In his second interview with Isabella, the real Angelo reveals himself as the clever seducer. To the observer who may have mistaken the earlier Angelo for an authentic personality, he is now shockingly different from the pompous, grave fellow who judged himself incapable of Claudio's sin. With wonderful art, he approaches and retreats, and again approaches and retreats in his calculated onslaught against Isabella. With characteristic irony, Shakespeare lets Angelo center his final appeal to her in the weakness of human nature. The simple truth that should have pardoned Claudio is now a bait for seduction:

> We are all frail.

But Isabella is now as immovable to his pleas as he once was to her pleas for mercy. When at last, in plainest language, he demands her body in exchange for her brother's life, Shakespeare again centralizes the theme of Angelo's unauthenticity of character, as expressed earlier by the Duke and by Angelo himself, in the epithet, "seeming." Driven to distraction by his apparent hypocrisy, Isabella cries out:

> Ha! little honor to be much believ'd,
> And most pernicious purpose! Seeming, seeming!

"Seeming" here has a double-entendre for Angelo: his first "seeming" was the unconscious falsehood of his unauthentic self; his "seeming" now is the hypocrisy of his authentic self. But Angelo is now comparatively calm under Isabella's flaying accusations. He has faced the potentiality for evil in himself, he has deliberately chosen to pursue it, and he knows it.

Thus, as Act II ends, Shakespeare has worked a complete psychological change in Angelo. He has brought him to self-revelation, to existential discovery of himself. Shakespeare now has little more to say of Angelo. He does not appear at all in Act III and not again until the end of Act IV. Here Angelo speaks little, except to indicate his descent into greater depths of evil in violating his promise to save Claudio's life. Shakespeare allows him one more soliloquy, but now the dialogue is between Angelo's authentic will and the evil in human nature. He contemplates in himself the ease with which man, having once fallen, sinks more and more deeply into sin:

> Alack, when once our grace we have forgot,
> Nothing goes right; we would, and we would not.

With the expression "would" and "would not," the scene closes ironically with almost the identical words of Isabella in her first statement to Angelo in Act I:

>   I am
> At war 'twixt will and will not.

Both Isabella and Angelo have engaged in authentic existential struggle, but for the time being, the "will" has triumphed in one, the "will not" in the other.

In the final Act of the drama, when Angelo's wickedness is at last exposed, he breaks down completely and, full of remorse, begs for the punishment he deserves. Here he is pathetically true to his earlier boast that he would censure himself for Claudio's sin if he himself were guilty of it. Angelo makes no plea for mercy, recognizing only too well that he has shown none and deserves none. He is a man who has sinned and is sorry for it. What is essential to note here is that there can be no "sudden conversion" or self-recognition on Angelo's part in this final act. His authentic self-discovery has already occurred in Act II: the sudden "explosion" of his unauthentic will initiated by his encounter with Isabella, when his "glassy essence" cracked, has already revealed him to himself. In short, Angelo's repentance in Act V must be taken at face value or it has no meaning at all.

Shakespeare has often puzzled critics because of the apparent injustice of the pity and mercy he permits Isabella and the Duke to grant to Angelo at the close of the drama.[23] Yet such mercy, as revealed by existential psychological analysis of Angelo's character, is appropriate (even aside from both the matter of equity and the Christian coloring of the play). When Isabella pleads with the Duke for Angelo's life, she goes straight to the heart of the matter with her usual intuitive rightness:

> I partly think
> A due sincerity governed his deeds,
> Till he did look on me: since it is so,
> Let him not die.

Isabella claims only "sincerity," no other virtue, for the earlier, unauthentic Angelo. And her claim is valid. Angelo is not a tragic hero like Macbeth, fall-

23. See, for example, Bradley, *op. cit.*, Lecture II.

ing because of a tragic flaw in his armor. Nor is he a cunning villain like Iago, plotting evil from the very beginning of the drama. He is a man who has never known himself as an authentic human being until his encounter with Isabella. It is an existential truth that man becomes himself only in true encounter with his fellow man. It is doubtful that Angelo has ever encountered another human being in depth until his meeting with Isabella. Then he becomes an authentic man for the first time, unlearned and unschooled in acting as a man. The Duke, as a God-figure, has put his virtue to the test. Overwhelmed by his entirely new situation, Angelo first discovers himself and then falls. In due time, he repents sincerely, seeking no mercy even after Isabella pleads for him. When the ancient Lord Escalus expresses sorrow at Angelo's fall from grace, he answers:

> I am sorry that such sorrow I procure;
> And so deep sticks it in my penitent heart
> That I crave death more willingly than mercy.
> 'Tis my deserving, and I do entreat it.

Both the unconscious and the conscious "seeming" are now ended. Angelo is no villain: his story is one of pathos, not tragedy; he deserves mercy, not death.

And this is precisely why Shakespeare's happy ending should not be the puzzle to critics that it sometimes has been.[24] As the character of Angelo is developed psychologically, death as punishment for him would have been completely lacking in inevitability. Conversely, the happy ending for Angelo and all

24. *Ibid.*

concerned, brought about by the Duke who watches
so carefully over all, is precisely appropriate. Moreover, no one in the play has suffered permanent injury
or death because of Angelo's fall; a tragic ending,
therefore, would have lacked probability.

Aside from the happy ending, it has also been
objected that Shakespeare pursues tragedy for the
first two Acts of *Measure for Measure*, and then, with
more or less artistic invalidity, pursues comedy for
the last half of the drama.[25] Yet Shakespeare's treat-
ment of Angelo's character demands a grave and
serious tone during the first two Acts, even though
the play is a comedy. Angelo's existential discovery
of himself is precisely central to the first two Acts of
the play. They close with his magnificent self-recognition. If it be objected that self-discovery occurs
much later in Shakespeare's tragedies, such as *Othello*
and *Lear*, one can only answer that in *Measure for
Measure* Shakespeare was not writing tragedy. If it be
objected that in comedy, too, the recognition scene
should occur later in the drama, one can only answer
that it is dangerous to impose patterns on genius.[26]
Recognition had to occur sufficiently early in the
drama to allow Angelo time for his subsequent sin
and repentance. If Angelo had not discovered himself
until the final Act, tragedy would have been inevitable. After the first two Acts, incident and situation,

25. E. M. W. Tillyard, in *Shakespeare's Problem Plays*
(Toronto, 1949), discerns an abrupt change of tone and technique
half-way through the play. See John Russell Brown, "The Interpretation of Shakespeare's Comedies," *Shakespeare Survey*, 8 (Cambridge:
The University Press, 1955), p. 12. See also Murray Kreiger,
"*Measure for Measure* and Elizabethan Comedy," *PMLA*, LVI
(1951), 775-84.

26. See Leech, *op. cit.*, pp. 66-67.

as determined largely by the Duke, are important in the further complication and denouement of the plot. No further revelation of Angelo is necessary until his final repentance. And the tone of the developing situation is rightly one of comedy, not tragedy, since mercy and reconciliation are the appropriate culmination of the plot. The cycle of false will, authentic will, moral fall, and repentance is now completed in Angelo. As the play closes, he is a complete human being who has experienced both psychological fulfillment and moral regeneration. In terms of our earlier analysis, Angelo has undergone death, existential crisis, and rebirth.

EXISTENTIAL RESOLUTION OF THE PROBLEM

It is the thesis of this Chapter that Angelo, in Shakespeare's *Measure for Measure*, is at the beginning of the drama a character of unauthentic will who is closed to reality, and that his existential encounter with Isabella suddenly breaks down his resistance to reality, exposing his authentic self. From the existential psychological point of view, Angelo as the play opens is not unethical: he is a man who is incapable of openness to his lived experience. And to the degree that he lacks openness, he is neurotic. Therefore it is surely inadequate to describe him—as has often been done—simply as a virtuous, though vain, untried, and overly-precise man, who is suddenly overcome by irresistible temptation and plunged more and more deeply into evil. If Angelo were only this, he would be merely a "well known type of dra matic character." [27] And we should be hard put to account for the depth of interest his character has aroused, particularly in contemporary readers who are dissatisfied with so facile an analysis of a personality so complex. Angelo's repressions lend themselves well to Freudian analysis, to be sure, but the latter explains not at all his sudden change from a man closed to reality to one open to his lived experience and willing to assume full moral responsibility for his authentic decisions. The existential psychological construct of authentic will throws a clear light on Angelo's self-discovery and sudden moral fall—a complex character development which unfortunately has been seen too often in only one dimension as the further fall from grace of an already proud man. In a sense, Angelo never lived as a real person until the "explosion" of his unauthentic will in his encounter with Isabella. His fall is his first act as an authentic human being. And he gains both maturity and moral regeneration in his repentance after his more or less "felix culpa."

As we have said, the existential approach to literature is a multi-vision. It is now clear that the "Christian" interpretation of *Measure for Measure*, which approaches the play as a comedy in the medieval tradition with the Duke as Providential Father and the "felix culpa" theme as central, is a partial vision of the core of meaning of the drama. Existential psychological analysis of the character of Angelo

27. See Thomas Marc Parrott, *Shakespeare: Twenty-three Plays and the Sonnets* (New York: Charles Scribner's Sons, 1953), p. 592.

reveals that the "felix culpa" theme is only one aspect—a secondary aspect—of a drama centered in the development of a rich and complex character. On the other hand, the "dark" interpretation of the drama, while it is understandable and illuminating as a protest against a "Christian" interpretation which leaves so many central moral questions go shockingly unanswered, cannot be accepted in its misunderstanding of the central spirit of Shakespeare's play. It inevitably results in a reading of Angelo's character as despicable in the extreme.[28] Both the "Christian" and the "dark" interpretations err in their over-emphasis of the moral problem of the drama. Existential analysis reveals that a central theme of the play is Angelo's discovery of his self-identity through a breakdown of his unauthentic functional will and his consequent acceptance of reality. Reality brings with it his conscious fall and his decision for repentance. In the light of this central theme, the moral question is answered: Angelo is no ingrained scoundrel; he deserves the mercy he receives. The questions of structure and genre are also answered: the play is a serious comedy, with the first two acts properly grave in tone, and the last three moving gradually toward the happy ending of mercy and reconciliation.

The existentially oriented psychological approach to Angelo's character is thus seen to throw light on a highly complex problem of interpretation in *Measure for Measure.* Such an approach uncovers an irreducible core of meaning which helps to give unity and lucidity to partial visions of the reality of the

28. See, for example, Dunkel, *op. cit.*, p. 284.

drama based on particular angles of vision. It demonstrates, moreover, the manner in which psychological constructs may illuminate the analysis of the literary critic.

To be sure, in order to complete the multivision of *Measure for Measure*, it would be necessary to pursue existential psychological analyses of the characters of Isabella, the Duke, Claudio, and Lucio, and to consider the core meaning of the sub-plot of the play. Even with such analysis completed, the existential critic would still be aware of his own limitations: just as it is impossible to comprehend at once the whole of reality, so it is impossible to comprehend at once the total implications of a work of genius. The history of the criticism of *Measure for Measure* only moves toward such understanding. Existential psychological analysis of Shakespeare's Angelo suggests that similar character analyses may throw new light on other great works of literature, especially on those masterpieces which by their very richness of life have stimulated the most intense literary controversy.

ANNA IN TOLSTOY'S
ANNA KARENINA

"WHEN you read Tolstoy, you have an impression of looking out through a window upon the real world," Stefan Zweig once wrote. Tolstoy himself confirmed the authenticity of this statement in theory when he declared that the essential quality of a writer is "not to lie." He confirmed it in practice in his novels, in which, with the genius that conceals the labor of art, he wrote as a lucid and exact observer of reality, relating all that he saw and felt as he responded to existence. Precisely because he considered himself not a fiery prophet but a humble witness to reality, Tolstoy was one of the most clear-sighted human psychologists who ever lived. His understanding of personality in depth is only beginning to be appreciated in our time.

Of all the superb characters given life by Tolstoy, perhaps Anna Karenina is his most sympathetic incarnation of the dark complexities of human nature

struggling for identity and fulfillment. Tolstoy stated
that in writing *Anna Karenina* he wished to embody
the destructive power of the passion of love. If the
fatality of *War and Peace* is the horror of war, then
the fatality of *Anna Karenina* is the "folly of the
senses." But it is much more than that. *Anna Karenina*
is a window through which the reader looks upon the
world of encounter of all other human beings and of
himself. Anna herself is a masterful embodiment of
existential struggle culminating in personal disaster
with which the sensitive reader identifies so completely that he feels he has always known what the
genius of Tolstoy reveals to him. Moreover, *Anna
Karenina* is perhaps the most superb study of the
psychology of woman ever written. Not one of
Shakespeare's heroines—not Desdemona, Cordelia,
or Ophelia—is so completely feminine as Anna.

It is the purpose of this Chapter to interpret
the development of Anna Karenina's character
throughout her existential psychological struggle,
from the moment of her first encounter with her
lover, Count Vronsky, until her desperate suicide.
Analysis of the novel reveals that Tolstoy centered
his creation of Anna's personality within five complex
crises of increasing emotional intensity, culminating
in her anguished self-destruction. Each of the crises is
grounded in encounter with her lover, Alexey Vronsky. And all of them define, in a widening crescendo,
her existential conflict to maintain her personal identity while attempting the impossible task of pursuing
two completely incompatible projects of existence.
Anna Karenina's tragedy is universal in its significance, for it gives artistic representation to the

struggle endured by all men who in greater or lesser degree refuse to accept the very real limitations of their existence.

NEGATIVE CRISIS IN *ANNA KARENINA*

In the opening chapters of *Anna Karenina* we watch with fascination as Anna, a faithful and reasonable wife, an affectionate mother, abandons herself quite suddenly to a turbulent love affair. When Anna encounters Vronsky by chance at a railway station, she is ironically engaged in a successful mission to bring stability to the marriage of her brother Stefan whose wife has been about to divorce him. The mutual appeal of the handsome young Count and the beautiful, charming Anna is immediate—the more so, as we discover later, because no real love exists between Anna and her cold, precise, punctilious husband, Alexey Alexandrovich, twenty years her senior. A few days after the first meeting of Anna and Vronsky, the two find themselves together at a ball and at once become oblivious of everyone and everything except their mutual captivation. Tolstoy allows the reader to observe the relationship between the two through the eyes of the young girl Kitty, who up until now has been the center of Vronsky's romantic attention:

> . . . . on Vronsky's face, always so firm and independent, Kitty saw . . . a look of bewilderment and humble submissiveness, like the expression of an intelligent dog when it has done wrong.
>
> Anna smiled, and her smile was reflected in him. She grew thoughtful, and he became serious . . . She was fascinating in her simple black dress, fascinating were her round arms with their bracelets, fascinating was

her firm neck with its thread of pearls, fascinating the
straying curls of her loose hair, fascinating the graceful,
light movements of her little feet and hands, fascinating
was that lovely face in its eagerness, but there was something terrible and cruel in her fascination.

Vronsky's sudden change from independence of spirit
to a slave-like attitude of submission, evidenced even
in his facial expression, is the obvious complement
to the "terrible and cruel" triumph of the usually
gentle Anna.

After Vronsky and Anna have left each other,
and Tolstoy allows us to glimpse each of them alone
in individual fantasy, we realize the supreme discrepancy in their attitudes toward their own existence,
and we experience a foretaste of the depth of potential
tragedy in their mutual bewitchment. Vronsky, who
is light, likable, and vain, centers all his fearful energy
in his desire for Anna and his hope of seducing her.
He "kept increasingly going over every position in
which he had seen her, every word she had uttered,
and before his fancy, making his heart faint with
emotion, floated pictures of a possible future." The
submissive slave is now "more haughty and self pos-
sessed than ever," and Tolstoy is wonderfully realistic in describing Vronsky's exclusive and inordinate
preoccupation with his desire:

. . . . He looked at people as if they were things. A
nervous young man, a clerk in a law-court sitting opposite him (in the railway carriage), hated him for that
look. The young man asked for a light, and entered into
conversation with him, and even pushed against him, to
make him feel that he was not a thing, but a person. But
Vronsky gazed at him exactly as he did at the lamp, and

the young man made a wry face, feeling that he was
losing his self-possession under the oppression of this refusal to recognize him as a person.

For Vronsky, there is no personal problem in
his sudden passion except that of winning Anna. No
question of moral or social obligation obstructs the
comparatively simple road to his desire. To be sure,
he does not really know Anna: his complete fascination is for her immediately perceived charm and
vitality. Just what Anna's private personality, her
deepest subjectivity might be, never even crosses
Vronsky's mind. He is not even curious about her: he
simply desires her. Vronsky merely follows his in-
stinctive reactions, as he has done all his life, adhering
only to a private and convenient code of action of his
own design. For Vronsky, then, there is no question
of interior conflict, of crucial decision or commitment.

For Anna, however, the case is quite different.
Sitting on the same train as Vronsky in another carriage, she is undergoing an acute emotional crisis.
Conscientiously attempting to suppress the image of
Vronsky which hovers at the edge of her consciousness and the eager excitement she feels, she suddenly
becomes ashamed. And at once she enters into a fitful,
nervous dialogue with herself:

"What have I to be ashamed of?" she asked herself
in injured surprise . . . There was nothing . . . She
remembered the ball, remembered Vronsky and his face
of slavish adoration, remembered all her conduct with
him: there was nothing shameful. And for all that, at the
same point in her memories, the feeling of shame was intensified, as though some inner voice, just at the point
where she thought of Vronsky, were saying to her,

"Warm, very warm, hot." . . . "Well, what is it?" she
said to herself resolutely . . . "What does it mean? Am
I afraid to look it straight in the face? . . . Can it be that
between me and this officer boy there . . . can exist any
other relations than such as are common with every acquaintance?" She laughed contemptuously. . . .

But Anna cannot repress the awareness of Vronsky
that forces itself to her consciousness, nor can she
deny her rare delight at the thought of him. Her
"nerves were strings being strained tighter and
tighter . . . She felt her eyes open wider and wider
. . . something within oppressing her breathing,
while all shapes and sounds seemed . . . to strike
her with unaccustomed vividness . . . She was un-
certain whether the train were going forwards or
backwards, or were standing still." Anna, says Tolstoy, was afraid of giving way to her new and delicious delirium. "She felt as though she were sinking
down . . . But it was not terrible, but delightful."
Startled at the intensity of her reaction, she at once
begins to reason with herself. "What am I myself?",
she asks, suddenly aware of a totally new dimension
in her personality. "Am I myself or some other
woman?" A powerful force drew her toward her
ecstatic delirium, says Tolstoy, but yet she knew that
"she could yield to it or resist at will."

    And precisely at this point we witness the
crucial moment for Anna's future. Unlike Vronsky,
she is consciously faced with a critical decision and
she knows it. She realizes, even in her intense emotional excitement, that she can "yield or resist at
will." Skirting a new mode of existence opened up by
her passionate encounter with Vronsky, she is aware

that if she surrenders she will be "another woman."
She is not yet aware, however, that the "other
woman" will be a living challenge to herself, to her
deepest subjectivity. Yet she questions who she is,
wonders indeed which of the two women *is* herself.
And this sudden loss of identity so overwhelms her
that she temporarily loses contact with her immediate
reality. Leaving the train at this crucial moment,
Anna briefly meets Vronsky, who has deliberately
followed her, hoping for such an encounter. At once
he seizes his opportunity to protest his absolute devotion to her. Anna returns to her carriage, panic-
stricken but blissful. Her fantasy of Vronsky now continues, more glowing and exhilarating than before.
Not yet yielding to the "other woman," her violent
attraction to Vronsky steadily overpowers her. When
at last Anna meets her husband at the end of her
journey and at once feels a new revulsion toward him
coupled with a novel feeling of hypocrisy within herself, the reader knows that the "other woman" is well
on her way to success in the decision which will soon
force itself upon Anna. Even such personal details as
the size of her husband's ears, which she has never
been conscious of before, now irritate her beyond
endurance.

Anna's questioning of her own identity and
her awareness of a new dimension in her personality
are central to Tolstoy's artful description of this first
great moment of crisis in her life. Up until now, Anna
has clearly followed the mode of existence of a faithful wife; she has lived her life in moral and spiritual
dimensions unknown to Count Vronsky. But now a
new mode of existence, completely incompatible with

that which she has pursued unquestioningly for years, is suddenly and powerfully present to her. From the start, Tolstoy emphasizes the fact that Anna's life as wife and mother is integrated with the very core of her being: the attractive role of Vronsky's mistress is that of—in her own words—"another woman." And thus Tolstoy implies that any attempt on Anna's part to reduce her subjectivity to an alien mode of life will lead to inevitable tragedy.

INCOMPATIBLE MODES OF EXISTENCE

For a few weeks Anna attempts to convince herself that she will remain faithful to her husband, and she makes a feeble effort to suppress her intense excitement at Vronsky's successful efforts to see her. But one day when she expects to see him and he does not appear, she admits to herself with sudden pain that his pursuit of her has become the total interest of her life. Again she is shocked, for she has repressed the fact that Vronsky has become for her not a casual interest, not just an object of desire, but the whole of her being. Psychologically, the transference of her feelings is already complete, though in reality she still scarcely knows Vronsky as a person. When Vronsky next protests his love, she throws him into unexpected ecstasy by encouraging him. Anna's own immediate reaction to this episode is to lie to her husband, closing herself completely to him, and feeling triumph in her guilt.

A few months later, when Anna finally yields to Vronsky, Tolstoy presents a thoroughly realistic account of her pitiful failure to enter at once upon two incompatible modes of existence. Despite all the rapture of the "new woman" in her surrender to Vronsky, Anna experiences a powerful shame and humiliation she has never known before. In her despair, she calls Vronsky her "accomplice in horror," and when he exclaims ecstatically over their happiness, she silences him. Even Vronsky becomes strongly aware of their deception of Anna's husband, and in the very consummation of his desire he feels a strange and unnamable "loathing." The lovers are acutely conscious of their shame at those moments when they meet in the presence of Anna's little son. In him they perceive a kind of compass showing them the direction of their lives, but they repress this knowledge, says Tolstoy, because "they do not want to know."

Anna now involves herself completely in her neurotic attempt to be at once both her real self and the "other woman" whom Vronsky loves. From the very start, the conflict within her manifests itself in numerous deviations. She represses her guilt for her unfaithfulness to her husband; yet the greater her deceit, the greater the evil she sees in him simply *because* she is deceiving him. She rejects any positive step toward seeking a divorce because the real Anna wishes to protect her son. Yet when Vronsky reminds her of her impossible situation, she refuses to face it, leading him to wonder if she is really the woman he loves. At the same time, she passionately declares her love for him, confessing her hatred for her husband and her love for Vronsky with equal intensity. Yet, there is hysteria in Anna's protestations. Psychologically, she is balancing herself on a tight rope, attempting the impossible task of being at once the woman she is and the woman she has chosen to become.

When Anna discovers that she is to bear
Vronsky's child, her lover agains begs her to confront
the reality of her situation. But she is passionately
resentful toward him, insisting on living only in the
delight of her immediate present and blocking out all
thought of her future. The authentic Anna breaks
through in a moment of rage, however, and she finds
sudden release in exposing to her husband her unfaithfulness to him, her hatred for him, and her love
for Vronsky. Then, in her terror and shame, she conceals her confession from her lover because she again
fears having to face the reality of their relationship.
In the frightening insecurity of her situation, she now
transfers her doubts to her lover and begins to feel
neurotic anxiety concerning his love for her. Though
Vronsky treats her with greater love and respect than
ever before, it is easy for Anna to convince herself
that he is growing tired of her. Her pregnancy is now
the source of a new devastation of soul and of the
second great emotional crisis of her life.

Just as in her earlier moments of crisis, Tolstoy once again describes Anna's crucial emotional
experience as manifesting itself in a loss of contact
with reality as well as in an agonizing spiritual
struggle:

> Anna sat in the same position, her head and hands
> hanging aimlessly, and every now and then she shivered
> all over, seemed as though she would make some gesture,
> utter some word, and sank back into lifelessness again.
> She repeated continually, "My God! My God!" But
> neither "God" nor "my" had any meaning to her . . .
> She began to feel anguish at the new spiritual condition,
> never experienced before, in which she found herself. She
> felt as though everything were beginning to be double in

her soul, just as objects sometimes appear double to over-
tired eyes . . . Whether she feared or desired what she
longed for, she could not have said.

"Oh, what am I doing?" she said to herself,
feeling a sudden thrill of pain in both sides of her head.
When she came to herself she saw that she was holding
her hair in both hands, each side of her temples, and pull-
ing it. . . .

The pattern repeats itself: as in her first interior dialogue, before yielding to Vronsky, Anna
experienced a fearful impression that she had lost her
identity and become another woman, so now she feels
that everything is "double" in her soul. The schizoid
split in her existence forces itself into her consciousness. And the anguish she has been suffering deep
within her unconscious finds pre-reflective expression
when she painfully tears her own hair, unaware of
what she is doing. Now again she loses touch with
reality, and when she regains consciousness she once
again comes face to face with the necessity for making
a decision. Impulsively she declares that her son
means more to her than her lover or her husband; she
resolves to leave home with her boy at once, without
knowing or caring where she will go or what she will
do. But Anna's will is now weakened, and in any case
her decision is too capricious for execution. So she
changes her mind and sends for her lover to tell him
of her confession of unfaithfulness to her husband.

The encounter which follows between Anna
and Vronsky is a critical one in their relationship. In
her deepest consciousness she is veering back and
forth between love and fear, decision and indecision.
Frightened by her own uncertainty, she now depends

completely on Vronsky and decides to give up all, even her son, and go away with him. But in the insecurity of her position she has become pathetically vulnerable to every word and slightest gesture of her lover. As she tells Vronsky her sad little story, she misreads the expression of his face and imagines she discerns a new coldness toward her which he does not in the least feel. When she reacts to this fantasy by violently protesting her love for him, the bewildered man is momentarily unable to respond to her. Thus the equilibrium between her two modes of existence is perilously maintained, and Anna remains balanced on her tight rope, continuing the schizoid existence which is slowly driving her to despair.

CONFLICT AND EXISTENTIAL DECISION

Once Anna's fear that Vronsky's love for her is growing cold has taken root in her fantasy, it rapidly assumes monstrous proportions. At first Vronsky unconsciously satisfies her neurotic need for reassurance, but his passionate avowals of love only increase her demands for his continual protestations. In her romantic fancy, moreover, she finds it necessary to divinize him. "Every time she saw him," writes Tolstoy, "she was making the picture in her imagination (incomparably superior, impossible in reality) fit with him as he really was." Fearful of losing her dream, Anna cannot bear to let Vronsky out of her presence. Inevitably she drives him to deceit by her demands for an account of every moment of his existence. Her lover remains patient until, anguished by her jealousy, Anna suggests that he may be unfaithful to her. Vronsky cannot help reacting coldly to her irrationality, and now he becomes instinctively aware that his greatest happiness is behind him. Paradoxically, however, he feels more bound to her than ever before. Every encounter of the two lovers is now basically a bitter conflict, and each seems to be driven by a demoniac desire to torture the other. Moving unconsciously toward self-destruction, Anna now threatens Vronsky with a prediction that she will die at the birth of her child, and she begins to feel that death will be a happy resolution of her suffering. Meanwhile, she is still living in her husband's house, still presenting herself to the world as her husband's wife.

The birth of Anna's daughter precipitates the third crisis in her life. As she has anticipated, she lies critically ill, and in her delirium the "two women" in her struggle for ascendancy. When death seems certain, the deepest subjectivity of Anna as wife emerges with magnificent clarity. She is unaware of her lover's presence and begs her husband to come to her. Humbly seeking his forgiveness, she gazes at him with triumphant tenderness:

> "Don't be surprised at me. I'm still the same . . . But there is another woman in me. I'm afraid of her; she loved that man, and I tried to hate you, and could not forget about her that used to be. I'm not that woman. Now I'm my real self, all myself. I'm dying now, I know I shall die . . . Only one thing I want: forgive me, forgive me quite . . . No, you can't forgive me! . . . No, no, go away, you're too good!"

The split in Anna's personality now no longer exists. Every word she speaks is in praise of her husband, in condemnation of the life she has lived with Vronsky. Feeling that he has lost her completely, her lover goes off alone and attempts to take his own life.

But Anna's conflict is not destined to be resolved so simply. Almost against her own will, she recovers. And as she slowly gains strength, the unfaithful Anna again emerges, the old love for Vronsky and loathing for her husband return. In the face of her recent repentance, her situation is now utterly unbearable, and she contemplates suicide as her only release—until the day that Vronsky returns and she again surrenders to him. But even as Anna leaves her husband and her son to go away with her lover forever, she perversely protests that it would have been better had she died. Anna agrees with Vronsky that it is their destiny to be together as long as they live, but she declares, white with fear, that there is something terrible in the renewal of their love. When Vronsky asserts that their love will be strengthened by the "something terrible" in it, she resolves to bury the old Anna forever and to be her lover's mistress and only that. In her struggle between two incompatible modes of existence, the balance now swings in favor of that manner of life which is antithetical to her most profound subjectivity.

DISINTEGRATION OF PERSONALITY

For a time Anna seems to be successful in repressing all consciousness of the woman she once was. Living abroad with Vronsky, she attempts to give herself completely to her delirious dream of love. She declares herself to be radiantly happy

beyond all her hopes. She "forgets" the fearful fact
that she has abandoned her husband and son. Her
"complete ownership of Vronsky is a continual joy"
to her; she can find nothing in him that is not superbly
fine. Indeed, she is more foolishly fascinated than an
adolescent in love for the first time. There is only one
dark cloud over her "happiness," and that is her fear
of losing Vronsky's love. In short, she can maintain
her new mode of life only by intensifying it so in-
ordinately in her fantasy that it drowns out all awareness of the past which is buried in her unconscious.

Meanwhile Vronsky, having given up both
his military career and his social life for Anna, is less
than perfectly happy. Stricken with *ennui*, he becomes
successively interested in politics, in books, and in
art. The more Anna attempts to possess him completely, the more restless he becomes. And the more
he seeks an outlet in interests beyond his love for her,
the more jealous she becomes. In a vicious circle, the
reactions of each of the lovers goad the other to
fortify his defense of his own position.

Just at this point in his narrative Tolstoy
ironically reveals how completely unsuccessful Anna
has been in transforming herself into the "other
woman," and how little Vronsky knows or ever did
know the real Anna. While the two are in Italy, they
engage a famous artist to do a portrait of Anna.
Vronsky is amazed at the painter's success:

> It was strange how Mihailov could have dis-
> covered just her characteristic beauty. "One needs to
> know and love her as I have loved her to discover
> the very sweetest expression of her soul," Vronsky
> thought, though it was only from this portrait that

> he himself learned this sweetest expression of her soul.
> But the expression was so true that he . . . fancied he
> had long known it.

Here Tolstoy, speaking directly as author to reader,
reveals unequivocally that Vronsky has never known
the true Anna. Moreover, he declares with biting
irony that a sensitive artist who has never even seen
her before is able to grasp the "expression of her
soul," while her lover is grossly unaware that the
stranger is revealing the subjectivity of Anna to him
for the first time. Vronsky does not even suspect that
the captivating woman he loves is a role Anna has
assumed only for him, repressing her true self whom
he will never really know intimately.

At about the same time that her portrait is
completed, the real Anna breaks through her repressions in a sudden irrepressible longing to see her
son again. Now she hesitates to tell Vronsky of her
desire for fear that his certain reaction of indifference
may lead her to hate him. The one thing she cannot
bear to lose—for it alone enables her to maintain her
psychological balance in her schizoid existence—is
the mutual passion of herself and Vronsky. She understands intuitively that she cannot reveal to her lover
her craving to see her son, for the Anna who loves
her son is not the Anna who adores Vronsky. And so
she sneaks away quietly to visit her little boy in one
of the happiest and yet saddest moments of her life.
Now she confesses to herself with chagrin that she
loves her son with the most elemental passion of her
nature, while she is almost incapable of affection for
her own and Vronsky's little daughter. What she does
not realize is that her son is truly her child in the most

primordial sense, while her daughter is the child of
the "other woman," the intruder who has taken over
her personality and her life.

Now Anna returns again to Vronsky, clinging
more and more desperately to her love for him, unaware that her slavish dependency is her last and terrible defense against a complete disintegration of her
personality. And so the "other woman" becomes
more and more madly possessive of Vronsky, alter-
nating between passionate outbursts of love and despairing accusations of his failure to love her. She is
offended at his smallest imaginary slight to her; she
confronts him again with the suspicion that he loves
another woman; she resents every thought or word
of her lover that is not centered absolutely in herself.
Slowly she drives him to fury, to indifference, almost
to hate. As their conflict deepens and Anna senses, in
a pre-reflective way, that there is no real bond between her profoundest self and Vronsky, she strives
more and more to bewitch him with the "other
woman." Anna now gives endless care to her alluring
appearance; she flaunts her beauty before Vronsky
until he becomes utterly unmoved by her charm and
appalled at the vulgarity of her demands. As Anna
sinks to mere commonness in her efforts to hold him,
Vronsky develops a finely sensitive revulsion toward
her cheap appeals. And thus is brought to a headlong
climax the fourth crisis of Anna's life. Each of her
crucial emotional experiences has been successively
more fraught with terror, and Anna is now sometimes
conscious, for all her desperate grasping at the last
straw of her passion, that she is headed for destruction.

As in each of her previous crises, Anna's fourth crucial moment is marked by a temporary lack of contact with immediate reality. As Vronsky's mistress and a "fallen woman," she has long been aware that she is no longer accepted in the Moscow society in which she has formerly moved with casual sureness. But one night, driven to distraction by Vronsky's apparent lack of love for her and the vulnerability of her social position, she dons a low-cut gown in extravagantly bad taste and goes to the opera alone—literally "asking for insult," as Vronsky declares. Her lover wonders if she is mad, but Anna indulges her caprice and so suffers the open insult she has courted. Only interminable reassurances of Vronsky's love, "which seemed so vulgar to him that he was ashamed to utter them," are able to calm her after her "hideous" experience. Worst of all, she has driven Vronsky even further away from her. To be sure, Anna does not realize what dark force has driven her to seek public punishment in so masochistic a fashion. Nor does Vronsky know that the real Anna is thus cruelly punishing the "other woman." And so the schizoid struggle within her personality mounts to reckless tension as she strives feverishly to repress it from her conscious awareness.

EXISTENTIAL DESPAIR AND CATASTROPHE

Anna and Vronsky now resolve to live at his estate in the country, removed from the hypocritical society of Moscow, hopeful of finding peace at last. Tolstoy lets some months pass for them in their new situation before he allows the reader to observe Anna again, this time from the point of view of her sister-

in-law Dolly, whose marriage Anna ironically res-
cued from destruction on the very day that she first
encountered Vronsky. All that Dolly sees on her visit
to Anna points to a slow and pathetic disintegration
in the personality of her friend. Like Shakespeare's
queen, Anna protests her happiness too much. She is
more beautiful, more charmingly groomed, more
sophisticatedly poised than ever before. But Dolly
notes that her charm has a brittle quality of frivolity,
that she carries on a cheap flirtation with a loose-
minded house guest, that she continually displays an
unpleasant coquetry with Vronsky, that she has engaged a disreputable-looking nurse for her baby.
Most peculiar of all, she acts like a guest in her own
household and is only a rare visitor to her little girl's
nursery. When Dolly asks her how many teeth her
baby has, she is amazed to discover that Anna doesn't
know! Observing her closely, Dolly becomes aware
that Anna has acquired a symbolic habit of half-
closing her eyes when any topic is broached which
might recall her from the experience of her immediate
present. Dolly's suspicion of a radical change in her
friend is confirmed when Anna confides in her that
she will have no more children because she must remain beautiful to hold Vronsky's love.

As her visit progresses, Dolly feels an insur-
mountable barrier between herself and Anna. In the
one conversation in which they speak to each other
with complete openness, Anna confesses that she cannot allow herself to think of her situation or she will
be driven mad by the prospect of a divorce and the
fear that her son may despise her. So she permits her
mind to dwell only on her personal appearance, her

passion for Vronsky, her absorption in the task of keeping complete possession of him. She contemplates with terror the slightest deviation from her immediate mode of existence. Because she cannot tolerate the unutterable tension of living the role she has adopted, Anna now relies on morphine for relief. When Dolly finally leaves Vronsky's house with a sense of grateful release, she feels that she is departing from a theater where everyone present has acted out a flamboyant role.

Meanwhile, Vronsky feels more and more like a caged animal caught in Anna's "loving" snares. He can scarcely breathe without precipitating quarrels and recriminations. Reacting quite normally to Anna's suffocating possessiveness, he desires his freedom and independence above all. And Anna herself feels the coldness which he cannot restrain as cruel indifference. When Vronsky informs her unequivocally that he is weary of her factitious efforts to fascinate him and that he feels persecuted to the point of cruelty, Anna summons all her courage and decides to seek a divorce from her husband and bind herself to Vronsky forever by marriage.

While she awaits her husband's answer, Anna grows more and more desperate in her struggle to obliterate her real situation from her consciousness. The very possibility of a divorce exposes her to the deepest dread of all—that of losing the love of her son. And yet divorce is the only means—in her distorted view—to maintain Vronsky's love, essential to her very existence in the role she has chosen. Thus her despairing solution only complicates her dilemma. Anna is now a frantic creature floundering in a labyrinth. To prove to herself that she is still lovable, she strives to arouse passion in every young man that she meets. To repress her guilt because she cannot love her own little daughter, she adopts an English girl and educates her in Vronsky's home. To soothe her anxiety over the useless life she leads, she even writes a story book for children. But none of these pursuits arises from any real commitment, and they all bore her. When Vronsky accuses her of using the English girl as an unnatural substitute for her own little daughter, Anna breaks into violent outbursts of fury which he cannot even comprehend. Allegations and insults on both sides multiply. And Anna's jealousy expands like a net over the whole of their existence.

In her lucid moments, Anna now realizes that she is killing the very passion which is the sole and fragile screen shielding her from complete emotional disintegration:

> And perceiving that, while trying to regain her peace of mind, she had gone round the same circle that she had been round so often before, and had come back to her former state of distraction, she was horrified at herself. "Can it be possible? Can it be beyond me to control myself?" she said to herself, and began again from the beginning.

In such brief periods of light, Anna approaches Vronsky with penitence and tenderness, but the vicious circle begins again and the breach between the two widens and widens until, even to the detached observer, there is no exit for Anna. At last she convinces herself that Vronsky hates her. To be open to such a reality is impossible to her: she resolves that she must die to punish her lover. Thus Anna enters into the fifth and final crisis of her increasingly unbearable existence.

Taking opium to fortify her, Anna now threatens Vronsky with the ominous prediction that he will regret his cruelty to her. With pitiful irony, Vronsky decides, at the very moment in her life when Anna needs him most, that since he has tried everything possible to help her without success, the only solution left to him is to ignore her. So he goes away and leaves her alone, desperate in her conviction that she has lost everything. As Anna yields to cold panic, her consciousness bursts its restraints. At first she loses contact with the ordinary, everyday realities about her. Then she confuses her little girl with the son she has lost. Sick with dread, she asks herself if it is possible for her to live without Vronsky, but she cannot bear to answer her own question. When at last she dares to analyze her immediate feeling, she discovers with horror that she actually hates Vronsky as he hates her. Her terror mounts as she realizes that she hates not only Vronsky but everyone and everything that she has ever known. The whole world has become for her a hell in which everyone hates everyone else. Sinking into nothingness, Anna grasps at a last possibility to save her identity. She sits down and writes a poignant telegram to Vronsky:

"I was wrong. Come back home. I must explain. For God's sake come! I'm afraid."

When Vronsky fails to answer her note at once, she shudders with fury:

> "Then, since it's so, I know what I must do. I'll
> go to him myself. Before going away forever, I'll tell him
> all my hate. Never have I hated anyone as I hate
> that man!"

As Anna sets off in her delirium for the railway station, she notes that a fat, ruddy gentleman has
mistaken her for an acquaintance and bowed graciously to her. The simple incident fills her with self-
scorn:

> "He thought he knew me. Well, he knows me as
> well as anyone in the world does. I don't even know my-
> self. I know my appetites, as the French say . . . We all
> hate each other . . . The struggle for existence and
> hatred is the only thing that holds men together. . . ."

Thus Anna enters further into demoniac dialogue
with herself. For the first time, she turns the glaring
light of her sharpened perception to a cruel analysis
of her relations with Vronsky:

> "What is it he sought in me? Not love, but the
> satisfaction of vanity. Yes, there was the triumph of suc-
> cess in him . . . He boasted of me . . . Now that's
> over. There's nothing to be proud of, but to be ashamed
> of." . . . She remembered his words, the expression of
> his face, that recalled an abject setter-dog, in the early
> days of their liaison. . . .

> "My love keeps growing more passionate and
> egoistic, while his is waning and waning . . . He is
> everything to me, and I want him more and more to give
> himself up to me entirely. And he wants more and more
> to break away from me . . . If I could be anything but a
> mistress, passionately caring for nothing but his caresses;
> but I can't and I don't care to be anything else. And by

that desire I rouse aversion in him, and he arouses fury in
me . . . And where love ends, hate begins. . . ."

Thinking of her son, Anna declares:

> "I thought, too, that I loved him, and used to be
> touched by my own tenderness. But I have lived without
> him, I gave him up for another love, and did not regret
> the exchange till that love was satisfied." And with loath-
> ing she thought of what she meant by that love. And the
> clearness with which she saw life now, her own and all
> men's, was a pleasure to her . . . "We are all created to
> be miserable, we all know it, and we all invent means of
> deceiving each other. And when one sees the truth, what
> is one to do? . . . I will punish him and escape from
> everyone and from myself."

Only the "other woman" is speaking in these last
words. Anna's subjectivity is so buried, the role she
has assumed becomes so drastically magnified, that
the reader feels a sharp split. In Anna's absolute
aloneness and nothingness, in her complete usurpa-
tion by the woman she is not, only one ending is now
possible.

At the very moment that she suddenly drops
on her knees before the approaching railway train,
Anna is terror-stricken and cries out:

> "Where am I? What am I doing? What for?"

And the real Anna answers from the deepest core of
her being:

> "Lord, forgive me all!"

The inevitable destruction is accomplished. Just as
Anna's true subjectivity emerged when she was close

to death in childbirth, so now her unique self emerges at the moment of her suicide. In the hour of the final crisis, it is not the mistress of Vronsky who triumphs, but the Anna who wears no masks and plays no roles.

TRAGEDY OF UNAUTHENTICITY

From an existential psychological point of view, *Anna Karenina* is a superb study of a finely sensitive and beautiful woman who attempts the impossible—to pursue two completely incompatible projects of existence. The novel is tense with the struggle for ascendancy of the two personalities in the "double" woman. Now the wife and mother is in conscious triumph; now the passionate mistress who counts all other loyalties well lost for her love. But when the one woman is in conscious domination, the other is all the more powerful in her dark, unconscious force. Only self-destruction brings the contest to violent conclusion. Early in the novel Tolstoy lets his reader know that Anna's life as wife and mother is identified with her most profound subjectivity. But the role of Vronsky's mistress fascinates her so powerfully that she becomes a powerless victim in a series of schizoid crises driving her to further and further withdrawal from reality.

Anna's struggle is acted out chiefly on the ground of her encounter with her lover, Vronsky. Because she has assumed an unauthentic role to live out her passion for him, the encounter of the lovers is a mad cycle of desire and hate, increasingly intense as it promises over and over again a fulfillment impossible of attainment. In all their efforts to grow to closer intimacy, Anna and Vronsky are increasingly frustrated until they experience complete despair. What neither consciously realizes is that Anna loves and is loved by Vronsky only in the role of mistress which she has adopted exclusively for him. Her true subjectivity, which the sensitive portrait painter can divine at once, is never really known to Vronsky. And so he never satisfies her. Nor is the real Anna even known to herself—as she herself declares—except when she is face to face with death.

Anna's existential attitude toward life as she contemplates suicide is close to that of certain pessimistic twentieth century psychologists, especially in her final, lucid stream of consciousness when she enters into a new dimension of existence which is absolute despair. As Anna looks back over her years of suffering, the reader sees the source of her struggle in a failure to be open to reality from the moment of her first encounter with her lover. Her life as Vronsky's mistress has been almost completely unauthentic. Indeed, authenticity would at once have negated such life for her. But Anna has chosen to play a role and has then attempted to repress her authentic personality from crisis to crisis. She dares to unveil reality only at the moment of her death.

It is interesting to note that the hell of hate which Anna experiences as she finally confronts the reality of her relationship to Vronsky is also expressed in terms similar to those of certain twentieth century phenomenologists of hate. Tolstoy declares over and over again that Anna judges Vronsky's loss of love for her by the "coldness of his glance" which she interprets as hatred. His "stare of hatred" reduces her to an object in his eyes. Since she exists only for him, she feels that her life loses its meaning completely under the domination of his hatred. His stare indeed destroys all her potentialities, for not only does he now no longer love but hate her: he causes her to be incapable of loving so that she hates him in turn. And Anna's ultimate conclusion is that what is true of her experience is true for all men, and love itself is impossible. As she rides in her carriage to her death, Anna looks about her and exclaims:

> ". . . . I don't know these streets at all. Hills it seems, and still houses, and houses . . . And in the houses always people and people . . . How many of them, no end, and all hating each other!"

All men hate, and they are finally bound together only by their hate, and the man who openly faces reality achieves an intellectual pleasure in the contemplation of this truth. For Anna, the only solution is suicide. She will punish Vronsky by becoming the thing that his hatred has caused her to be.

But herein lies the tremendous paradox of *Anna Karenina*. For the Anna who thus reduces her life to the nothingness of hatred and self-destruction is not the authentic Anna. She is the role-player, the actress, the "other woman," the "double," the destructive element in Anna's schizoid existence. The woman who cries out for forgiveness in the act of suicide is the real Anna in the very core of her being.

And what is the real Anna's attitude toward existence? It is that of the woman who is primordially loving. This is the Anna who transcends herself, who breaks away from her fascinated self-centeredness to beg her husband's forgiveness. The Anna who hungers to see her little boy, who would rather die than experience the hatred of her child. This is the Anna who is clear-sighted enough to deny that she is happy in the very act of surrender to her lover, who finally knows that her self-regarding passion for Vronsky is not love but hatred—hatred for herself, for him, and for all men. In short, the authentic Anna realizes ultimately that love is not self-centered but creative. Neither she nor Vronsky has ever truly caused the other to be. Anna has reduced herself to a series of predicates for her lover, and he has finally known her only in her facticity. They have never given themselves to each other in the fullness of being in which authentic lovers mysteriously participate.

Anna is most genuinely human, most happy, in her encounters with her little son, in which both of them experience the creativity of spontaneous love. Tolstoy leaves no doubt in our minds, either at the beginning or the end of the novel, that Anna is a woman who fundamentally desires the fulfillment of creative love. But Tolstoy is writing a tragedy, not a comedy. And so Anna breaks through to the truth of her existence only at the end of a long series of tragic crises, in which the authentic Anna finally casts out the false one by destroying her. Because the tale is tragic, the real Anna must destroy herself too. Because she is a child of Eve, her knowledge of the meaning of existence is dearly bought.

MARCHER IN JAMES'
THE BEAST IN THE JUNGLE

HENRY JAMES' *The Beast in the Jungle* has been recognized as one of the greatest *nouvelles* ever written for both its artistry and its depth of psychological insight. As T. S. Eliot said of James, he "has a kind of sense, a receptive medium which is not sight. Not that he fails to make you see, so far as is necessary, but sight is not the essential sense. He perceives by antennae: and the 'deeper psychology' is here." What Eliot calls the "deeper psychology" is the existential approach to life which made the James family—Henry, Sr., Henry, Jr., and William—the only psychologists of the early twentieth century in America who developed a consistent underlying structure which gave unity to their concern with man in his immediate existence. I say "the James family," for who will assert that Henry and his father were less existential (or psychological) in their approach to life than William James?

The world of Henry James is an existential world: in it the drama of situation precedes "fate"; nothing is unchangeable; man exists only in relation to other men and to the world. Man becomes what he is, not through some outside force, but by what he himself makes of his own experience. James' *The Beast in the Jungle* is perhaps his most penetrating presentation—through the power of negation, to be sure—of man's existential situation. In this *nouvelle*, James analyzes in a definitive manner the un-man, the man who negates his life by refusal to exist. And, paradoxically, he implies a consummate image of the fullness of human existence in this man's anguished loss of what-he-might-have-been.

The Beast in the Jungle is the story of a man who lives a life of futility—a death-in-life—because in his pride he feels that he is marked by destiny for some strange and rare experience. He wastes his life in waiting, unaware of the redeeming love that is every day offered to him, only to discover in the end that his unique distinction is that *nothing* has ever happened to him. Psychologically speaking, he is fixated early in life in existential transference to his own impregnable ego. His fear of encounter with the beast in the jungle of his own psyche, with the demon of his "other self," has its central source in this transference which diminishes his capacity for openness to reality, encounter with other human beings, and the decision which alone would make him truly human. Ultimately, his life is a death-in-life because he is incapable of giving or receiving love, and therefore incapable of accepting redemption.

EXISTENTIAL TRANSFERENCE TO EGO

As the story of *The Beast in the Jungle* begins, John Marcher, a well-to-do London bachelor of thirty-five, renews his acquaintance, quite by accident, with May Bartram, a woman of thirty, with whom he feels an immediate and vague rapport as of a thread of past experience which he cannot at once identify. Without a direct sign from her, he nevertheless senses that *she* has not lost the thread of their relationship, even if he cannot trace its source. Very soon the reader discovers, through John Marcher as the central intelligence of the story, the extreme discrepancy between the attitudes of the young man and woman toward each other. May remembers everything about their past acquaintance, down to the smallest detail. Marcher remembers almost nothing. This fact might seem ordinary enough, revealing only May's intense interest in Marcher, which soon becomes an incipient and completely unselfish love for him. Not loving her, Marcher would hardly be expected to recall the fine points of a casual meeting with a woman he has not seen for ten years.

But then Henry James drops a small psychological bombshell. May Bartram reminds Marcher that ten years ago he disclosed to her the central secret of his life. Unaccountably, he has forgotten that he once drew her—a girl he scarcely knew—into his most intimate confidence. Marcher is certain that he has never revealed his secret to anyone else, and May immediately assures him that she has guarded his confidence and always will.

The reader now becomes uncomfortably aware that Marcher is not at all interested in May Bartram as a person. As their conversation progresses, it becomes increasingly evident that his seeming interest in her centers only in the fact that she has so long remembered *him*. Their entire discussion is concentrated on him and his secret: his "peculiar distinction" or "sense of being kept for something rare and strange, possibly prodigious and terrible, that is sooner or later to happen to him." When May states that his revelation to her was really "very simple," Marcher is offended. Careful to safeguard the rarity of what is to happen to him, he questions whether she really understands. Because she is strongly aware that Marcher has already waited more than a decade for the "great thing" to happen, May quietly asks whether it is "something he is merely to suffer." In reply, Marcher attempts to impress her with the unique and dreadful character of his anticipated fate:

> "It is something to wait for—to have to meet, to face, to see suddenly break out in my life; possibly destroying all further consciousness, possibly annihilating me; possibly, on the other hand, only altering everything, striking at the root of all my world and leaving me to the consequences, however they shape themselves."

May remains sympathetic and accepting, but the reader begins to feel ambiguously uncomfortable once more at the tone of morbid self-centeredness in Marcher's description. Now again May attempts, in a wholesome, intelligent manner, to bring Marcher's apprehension into the common light of day, to relate it to the reality of ordinary, but dear and precious human experience. "Isn't what you describe," she asks, "perhaps but the expectation—or at any rate the sense of danger, familiar to so many people—of falling in love?" Marcher's reply confirms the reader's suspicion of his unconscious conceit. After long thought, he answers, "Of course, what's in store for me may be no more than that." The casual manner in which he brushes off the experience of love as trivial can only be interpreted as an almost ludicrous lack of insight. And the matter-of-fact quality of his unawareness prompts the added suspicion of a deep wound in his personality.

May Bartram remains unperturbed, blandly asserting that if Marcher has never felt love as overwhelming, he has never been in love! Love, Marcher declares in answer, is not what *his* destiny is to be. And then May probes his unconscious wound by inquiring, "You want something all to yourself—something that nobody else knows or *has* known?" But Marcher is all unaware of her indirect reference to his egotistic exclusiveness. He merely elaborates on his strange presentiment, on the uniqueness of the experience that is to be his. As James subtly remarks, "He liked to talk of it."

Now May tries another approach. Three times she asks Marcher if he is afraid of his rare destiny. Twice he evades her question, finally declaring that he doesn't know. He pleads with her to "watch with him" as he awaits his unspeakable fate. And May, who is now obviously drawn to him for himself alone, promises to be with him in his unusual adventure. Throughout the entire conversation,

Marcher has not once shown interest in May as an individual. He relates to her merely as the person who has covertly shared his foreboding for so long, and consequently assumes importance in his eyes. And thus closes the first scene of James' strange little drama.

On a symbolic level, May Bartram represents what Henry James would have called "the second consciousness" of Marcher. As such, she will carry on a dialogue with him throughout the story. She will devote herself to him absolutely. From a psychological point of view it is significant that Marcher has "forgotten" that he confided his great secret to her: the very fact that he told it should have rendered the telling unforgettable, for it is at the center of his conscious existence. The importance of his forgetting, to be sure, is that it reveals a strong repression in his life of the deepest psychological meaning of the secret. Moreover, Marcher is never to become aware of May's ultimate sacrifice of herself to his egotism. On a surface level, she is to be present to him always; on the deepest psychological level, he is never to encounter her.

From a narrative point of view, James presents in this first scene a long foreground to the central rising action of John Marcher's story. He and May Bartram are not yet concretely realized as rounded characters. If nothing seems to happen in the scene except an ambiguous conversation, one must remember James' difficult dramatic problem: to give reality to a character who exists only in his own enclosed ego. May is spontaneous, intuitive, open to reality, but long before the story begins Marcher has transferred to his own ego all his natural reaching out toward life. It becomes increasingly clear that his existential transference is strongly fixated in his personal presentiment concerning his future.

In his Preface to *The Beast in the Jungle,* James explains how he attempted to reveal the "extreme" in the character of Marcher.[1] The latter's fixation on self so divorced him from reality that his fate, as conceived in his fantasy, could disclose itself to him only in "a rare distinction, an incalculable violence, an unprecedented stroke." Therefore Marcher, according to James, reveals at once the extravagance of apprehension and of confidence. Nothing that either he or May can conceive is either damning enough or sublime enough for him. He dismisses all human experience—including love—as too common. Therefore he appropriates no experience as his own. Yet he guards his secret, and expects May to guard it too, because of his dread of imputed pride or pusillanimity. The result is that he enters upon a career of great negative adventure. If his apprehension of his fate is extreme, so is his egotistic certainty that the unspeakable event will happen. The fear and the confidence are really two sides of the same coin.

In a sense, Marcher may be said to incarnate the isolation and frustration of unfulfilled humanity. His inability to face reality—later in the story to be symbolized in the beast or demon—reflects the failure of man to transcend the transferential stages of his existence. In Marcher's consciousness, and

1. Henry James, "The Altar of the Dead," in *The Art of the Novel* (New York: Charles Scribner's Sons, 1934), p. 246.

consequently in his personality growth, he is to remain existentially immature to the end.

DEMON AS BEAST IN THE JUNGLE

As the second scene of James' story opens, Marcher complacently accepts May Bartram's consent to await with him the occurrence of his great experience. The two are, says the author, "afloat together." Marcher treats May as a "mere confidant," while "careful to remember that she also has a life of her own." James now executes a subtly ironic explication of the encrusted selfishness of Marcher. The latter regards himself as a "disinterested person" in society, carrying his "concentrated burden" ever so quietly. When he hears others speak of experiences which have "unsettled" them, he has moments of temptation to tell them what it really means never to have a settled hour in one's life. Because he listens graciously and civilly to others despite his own secret suffering, he considers himself to be "decently—perhaps even a little sublimely—unselfish." Though he permits himself to be "just a little selfish" with regard to May Bartram, he doesn't *really* believe that he is so. He takes their close relationship completely for granted, meanwhile, never for a moment contemplating marriage. After all, his unique fate is not "a privilege he can invite a woman to share"! He is alone, different, untouched. Something or other lies in ambush for him "like a crouching beast in the jungle." Amid the twists and turns of the months and the years, the definite point he awaits is the inevitable spring of the creature.

Despite the exceptional secret he carries with

him, however, Marcher declares himself unwilling to burden others with tenseness or solemnity. And so he assumes, even toward May Bartram, a false gaiety. For example, when she acquires a lovely house in London, he remarks facetiously that perhaps this is the "great thing" that is to happen to him. But when she retorts that such a trifle can hardly be the climax to so special a suspense, he wonders, with exquisite insensitivity, whether she has a larger conception of his singular fate than even he himself has! As time slowly passes, Marcher is all the while subtly flattered that May, like himself, is absorbed in his life, judging it, forecasting it. When the two speak of what is to happen to him, they now refer to it only as "the real thing." Meanwhile May accepts his aloofness, she accepts his false gaiety, she accepts all that he is and even seems to him to make his life her own.

Gradually Marcher's behavior becomes, before the world, a long act of dissimulation. He wears "a mask painted with a social simper." And inevitably May, too, is forced, as the watcher of his fate, to give a false account of herself to the world. In her personal response to Marcher, however, her whole attitude is a virtual statement of her love for him; but his awareness of her passion, like every perception except his intense concentration on himself, is crowded out of his consciousness. To prove to himself that he has not sunk into "real selfishness," he makes a point of practicing special social amenities in their relationship. For example, he offers her rare little gifts as tokens of his esteem and gratitude.

Once when he brings her a gift on her birthday, May remarks that their habit of indispensable friendship makes him, so far as other people are concerned, "indistinguishable from other men." But Marcher is not concerned with other men. As long as he and May know of his uniqueness, he is satisfied. He responds, however, by asking her whether she ever feels that her absorption in his plight is not being particularly repaid. Sensing that his question is a projection of his own unconscious doubt, May asks him whether he too feels unrequited—especially since he has waited so long for the beast to spring. Marcher answers significantly: "It isn't a matter as to which I can choose . . . It isn't one as to which there *can* be a change. It's in the lap of the gods. . . ." May agrees that one's fate must come, of course, but adds pointedly that Marcher's "was to have been so exceptional . . . so particularly *your own.*" Immediately Marcher seizes upon her phrase "was to have been," accusing her of no longer believing that something rare and strange awaits him. But May reassures him; she is more certain than ever that her curiosity concerning his fate will be only too well repaid.

In the closeness of their companionship, these two now tend to view their predicament more gravely. As their middle years slip slowly away, Marcher begins to ask obscure questions concerning his future. Projecting his own anxiety to May, he asks whether she has grown fearful of the future. May admits ambiguously that there have been days when she thought *he* was afraid. Extremely weary of the long suspense of waiting, it seems to Marcher that his fear has lost itself in the jungle of his life. He yearns for the consummation of his fate. But May declares that he has become so accustomed to danger that he is indifferent to it. She concludes, with almost comic irony, that "his attitude could not well be surpassed." Misinterpreting her with a kind of double irony, Marcher naively asks whether she regards him as heroic. "Call it that," May answers enigmatically. When he pursues the point, obviously to satisfy his own doubts, and asks her whether she considers him a man of courage, May parries the question, responding, "That's what *you* were to show me." Marcher declares that a man of courage always knows what he is afraid of, while he himself is unable even to name his fear. Indirectly, he is begging May to reassure him of his courage. May does so, but emphasizes the fact that he still has seen nothing of his fate. Her cryptic attitude leads him to assert impulsively that she *knows* what is to happen to him, but is afraid to tell him. His fate must be so appalling, he declares, that she is guarding the truth from him. Then, as a sudden climax to the scene, May answers, "You'll never find out."

In this second section of James' story, three main psychological implications emerge. The first is the overt reference to the "beast in the jungle"; the second is the fear motif which is the thread of all the interactions between Marcher and May; and the third is her indirect and his direct allusion to the possibility of *choice* with regard to his life.

The identification of the beast is crucial to the understanding of the above circumlocutory dialogue. The symbols of both the beast and the jungle are found elsewhere in the writings of Henry James.[2]

2. See Leon Edel, ed., *The Ghostly Tales of Henry James* (New Brunswick: Rutgers University Press, 1948), p. 669.

They are always associated with a sense of unutterable fear. The beast is an "awful agent, creature, or
presence" which comes from within the mind and is
projected and attached to the image of the crouching
tiger. James once wrote of encountering such a horrible creature in a nightmare. Moreover, his sister
Alice, who suffered a mental breakdown, recorded in
her journal that her head "felt like a dense jungle
into which no ray of light had ever penetrated."
Again, in "The Turn of the Screw," the governess
describes the onset of her ghostly apparitions as a
"hush in which something gathers or crouches. The
change was actually like the spring of a beast."

Perhaps the most significant key to the symbol
of the beast, outside of the *nouvelle* itself, is found in
James' short story, "The Jolly Corner," which is
closely related in theme to *The Beast in the Jungle*.
The protagonist of "The Jolly Corner," Spencer
Brydon, speaks of "a strange *alter ego* deep down
within me" which is "monstrous . . . quite hideous
and offensive." It requires boundless nerve and patience to stalk this cunning prey, "at bay more
formidable than any beast of the forest." This "fanged
and antlered animal," the opposed projection of
Brydon's self, the agent of his shame, is capable of
driving him to self-destruction. And interestingly
enough in its implications for later psychoanalysis,
James' protagonist feels that he can "cultivate" his
conscious perceptions in order to prepare for concentrated combat with his savage "other self." When
Brydon finally encounters the beast face to face, it is
"evil, odious, vulgar,"—"a rage of personality before which his own collapsed." Yet the beast is, he

declares, "a man of his own substance." He can conquer it only by tracking it down "like a big game
hunter" and confronting it. After his encounter with
it, which results in a kind of temporary "death" for
Brydon, he is at last able to assert his own independence.

It is clear that John Marcher's beast is his
"other self" lurking in the depths of his own psyche.
The "beast" is the "demon" which every man must
discover in himself and acknowledge as his own before
he can be free and therefore truly human. It is Jung's
"shadow." The nature of the beast for which Marcher
watches is indeed unknown to his consciousness. But
the horrible creature defines the inexplicable fear
which runs through his whole life, and especially
through his relationship with May Bartram, his
"second consciousness." Henry James was deeply
cognizant that man's demon, which he calls "alter
ego," is charged with evil. For the average person
this demon is frightful enough, but for a man like
John Marcher, a victim of unconscious obsession, it is
an agent of heart-rending anxiety and unutterable
fear. In his notebooks, James describes *The Beast in
the Jungle* as the story of a man "haunted by fear,
more and more, throughout his life, that something
will happen to him, he doesn't know what." [3] Only a
woman, he adds, will help him to see *what* his fear is.
Only she will see his life *as it is*, the reality of it.
But despite all her efforts, despite *her* complete ac-

3. *The Notebooks of Henry James*, ed. by F. O. Matthiessen
and Kenneth Murdock (New York: Oxford University Press, 1947),
p. 311.

ceptance of his other self, he will not see the truth of
his existence until it is too late.

James never overtly identifies the "beast" in
the story as the demon or shadow of Marcher's own
monstrous egotism. Indeed, the sometimes matter-
of-fact way in which Marcher discusses the beast who
haunts him increases the grotesque terror of the
story. James believed that reality in fiction must be
close to the reality of life, in which every man who
is at all capable of spiritual growth faces the darkly
ambiguous situation of the evil of his own nature.
James did not think it necessary or even artistic to
present every detail of this human conflict. As Leon
Edel suggests, the reader is given a "blank check." [4]
And what James calls the "process of adumbration"
is, in a sense, a collusion between the fictional character and the reader. The latter must enter into
Marcher's fantasy and partake of *his* reality. Henry
James' art is the means of entrance. To be sure, the
reader's understanding of Marcher's beast depends
to a great extent on the depth at which he has discovered the demon in his own nature and in that of
all men. The beast, therefore, can be interpreted on
many levels; the fear can be experienced in innumerable degrees of depth. Marcher is perhaps the
most wounded of all of James' impotent heroes, for
he is afraid of his own life, completely identified with
his own fear.

The ontological basis of the fearful symbol of
the beast may be found in the philosophy of Henry
James, Sr., which, as Quentin Anderson has pointed

4. Edel, *op. cit.*, p. xxix.

out, James adapted to his fiction.[5] The two Jameses, father and son, saw man as an "event" or psychic dynamism. For them, man moves between two opposing poles in his own psyche. Human nature *is* the relationship between "the dove and the serpent." Therefore, life is dramatic in essence. The ultimate fear is the fear of the other self. As Henry James, Sr., so strikingly asserted, neither a good dove nor a good serpent can ever be a man. Self-love and brotherly love in man remain in uneasy equilibrium. When self-love dominates, it isolates. John Marcher is isolated in his selfhood. Thus is his existential transference defined. Only by accepting the beast in his own nature—as May accepts it—can he become fully a man. But this Marcher is not able to do.

Besides the identification of the beast and the definition of the fear, the third concept which emerges as the story of Marcher progresses is the problem of will and decision. Because May knows intuitively that nothing is going to *happen* to Marcher, that the beast will not spring so long as he waits for it to spring, she suggests to him the futility of waiting. He replies that he *has* to wait: "It isn't a matter as to which I can *choose*. . . ." In this scene May Bartram proposes indirectly, indeed personifies, the life Marcher might choose, the possibility of real experience. But he sadly lacks the ability to make the decisive gesture of reaching out for life, of taking his destiny into his hands. His ultimate failure is to do nothing, to be nothing. This paralysis of will is crucial to any understanding of his failure to en-

5. Quentin Anderson, *The American Henry James* (New Brunswick: Rutgers University Press, 1957), pp. 161-62.

counter the "beast" of his other self until it is "too late." Here, to be sure, is a moral situation, but a psychological one as well.

Existentially, Marcher renders himself incapable of decision. The existential psychological approach to man holds that will and decision cannot be left to chance or to "waiting for something to happen." [6] Will is, in fact, at the center of man's existence. But throughout his life, Marcher never consciously chooses a way of acting. In fact, he denies that he *can* choose. Because of his insulated ego, he lacks the crucial power which alone makes man "truly human." First of all, Marcher lacks fundamental awareness of his situation. Consequently, he is incapable of the self-consciousness necessary to translate experience into the insight required to will. Ultimately, he is incapable of decision, of responding to reality as it is, because decision and responsibility depend on will. They are forms of consciousness moving toward self-realization, integration, and maturity. These John Marcher cannot achieve. And so he is destined to remain bound by his fixation until the self-revelation that comes at the very close of his life.

UNAUTHENTIC SELF-DIALOGUE

The third section of *The Beast in the Jungle* is a transition to and preparation for the fourth and climactic scene of the story. It has already been pointed out that, so far as overt action is concerned, little happens in the complication of the plot, for

6. See Rollo May and Adrian van Kaam, "Existential Theory and Therapy," *Current Psychiatric Therapies*, III (1963), 74-81.

Marcher's psychological state precludes significant action. The inward movement of the third scene is the growth of Marcher's incipient doubt as to the consummation of his rare destiny. This is accompanied by a constant, expanding development of his outrageous selfishness.

James opens the scene with reference to Marcher's "occasional warnings against egotism." He maintains his "consciousness of the importance of not being selfish" by such little sops to his vanity as inviting May Bartram to attend the opera more frequently. He continues to accept as a matter of course the endless evidences of her complete absorption in his life. Repressing his sense of guilt that their relationship over the years has caused tongues to wag, he one day asks May how she has escaped "being talked about." May replies that she *is* the subject of gossip, but adds that her only concern is to help Marcher "to pass for a man like another." The *double entendre* of her remark escapes him, for he is too conceited to be aware of her dilemma. He sees only the beautiful gesture of her devotion, and she demands nothing of him. More and more he suspects that, because of her exclusive interest in him, and because of the "finer nerves" that women have, she must know his destiny. And with this thought a new apprehension arises in him, the dread of losing her by catastrophe *before* he meets his unutterable fate. Almost simultaneously, May informs him of an illness which has begun to drain her vitality.

In perhaps the finest ironic passage in the entire narrative, James now pursues Marcher's interior dialogue. In order to safeguard his "unselfishness"

in the face of his sudden fear of losing May completely, he proceeds to translate the direct menace
of his possible loss of her into a perverse and self-
flattering statement: "What if she should have the
misfortune to die before knowing *his* fate?" As May's
illness slowly develops, however, Marcher's sole
concern is to find out before it is too late what she,
through her feminine insight, may know of his destiny. With mounting fear, he becomes almost ludicrously aware of change in her. One day he suddenly
declares that she "looks" much older: he suspects
that she has been older for a long time, but "he has
just simply not noticed it"! On another day he has
the appalling thought that perhaps the unique experience destined for him is the loss of his charming
companion. But this possibility he dismisses as "an
abject anti-climax" to the imminent great event of
his life. If nothing but this should happen, he would
be "the most grotesque of failures." He is waiting for
"quite another thing." And then a further thought
suggests itself—fearful possibility!—what if it is
too late for anything at all to happen to him? Would
it not be a stupendous failure "not to be anything" at
all? For the first time, Marcher consciously doubts
the uniqueness of his destiny. Could he possibly have
been "sold"?

As the story now moves toward its climax,
Marcher begins to dally with the possibility that his
whole life may have been a singular fantasy, an erratic waiting for something never to happen. However, he only skirts the edge of this thought, quickly
repressing it and entering again into his fantasy
world. Yet this tiny ray of light is significant, for it

represents the first time that Marcher's thoughts actually verge on reality. When the idea for *The Beast in the Jungle* was germinating in James' mind, he wrote in his notebook, "What is there in the idea of *Too Late*—of some friendship or passion or bond— some affection long desired and waited for, that is formed too late? . . . A passion that might have been : : . And the wasting of life is the implication of death." [7] This is the situation that is clamoring for recognition in Marcher's consciousness while it is still, though late, not *too late*. But his consistent, undeviating fixation on self prepares the reader to expect not fulfillment but destruction in the climax about to be reached.

FIXATION IN EXISTENTIAL TRANSFERENCE

The fourth scene of the narrative culminates in the climax of Marcher's relationship with May, the first of the two great crises of his life situation. Because he is incapable of existential decision, both of these crucial scenes are precipitated not by himself but by others—the first by May Bartram and the second by a stranger. As May's now fatal illness grows worse, Marcher is filled with dread that she may die without revealing to him the knowledge of his fate which he senses that she possesses.

On a certain day he feels a critical change in her. She becomes for him an impenetrable sphinx talking across a strange gulf. With foreboding of her death, he dares to ask her, "What do you regard as the very worst that at this time *can* happen to me?" Even now May accepts without reproach his crude

7. *Notebooks*, p. 182.

manifestation of self-interest. She quietly reminds
Marcher that in the past they have together experienced great fears concerning his destiny, adding that
"some of them have been unspoken." Marcher answers that she knows something about him which she
must tell him, for now he fears only ignorance. May
concedes that if the thing she has never named should
happen, it *would* be the worst that could come to him.
He now cries out despairingly that if she gives him no
more light, she will be abandoning him. But May
answers firmly: "No! I'm with you still . . . I
haven't forsaken you." Understanding nothing,
Marcher begs her to tell him whether he will consciously suffer. And May promptly answers,
"Never!" In spite of all the gentle subtlety of May's
words, Marcher now protests, like a naive and stubborn schoolboy, that he still *doesn't know* what May
knows. She responds that even now, late as it is, he
still need not meet his awful fate, since it is not yet a
reality. Indeed, she pleads with him, declaring that it
is never too late. He does not reply, and the conversation would seem to have ended.

But suddenly, in a magnificently revealing
gesture, May offers herself to Marcher, offers herself
with superb beauty and without words. Even now
Marcher reacts to her revelation of love with a perverse, "I know nothing." Becoming suddenly very
ill, May can no longer conceal her anguish and
Marcher demands, "What then has happened?" She
answers sadly, "What *was* to."

Thus the climactic scene of the pathetic story
seals Marcher's fate. He has failed to accept May's
last and heroic offer to help him. All the efforts of

May's lifetime have not been sufficient to break through the barrier of his self-centeredness. In reading this quietly powerful scene, one becomes more and more amazed at Marcher's sheer inability to confront reality by the only possible means: encounter with another human being.

It is fascinating to observe how May Bartram provides a situation—and in fact has provided it for years—which is ideal for Marcher's communication of his inner self to her. Always, even when she almost despairs of helping him, she accepts him as he *was*, as he *is*. The strongest fixation might give way under such love; the other self, fierce though it might be, tracked down and encountered. In James' own words, recorded in his notebook, May is "understanding, perceiving, sharing, protective." [8] In the course of their relationship, Marcher really "has to tell her nothing." And despite all that May's insight reveals to her of his selfishness, she loves him for himself alone. With exhaustive patience, she attempts to build bridge after bridge to reach the man she loves, only to realize that all she can achieve is to help him "to pass for a man." Though she protests again and again that it is never "too late," Marcher remains deaf and dumb and blind.

It requires emphasis that if Marcher were capable of accepting May's love, he would be capable also of encountering his beast in the jungle. For Henry James believed that all who are open to reality engage in authentic encounter with the demon in their own personalities. And love is the open sesame

8. *Ibid.*, p. 181.

to the reality of encounter. May, as Marcher's "second consciousness," as his "conscience," would serve as his "bridge" to his demon. But he cannot love. He cannot, therefore, accept his guilt and open the flood gates of his existence to both the shame and the glory of his human nature. His refusal to be as other men, his desire for unique experience, excludes him from consciousness of the common guilt of mankind and from personal identity. He is his own jailer. Essentially, he refuses to exist. As Henry James, Sr., had written, neither the dove nor the serpent alone is man. Marcher cannot acknowledge the serpent in himself. Worse than this, he identifies being with his own ego, and remains fixated in falsehood.

SEARCH FOR IDENTITY

Marcher has yet to witness the death of May, however, and she has yet to follow the course of his failure to the end. As her death approaches, he once again begins to doubt his future: perhaps her dying, his consequent solitude may be the only destiny he awaits. But even now his invincible egotism rebels. Would not the death of a dear companion be "only the stamp of the common doom"? Well, he will bend his pride to accept the inevitable!

On Marcher's last visit to May, she attempts to set his mind finally at rest. "You've nothing more to wait for," she tells him. "It *has* come." He reminds her, with complete chagrin, that he has never yet been aware of the "thing," that it has not even touched him. "Ah," she replies, "your not being aware of it is the strangeness in the strangeness. It's the wonder *of* the wonder . . . It has made you all

its own . . . So utterly without your knowing."
But Marcher crudely pushes his point: "How can
the thing I've never felt at all be the thing I was
marked out to feel?" Unperturbed, May declares
that he has already suffered his fate—which is not
necessarily equivalent to *knowing* it! She adds sadly
that he simply does not understand, and begs him to
remain as he is—for she desires to save him from
pain. As she dies, she asserts her constancy: "I
would live for you still—if I could. But I can't."
Thus the woman whose whole life has been a deliberate sacrifice maintains her free decision to the
end.

After May's death, Marcher is wholly con-
vinced of the truth of what she has told him. He
believes that he has already met his fate, and the
element of suspense in his life is gone. Having accepted that the incalculable "thing" has happened,
he now lives entirely for the answer to another question: What *did* happen to him? Is his existence to
remain forever masked? He bends all his efforts to
"win back" the "lost stuff of consciousness." It
becomes for him "a strayed or stolen child to an un-
appeasable father." He travels over the world seeking
for what he has lost. And he vows that he will either
"win consciousness back or have done with it forever."

A total atmosphere of death hovers over this
fifth scene in James' complex analysis of John
Marcher's existence. To be sure, his life has always
been a death-in-life. Emotionally and spiritually
dead in himself, he has been alive only in May
Bartram. Now he begins to haunt her grave, pre-

ferring the company of the dead to that of the living. As the story nears its final climax, James creates a devastating picture of the long and frustrating years. The complete solitude of Marcher, his failure to reach out to any other human being, matches the futility of his present with that of his total past. Only physically alive, he is incapable of any type of human encounter, much less love. Remorse or regret is meaningless to him. He wastes his last years in searching for the secret he could not wrench from May, and in attempting to find peace at her grave.

CONFRONTATION WITH THE DEMON

Now, close at last to his own death, Marcher seeks distraction in a long journey to the East. In these closing pages of the novel, James pictures with superb subtlety the egotism that continues to govern Marcher to the end. Visiting scenes of romance and "superlative sanctity" in the depths of Asia, he still feels that "for a man who has known what *he* has known the world is vulgar and vain." He concludes, moreover, that all the things that he sees "cannot help being common" because he has become "common" to look at them. Indeed, he resents the fact that his travels rob him of his uniqueness, his "sense of difference" from other men. And so he returns again to "his own presence," which he finds only at May Bartram's grave. Though for everyone else he is nothing, he feels that at her tomb he is somehow everything. She is his point of orientation: he is dependent on her not only for support but for his very identity. And he holds fast to the conviction that, whatever has happened or not happened, he will ultimately discover his real situation.

After innumerable pilgrimages to May's tomb, after isolating himself more and more from common humanity, Marcher at last no longer desires to live. Standing one afternoon at May's grave, he longs to lie down on the slab, gratefully, forever. And then, without warning, the great revelation comes to him. As he raises his eyes with the response to death in them, he confronts the pain-ravaged face of a man at a nearby grave. The face is seared with passion and the anguish of loss. Overwhelmed with sudden envy, Marcher wonders what this other man *had* to make him suffer so and yet live. And the truth pours in upon him with unutterable intensity. No passion has ever touched *him*, John Marcher. All his life, he has existed *outside* his own life. He has never known the anguish of mourning a woman loved for herself alone, for he has never loved a woman. Nor has this devastating truth come to him through experience itself: it has "brushed him, jolted him, with the disrespect of chance, the insolence of accident."

He stands and gazes, in this flash of illumination, on the void of his life. May Bartram is what he has missed. This is the answer to all the past. Again and again she offered him the opportunity to transcend his doom, to love her. Then he would have lived. She lived—who can say with what passion?— for she loved him for himself alone. Whereas he never thought of her except "in the light of her use to him, in the chill of his egotism." Thus Marcher has precipitated his own fate—he has become *the man* in all the world to whom nothing on earth is to happen. Experiencing involvement in his own existence for the first time, John Marcher tries desperately to fix and hold his anguish, for this at least has something of the taste of the life he never lived:

> But the bitterness suddenly sickened him, and it was as if, horribly, he saw, in the truth, in the cruelty of his image, what had been appointed and done. He saw the Jungle of his life and saw the lurking Beast; then, while he looked, perceived it, as by a stir of the air, rise, huge and hideous, for the leap that was to settle him. His eyes darkened—it was close; and, instinctively turning, in his hallucination, to avoid it, he flung himself, face down, on the tomb.

For Marcher, knowledge has come at last. The truth, the "cruelty of his image," is his "other self," his demon, the lurking beast in the jungle of his life. The confrontation of the beast comes too late, and only physical death remains for the man who has never lived.

With the spring of the beast upon him, Marcher experiences the weight of reality annihilating his egotism. But it is significant that even now, at the moment of final revelation, he cannot find love. Even after the beast springs upon him, he throws himself upon the tomb not in passion but in despair. The moment he understands his fate, his life collapses. Perhaps the ultimate irony of his life is that its only *real* event is his understanding, not his regeneration.

The theme of Marcher's story, then, is the utter futility of a life without human encounter. His final recognition of the waste of a life not lived brings anguish, but not redemption. The catastrophic moment of enlightenment in the search for self-knowledge is sterile. Marcher breaks through his fixation on self too late to love. To be sure, he finds at last his long-lost consciousness. But this is not enough. For Henry James, only love is the ultimate redemptive force. Only the man who accepts the beast in himself acknowledges his need for redemption: and only the man who loves can accept his own inner demon. John Marcher encounters his beast in the end, but he does not reconcile the demon with the dove. So his existence ends in supreme defeat. May would have offered him love and redemption. "That," says Henry James, "is what might have happened, and what *has* happened is that it didn't."

FAILURE IN DECISION AND REBIRTH

The Beast in the Jungle may be experienced on as many levels as there are readers. Few will bring to the tale the depth of James' own insight. An understanding of James' novel from the viewpoint of existential psychology, however, illuminates many dark corners in the complex psyche of John Marcher. When one becomes aware, on the level of understanding personality in depth, that Marcher is fixated all his life long on existential transference to his own ego which stunts the growth of his personality, that his fixation diminishes the possibility of mature openness to reality, of human will and decision, and ultimately of human encounter, one can feel sympathy for this colossally conceited man. One can pity Marcher's failure to love, his death-in-life, and his loss of redemption. One can even understand, finally, why May Bartram loved him and sacrificed her life for him.

The reader may be reminded of another *nouvelle* by Henry James' good friend, Robert Louis Stevenson. Captivated one day by the idea of the "hanger back," the man who refuses to live full-heartedly, Stevenson set himself the task of writing the "case" for the type of man he least admired. In "Will-O-The-Mill" he created an extremely sympathetic portrait of an extremely dull man. Stevenson was not one-half the psychologist that Henry James was. Perhaps he learned through the genius of his friend who created John Marcher that even the most incredible egotist can deserve love.

CLAMENCE IN CAMUS' THE FALL

IN WRITING a tribute to Albert Camus immediately after his death, Jean-Paul Sartre called *The Fall* "perhaps the finest and least understood" of his books. One has only to read the interpretations of Camus' novel published since 1957 to realize the full implications of Sartre's statement.[1] *The Fall* is a novel, an anti-novel, and a mere monologue; it is humanist and anti-human; nihilistic and optimistic; existential-

1. See the following: Adele King, "Structure and Meaning in *La Chute*," *PMLA*, LXXVII (1962), 660-67; Louis R. Rossi, "Albert Camus: The Plague of Absurdity," *Kenyon Review*, XX (1958), 399-422; John Cruickshank, *Albert Camus and the Literature of Revolt* (New York: Oxford University Press, 1959), pp. 181-88; Germaine Brée, *Camus* (New Jersey: Rutgers University Press, 1961), pp. 131-34; Philip Thody, *Albert Camus, A Study of His Work* (London: Hamish Hamilton, 1957), pp. 74-81; Bernard C. Murchland, "Albert Camus: The Dark Night before the Coming of Grace," *The Catholic World*, CLXXXVIII (1959), 308-14; Henri Peyri, "Camus the Pagan," *Yale French Studies* (1960), 20-25; Gaëtan Picon, "Exile and the Kingdom," in Germaine Brée, *Camus, A Collection of Critical Essays* (New Jersey: Prentice Hall, Inc., 1962), pp. 152-56; and Roger Quilliot, "An Ambiguous World," in Brée, *A Collection of Critical Essays*, pp. 157-69.

ist and anti-existentialist; as classical as Voltaire and
as surrealist as Nathalie Sarraute. Its protagonist,
Jean-Baptiste Clamence, is a hero and an anti-hero;
John the Baptist and Lucifer; Christ and anti-Christ.
He is Camus himself, Jean-Paul Sartre, Sartre's caricature of Camus, and Camus' caricature of Sartre's
caricature of Camus!

There are many possible approaches to the
complex questions presented by *The Fall* (or created
by its interpreters). One is to state that its theme is,
precisely, ambiguity. Another is simply to treat
Camus' meaning as a problem in addition: one places
all the readings of the novel in one grand harem of
meaning, asserts that each has significance on a
different level, and totals them into one somewhat
meaningless whole. Neither of these two approaches,
both of which have been pursued, seems to do justice
to Camus' intent or accomplishment.

A warning which should be stressed at once
is that *The Fall* is an imaginative work of literature,
not a philosophical treatise. Camus, in his own words,
used "techniques of the theatre, the dramatic monologue and the implied dialogue, in order to describe
a tragic comedian." The presentation of the tragic
comedian in the protagonist, Jean-Baptiste Clamence,
is a masterpiece of satire and irony. Once when he was
asked whether there was an aspect of his work neglected by his commentators, Camus replied immediately, "Humor." [2] Perhaps not since Swift has
any modern writer offered so devastating and sar-

2. Quoted in Brée, Introduction to *Camus, A Collection of
Critical Essays*, p. 9.

donic a humor as that of *The Fall*. In fact, a comparison might be made between Camus and Swift, who was so often misread throughout the nineteenth century by critics who confused the dramatic voices of his satiric characters with the voice of Swift himself. There is much of philosophy in *The Fall*, of course, as in all great literary works. But in reading so ambiguous a novel, the dangers inherent in overlooking the aesthetic medium through which one must pass in order to isolate philosophic meaning are great. However, the present study is concerned primarily not with the philosophical but with the psychological meaning of the novel.

Once the reader has become aware of the implications of Camus' literary methods, many problems of interpretation are clarified. But difficulties in reading *The Fall* still abound. Precisely here the existential psychological approach becomes meaningful, for the novel has been interpreted from many apparently contradictory points of view, each of which uncovers some truth. The existential psychological method returns to a description of the fundamental human behavior of the fictional character, in this case the single narrator who develops the theme of *The Fall* with his own life as a point of reference. Thus it may be possible to integrate the various interpretations of critics of the work, insofar as they remain true to the novel itself, within its satiric framework. At the same time, an analysis from the viewpoint of existential psychology—not from that of existentialism—may offer a fresh, new view of the core meaning of Camus' novel.

PORTRAIT OF AN EGOTIST

The Fall is a dramatic monologue in the savagely satiric manner of Dostoyevsky's *Notes from the Underground*. Even more than Dostoyevsky's disturbingly gleeful narrator, the self-conscious Jean-Baptiste Clamence of *The Fall* is "the inheritor of a century of exploration of the 'I.' " A compulsive talker, he holds forth on the intensely interesting subject of himself in a marathon monologue of five nights' duration, his listener being an unidentified middle-aged gentleman whom he has cornered in the Mexico City, a cheap bar in Amsterdam. In the implied dialogue, the listener may well be you or I—the "hypocrite reader" of Baudelaire. It matters little to Clamence.

As the monologue opens, Jean-Baptiste introduces himself to his partner at the bar in quite courteous fashion. Almost at once he falls into a patronizing criticism of the illiterate bartender, punctuated by the declaration, "Mind you, I am not judging him." This equivocal statement is the prelude to the main theme of the novel. Clamence almost immediately informs his companion that his profession is that of "judge-penitent," which he does not define. From now on, suspense is maintained throughout the five-day monologue by direct and indirect references to this key word which is not clarified completely until the final day. Moreover, as the long tirade begins, Jean-Baptiste points out "an empty rectangle" on the back wall of the bar, marking the position of a displaced portrait which, again, is not identified until the close of the novel.

Jean-Baptiste now launches into a declamation which soon emerges in a pattern: a particular judgment is made, and it is at once expanded into a universal one. For example, Clamence has a weakness for fine speech, which might imply a cover-up for vilification; but then, "those who murder the language are not pure either." Or, the five million inhabitants of Paris have two passions: they fornicate and read the newspapers; but then, their vices are common to all "modern men." Again, the sterile society of the Dutch is ironically summarized in "a job, a family, and organized leisure activities"; but then, such organization is not just *theirs*—it is ours too!

After this careful amplification of vices to a universal plane, Jean-Baptiste goes on artfully to identify his listener with himself: both are sophisticated, open-minded, cultured bourgeois. And both are Sadducees because they do not share their possessions with the poor. Thus the parabolic nature of the monologue is implied. Now Clamence elaborates his own character: he is physically attractive, well dressed, well manicured, a man with a double profession—that of judge-penitent. But then, *all* human beings are "double." Here the motif of duplicity is initially emphasized. It is to be repeated with increasing artistic intensity throughout the story.

At this point the question naturally arises: Just who is Jean-Baptiste Clamence meant to be? Because of misinterpretations, it should be stressed at once that Camus protested the tendency of critics to identify him with his fictional characters. Moreover, as the reference to Sadducee suggests, Jean-Baptiste is less an individual than a stereotype. He represents

a certain type of postwar European—the disillusioned
humanitarian, morally broken, tortured by guilt, in
search of self-justification. Only ironically is he
Camus' mouthpiece. And in order to enter into his
complexity, a great deal is demanded of the reader.
True to character, Camus himself gives the best
clue to the identity of Clamence in the brief passage
from Lermontov which he places as an epigraph to
the novel:

> Some were dreadfully insulted and quite seri-
> ously, to have held up as a model such an immoral charac-
> ter as *A Hero of Our Time*; others shrewdly noticed that
> the author had portrayed himself and his acquaintances
> . . . *A Hero of Our Time*, gentlemen, is in fact a portrait,
> but not an individual; it is the aggregate of the vices of
> our whole generation in their fullest expression.

Clamence is no man and everyman. He is a composite
picture, a mask.

Jean-Baptiste now goes on to fill in the portrait of himself, the hero of our time. The setting
helps to define the character. Close by the Mexico
City is the Jewish quarter of Amsterdam, where
75,000 Jews were assassinated or deported by Hit-
ler's Gestapo. Here, precisely, is one of the causes of
the ugly distrust felt by the "modern man" of the
portrait. This is why the people of Amsterdam, like
the narrator, are "double." This is one of the reasons
why Amsterdam, a few minutes later, is compared
with hell: "Have you noticed that Amsterdam's concentric canals resemble the circles of hell? The middle
class hell, of course, peopled with bad dreams. . . ."
And not the city alone, to extend the figure, but the

whole modern world. Amsterdam is merely the tip
of the continent—symbolically, the densest, the darkest, the last circle, for Clamence has reached the
climax of the nightmare of his life. In *The Rebel*,
Camus speaks explicitly of the contemporary world
as hell. In our time, he implies, the newspaper readers
and the fornicators have reached the last circle—they
can go no further. Clamence can find no exit except
the perverse vocation of "judge-penitent."

Before bidding goodnight to his companion,
whom he has accompanied from the bar, Jean-Baptiste
strangely hesitates to cross a nearby bridge with him.
Why? Never, he confesses, does he cross a bridge at
night. What if someone should jump into the water?
Either he would run the risk of personal danger in
rescuing the unfortunate one, or he would burden
himself with guilt for not doing so. Clamence is now
foreshadowing the climactic revelation of the core of
his own guilt. In fact, all the threads of the ensuing
monologue are artfully woven together in this first
night's talk. Moreover, toward the end of the discussion, the one concept which later becomes the only
possible ultimate answer to the dilemma of the "hero
of our time" is proposed and rejected with bitterest
cynicism. After sardonically referring to the atrocious
murder of the Jews in Amsterdam, Clamence adds:

> I knew a pure heart who rejected distrust. He was
> a pacifist and libertarian and loved all humanity and the
> animals with equal love . . . He had written on his
> threshold: 'Wherever you come from, come in and be
> welcome.' Who do you think answered that noble invita-
> tion? The militia, who made themselves at home and dis-
> emboweled him.

For Jean-Baptiste Clamence, love is no solution.

In the brief pages of this first night's monologue, Clamence offers an implicit psychological revelation of himself. His talk is scintillating, patronizing, sarcastic: he is a consummate egotist. A ghoulish humor pervades the scene. The narrative technique of a one-sided conversation gives the reader the uncomfortable feeling that *he* is the listener, the companion who cannot get a word in edgewise. This response defines the vulgarity of Jean-Baptiste. He never listens. At certain points in the implied dialogue, he asks a question, but immediately answers it himself. And the reader almost catches himself interjecting: "But I didn't *say* that!" In this type of truncated dialogue, Camus is superb in uncovering clues to the character of the speaker. Although his companion never speaks, Clamence treats his implied point of view arbitrarily.[3] Thus the total effect is that of distortion, and the monologue takes on a surrealistic quality. In short, the second character is not even granted existence. He is totally dependent on Jean-Baptiste. Thus the latter's self-love is magnified and his subsequent confession of his vices becomes ironic.

Clamence, the reader soon becomes aware, is incapable of authentic communication. As the speaker rants on more and more compulsively, the suspicion grows that his endless talk alone renders his self-centeredness bearable. Jean-Baptiste's narcissism is the dominant truth to emerge, and as the reader listens to his charges that all men love themselves alone, he becomes increasingly conscious of the character's

3. See Cruickshank, *Albert Camus and the Literature of Revolt*, pp. 184-85.

neurotic projection. For all his self-love, however, Clamence is a fascinating character, partially because of the ambiguities of his personality. In any case, the listener desires above all to pursue the monologue. At the same time, he becomes gradually cognizant of an extremely grotesque quality in the whole performance. All the reader need do is detach himself, and at once he can laugh at the ludicrous stance of Clamence, in spite of all the quasi-serious, tragic implications of his harangue.

DUPLICITY PROJECTED TO THE INNOCENT

In the Mexico City bar the next night, Jean-Baptiste relates, after a long rising action, the crucial event of his life which marked the beginning of his "fall." Before he offers a graphic picture of this event, however, he must present himself in his "Eden" before the fall. Once he was a well-known Paris lawyer, famed for his justice to widows and orphans, scornful of the judges together with whom he pursued his high calling. Clamence's description of himself is melodramatically lacerating:

> My heart was on my sleeve. You would really have thought that justice slept with me every night. I am sure you would have admired the rightness of my tone, the appropriateness of my emotion, the persuasion and warmth, the restrained indignation of my speeches before the court.

After all, he was on "the right side." Crimes are committed, declares Jean-Baptiste, because no one can endure being wrong. One is reminded of an entry in Camus' *Notebooks*: "The need to be right is the sign of a vulgar mind." [4] So Clamence remained the smug defender of virtue. He accepted no bribes; he rejected flattery; he refused public honor. As a matter of fact, refusal was more satisfying to vanity than acceptance.

Jean-Baptiste indeed aimed *high*. He enjoyed his own nature to the full, and that nature was completely self-centered. He relished the comparatively subtle pleasures of giving up his seat in a crowded bus, offering his taxi to someone in a greater hurry than he, buying flowers from a peddler. The grinning clown in Camus rises to the surface as Clamence describes his charities:

> For instance, I loved to help blind people cross streets. From as far away as I could see a cane hesitating on the edge of the sidewalk, I would rush forward, sometimes only a second ahead of another charitable hand already outstretched, snatch the blind person from any solicitude but mine, and lead him gently but firmly along the crosswalk among the traffic obstacles toward the refuge of the other sidewalk, where we would separate with mutual emotion.

In short, Jean-Baptiste was master of his liberality, he was higher than vulgar ambition, he needed only to feel lofty—"especially if he were alone, well above the human ants." Admired by all, he was above the judges whom he judged, above the defendants whom he compelled to gratitude. He "freely held sway bathed in a light as of Eden." And his Paradise encompassed more than this: he was gifted, healthy, socially popular, completely in harmony with life. Indeed, he was so fully a man as to be a *superman*.

4. Albert Camus, *Notebooks: 1935-1942* (New York: Alfred A. Knopf, 1963), p. 32.

Now suddenly, in the midst of his ironic discourse, Clamence is reminded of the rarity of friendship and the hypocrisy of the living in the face of death. And, as in the first night's monologue, the duplicity of human nature becomes central to his thought. Man, he asserts, has two faces: he cannot love without base self-love. It is ourselves we really love, and not our friends, living or dead. We become bored, most of us, and this is the real source of our commitments. Jean-Baptiste's cynical meditation on friendship and death would seem to be a digression from his eulogy of his life in Paradise, but it is actually a prelude to the story of his fall.

Returning to his account of Eden, Clamence recalls a certain fine autumn evening when he walked up the quays of the Left Bank and crossed the Pont des Arts, feeling within himself a vast sense of power and completion. Suddenly he hears, behind him, a burst of laughter rising from the water. It is an oddly disquieting laughter. He turns quickly, but no one is there. His complacency shattered, he returns home with a feeling of vague unrest. When he looks at his smiling face in the mirror that night, it seems to him that his smile is "double." The laughter that Jean-Baptiste has heard is strangely unsettling because he feels instinctively that it is directed toward himself. Actually, it comes—a forgotten, malevolent force—from beyond his conscious level of thought and action. From now on, every time that he hears laughter, he will feel that it is directed in ridicule toward himself.

In this second day's monologue, Clamence does not explain the significance of the derisive laughter, but his "double" smile is the clue to its meaning. Also, a free association which he casually makes as he takes leave of his companion proves to be a key. Speaking of rogues he has defended, Jean-Baptiste declares: "If pimps and thieves were invariably sentenced, all decent people would get to thinking they themselves were constantly innocent . . . And in my opinion . . . that's what must be avoided above all. Otherwise, everything would be a joke." These last words of the evening's discussion are the first to suggest the denial of the possibility of innocence, a central theme of *The Fall*. The motif of the judge-penitent is caught up in the dialogue both before and after the account of the Eden episode, and the stage is set for the revelation of Clamence's fall, which is to be made on the third night.

The portrait which Jean-Baptiste draws of himself before the collapse of his unauthentic, ideal self is a superb picture of the egotist who has repressed the reality of his situation so completely that his conscious existence is a Paradise of false happiness. He is seemingly invulnerable because his neurotic defenses support his assumed role so magnificently. Moreover, a bored society which seeks sentimental and emotional release at all costs, even in the sacred rites of friendship, love, and death, is in collusion with Clamence in his fake manifestations of charity, justice, and benevolence. Because this society is sick in its pursuit of sham ideals, Jean-Baptiste's possibility of breaking through his abnormal self-centeredness to authentic encounter with his fellows is negligible. The irony of his posture

after his departure from his Eden, however, lies in
the fact that he is aware of the depths of his own
egotism, but still unaware of his falsehood in judging
others. He projects to all men not the self-love which
in varying degrees is a common failing of humanity,
but his own staggering egotism. The fact that there
is some truth in his judgment renders it more in-
sidious than if it were totally false. The self-indict-
ment of Clamence is nevertheless realistic: he has
sounded the rock bottom of his self-idolization, and
he is absolutely uncompromising in his self-accusation. He remains a paragon of self-love, and the
greater his self-condemnation, the greater the guilt
he can project to all men, thus maintaining his lofty
position above the "human ants."

        This theme is at the very core of *The Fall*. It is
first suggested in Jean-Baptiste's remark that "what
must be avoided above all" is that "decent people
think themselves innocent." In an interview printed
in the *New York Times* shortly after the publication
of *The Fall*, Camus stated that he modeled Clamence
on "an existentialist practice, a mania for self-accusation, so that they can accuse others more easily." He
was referring, of course, only to certain existential-
ists, particularly Jean-Paul Sartre, with whom he had
quarreled so violently over the principles enunciated
in *The Rebel*.[5] In the latter book also, Camus spoke
of the peculiar modern attack upon innocence when
he wrote, "On the day when crime dons the apparel
of innocence—through a curious transposition pe-

    5. See Nicola Chiaromonte, "Sartre versus Camus: A Politi-
cal Quarrel," *Partisan Review*, XIX (1952), 680-87.

culiar to our times—it is innocence that is called upon
to justify itself." [6] At still another time, Camus had
remarked, "People have insisted too much on the
innocence of creation. Now they want to crush us with
the feeling of our own guilt." [7] Jean-Baptiste, judge
of himself and judge of all men, is the arch-enemy of
innocence. In accusing himself, he accuses everyone.
And Camus, with an irony worthy of Voltaire, allows
him to pursue his damnation of himself to its caustic
end. Clamence is a tragic comedian, for he sees himself truly only in the evil of his nature, never in his
potential existential relationship to other men and to
the world. Therefore, to the detached observer he is
finally ludicrous in his self-castigation and self-love,
for he views himself and all men, not in reality, but
in the distorted mirror of a carnival playhouse.

SELF-DISCOVERY AND EXISTENTIAL SHAME

The third night's monologue of *The Fall*, like
a third act of Shakespearean tragi-comedy, culminates in the account of the climax of Jean-Baptiste's
life. Because he is a dramatic voice relating his own
crisis, the experience is a flash-back, presented with
graphic subtlety. For a time, Clamence partially represses the disturbing memory of the laughter he
heard on the Pont des Arts. But the repression finds
its own deviations. He becomes dejected, he has
"health problems," he finds it "hard to breathe." At
this point Jean-Baptiste swings his discussion cun-
ningly from his own difficulty in breathing to every

6. Albert Camus, *The Rebel* (New York: Alfred A. Knopf,
1957), p. 4.
7. Quoted in Thody, *Albert Camus, A Study of His Work*,
p. 78.

man's need to domineer, to enslave: "Commanding is breathing—you agree with me?" Everyone must dominate, he declares—if no one else, at least his dog. On a political level, domination is symbolized by the communique, which is now substituted for dialogue. Man must have slaves, but he must not admit it; so he calls them "free men." Clamence himself has always felt free and powerful simply because he has recognized no equals. He has conveniently repressed all evidences of superiority to himself. But from the moment that he hears the laughter of ridicule on the bridge, he begins to lose his extraordinary "ability to forget" and discovers a "few truths" about himself. "I was always bursting with vanity," he declares. "I, I, I is the refrain of my whole life, which could be heard in everything I said. I could never talk without boasting, especially if I did so with that shattering discretion that was my specialty."

Jean-Baptiste now creates suspense concerning the episode of the laughter by digressing on illustrations of his vanity and self-absorption. His demented monologue is clearly aimed at the conscience of his listener, his "hypocrite reader," in order to convince him of his own guilt and draw him into self-accusation. A down-to-earth account of being insulted as a "poor dope" by a motorist while stopping at a green light, for example, recalls to the reader apparently insignificant events in his own life which have caused him abysmal embarrassment and vindictive anger. And then Clamence craftily insinuates his own diagnosis of his fault: his *real* desire was to dominate the man who insulted him, to overcome him by force. In short, he has discovered in himself "sweet dreams of oppression." Whenever Jean-Baptiste is threatened, he becomes not only his neighbor's judge, but his irascible master, with a mad desire to strike down the offender to his knees. And what now of his vocation as defender of widows and orphans?

Clamence's second example of his domineering pride concerns his relations with women. In accordance with his constant projection of his own vices to all humanity, he now introduces his theme with the dogmatic assertion that "true love" occurs almost never—the rest of the time there is only vanity and boredom. Jean-Baptiste has conceived only "one great love in his life," and he himself is the object of it! For the rest, he has a "congenital inability" to see in love for woman anything but sensuality. Conquering a woman is a "game" in which love for self is verified by special powers of success. But the ultimate in Clamence's monstrous domination of others is revealed in his intensest sensuality, which is to conquer the woman he does *not* desire, to reduce her to slavery, simply because of her initial failure to desire *him*. Just at this point, however, Jean-Baptiste makes an even more subtle distinction in his analysis of his fundamental degeneration. In his sex life he cannot claim subterfuge, for "no man is a hypocrite in his pleasure": there selfishness screams aloud. Consequently he is more worthy, because more honest, in his private vices than in his professional flights on innocence and justice!

After these damning illustrations of his own degradation, Clamence sums up his spiritual state with lacerating sincerity. In order to live happily, it is necessary to him that others be so dependent upon

him that *they* do not live at all. The awareness of his
submission of others to actual slavery burst upon him
with a sense of shame for the first time when he discovered the source of the derisive laughter on the
Pont des Arts. The springs of this laughter he uncovers deep within his unconscious, in an incident
that occurred three years previously on the Pont
Royal. Crossing the bridge alone one midnight, he
suddenly became aware of a young woman leaning
over the railing, staring into the water. As he passed
on, he heard the sound of her body striking the water
and her cry of anguish. He hesitated but a moment
and then moved on into the night. Jean-Baptiste repressed the memory of his experience, but it lodged
itself invincibly at the core of his deepest unconscious.
Once recalled, it roused within him a shame which
harrowed him forever.

Up until the moment of Clamence's self-discovery, he is fundamentally a complacent, self-righteous Sadducee, living only in the good opinion of
others, existing superficially on the periphery of his
own life. The event on the Pont Royal is crucial because it proposes a central question: What does the
righteous defender of the poor and helpless do when,
alone in the night with no one to witness his decision,
he is faced with an unequivocal choice between selfishness and charity? Jean-Baptiste's decision is inevitable, granted the man that he is. Both the loneliness and the freedom of his choice provide the
perfect situation for the unmasking of his real self.
Clamence is literally forced by circumstance to face
the reality of his own cowardice. This is the essence
of his fall.

An interpretation of Clamence's fall as original sin or a lapse from grace, in Christian terminology, would be misleading. The symbols of Eden, free will, the fall, and judgment are carried throughout the novel, but only with ironic implications pervaded with ambiguity. "Eden," as already discussed, is the false happiness of the pharisaical Jean-Baptiste whose central psychological flaw is a fundamental lack of self-knowledge. His fall is not from grace, for he is banished from "Eden" through self-discovery, which is rather a movement *toward* grace. Moreover, for the non-believer like Clamence, whose god is himself, grace is mere irresponsibility, a refusal to bear the burden of one's own guilt. Jean-Baptiste's fall, then, is not original or actual sin: it is, as already suggested, the discovery of his own repressed cowardice. The moment that he hears the laughter of ridicule on the Pont des Arts, the symbol of his awareness of his own duplicity, he is filled with a sense of disquietude which he later identifies with repressed shame. ("I don't know how to name the odd feeling that comes over me. Isn't it shame, perhaps?") His human guilt is without reference to law, for he accepts no law except his own will. Therefore his shame is all the more painful because he has no standard for judging either innocence or guilt. Judgment without law is the hell of the godless "hero of our time" unmasked by Camus.

The so-called ambiguity of Clamence's fall, then, centers in a lack of a point of reference.[8] Am-

8. See Cruickshank, *Albert Camus and the Literature of Revolt*, p. 187, especially the reference to the relationship of ambiguity to downfall in Heidegger's *Sein und Zeit*.

biguity and falling are aspects of the same reality. Thus Jean-Baptiste is envisioned as continually falling rather than *fallen*. Falling without beginning or end, with no certainty to grasp *except* falling, is the essence of his hell. He describes this torture concretely when he declares, "Things kept slipping. Yes, everything slipped past me." It has been suggested that Clamence's constant talking is an attempt to arrest his fall. Thus uninterrupted monologue becomes a real psychological need for him, but not a cure for his anguish. As in the myths of Prometheus and Sisyphus, Jean-Baptiste is doomed to continue the action in which he is caught. His fall moves in the concentric circles of Dante's hell, as symbolized by the canals of Amsterdam. As the strange monologue continues, the reader realizes increasingly that Clamence has already reached the last circle of his fall, the densest darkness of his odious self-worship. And the hell of his shame is permanently before him in a bottomless pit.

The young woman on the bridge symbolizes, in addition to the exposure of Jean-Baptiste's false virtue, the inevitable death following the self-discovery of evil in tragedy. If Clamence were an Othello, his self-revelation would end in suicide. But he is no Othello: he is a "tragic comedian." And so his self-recognition provokes only nightmarish laughter, arising from his own unconscious. This is the dilemma of Camus' "hero of our time." He lacks the faith to repent and accept redemption in a Christian "happy ending," but he also lacks the high seriousness of the tragic hero necessary to release himself from personal hell through suicide. Thus Lermontov's and Camus'

"hero" is in truth an anti-hero. From the tragic point
of view, he is foolishly melodramatic; from the comic
aspect, he is pathetically farcical. The bizarre laughter
that sounds throughout *The Fall* is the grotesque response of the modern hero to his unique malady.

THE HELL OF EXISTENTIAL GUILT

For his own symbolic purpose, Jean-Baptiste
invites his compatriot, on the fourth day of their
acquaintance, to tour Marken Island and view the
Zuider Zee. Once there, he describes "a soggy hell
indeed," with millions of "invisible" doves in the sky,
but "never a head on which to light." Clamence is
now guiding his listener further into the depths of his
personal hell, "everlasting nothingness made visi-
ble," with no possible promise of the Holy Spirit.
Answering a protest of his companion against his
abstruse speech, Jean-Baptiste launches into a sustained image of the hell of his existence since his fall
began. The whole human race, now made up of his
accomplices in evil, is the object of his scorn. He
clings with ferocious tenacity to his conscious self-
love, even while his unconscious self-hate shouts
aloud for recognition. As his awareness of his guilt
and shame increases, he observes—in direct proportion—a gradual change in the attitude of others toward him. Because of his quickening vulnerability,
every new depth of vice he discovers in himself projects a vocation in other men to judge him. And thus
Jean-Baptiste identifies his enemies. The concourse
of his foes encompasses all his acquaintances, especially those he has chiefly obliged, and eventually
even people he has never met. Soon the whole world

hates him, the whole universe is laughing at him. And he knows experientially that to be judged is, for man, the unbearable, the unendurable. Yet, all men judge in order not to be judged, thus creating the reality which they seek to avoid. It is a perversity of existence that each man considers himself an exceptional case: the idea that comes most naturally to man is that of his *own* innocence.

This human paradox gives pause to Clamence and almost, but not quite, diverts him from his egotistic involvement to an objective consideration of the stubborn illogicality of human nature. Why, he asks, does man prefer a reputation for natural rather than acquired virtue? To the former, no credit redounds; to the latter, much merit. Yet man is adamant in desiring meritless "virtue" because the essential thing for him is to be innocent. Man *requires* that his misdeeds be provisional. He must dodge judgment. Only when he hears the grotesque laughter of his "double" self—laughter at his own fundamental duplicity— does man discover the truth about himself. Again paradoxically, this basic truth is discovered only after all other truths are known. Then man is at last able to see the reverse side of his virtues: his modesty which allows him to shine before men; his humility which permits him to conquer; his indifference which wins him love; his selfishness which emerges in generosity.

Passages like the one just described have led critics of Camus to declare that *The Fall* cannot be wholly satirical.[9] In their revelation of human nature, such observations as the above are too disturb-

9. See, for example, Thody, *Albert Camus*, p. 80.

ing, too disquieting in their aspects of truth, to be
ironic. In short, the conviction of Camus himself
here breaks through the voice of the tragic comedian
with a seriousness not to be mocked. Like all fine
satirists, Camus demands of his reader a versatility
of mind, a readiness to adapt to change of voice and
tone. Complexity and ambiguity are clarifying rather
than confusing to the total unity of *The Fall*, but the
mind of the reader must be as sharply flexible, almost, as Camus' own.

Clamence now returns to himself to elaborate
his self-accusations. Because of his fundamental duplicity, he declares himself to live his whole life under a double code. And despite his self-love, he cannot tolerate the two-faced Janus in himself. The
"absolute murder of truth" makes him dizzy. So he
must find an escape—somehow, he must evade judgment. Childishly, he contemplates all manner of
heinous atrocities. Because he feels a strong com-
pulsion to reveal himself, he takes to defending
thieves and cutthroats in order to expose "honest"
lawyers. He shocks even "the café atheists." He
draws the knife of ridicule on heaven, earth, and
hell. But he uncovers only what he has always
known: self-accusation alone is not enough to clear
himself.

In his mad search for escape from judgment,
Clamence goes so far as to seek the "true love" of
woman and, after that, chastity (with contemptuous
laughter sounding always in his ears). The perversity
of seeking the virtue he regards as fraud is now a
veritable caricature of his former "honest" perversity.
He discovers what he expects to find: he loathes

"love" and "chastity" is a bore. "Alcohol and women" are the only solace he deserves, he tells himself, but there is still another possibility: he will attempt to liberate himself from time and space through sheer debauchery, and thus achieve a kind of immortality. But his liver and his fatigue have their limits! Debauchery does serve to muffle the laughter, he discovers, and even to deaden judgment—temporarily. Then one day on an ocean voyage, he descries a dark speck on the deep, and the image of the girl on the Pont Royal returns once more, and he is certain that he is not cured. Now a macabre symbol arises in his fantasy to define the horror of his existence.

The epitome of the unendurable takes shape in his fancy as "the little ease." The latter was a ghastly dungeon cell constructed in the Middle Ages, neither high enough to stand up in nor wide enough to lie down in. The condemned prisoner had to live literally on the diagonal; thus every moment of his existence he discovered anew the consciousness of his guilt. Similarly, Clamence feels that he is permanently condemned to be judged, to live forever as a spiritual hunchback, his only possible solace centered in his faith that all men share his guilt. The certainty of the innocence of even one man might thus cause his reason to collapse in madness. For Jean-Baptiste, like Lucifer, can accept guilt only if he can condemn all men with himself. Only thus can he still dominate. For such mastery, he discovers, one does not need God. The judgment of man is hell enough.

At this point in the monologue, the possibility

of individual innocence demands clarification by Clamence. What is the meaning, for example, of the
crucifixion of Christ? Here Camus introduces a master stroke of biting irony. Christ was murdered, declares Jean-Baptiste, because he too was guilty—he
had survived as an infant only because the innocents
were slaughtered in his place. The sin of Christ,
then, is the crux of ambiguity: it is an "innocent
crime." Here is perversity of logic at its apex. Here
is the collapse of logic. And Clamence's conclusion
is expected: the order of the whole world is itself
ambiguous. Or, as Henry Adams once declared:
"Chaos is the law of nature; order is the dream of
man."

However, there is nothing to prevent irrationality and love from existing side by side. So
Jean-Baptiste is forced to admit that, though all men
create hell by judging, Christ judged no one. He
wanted to be loved, nothing more. Clamence is willing to admit that there are "a few" who love Christ,
very few. But he insists that there are *no innocents*:
all men are guilty before one another, and there is no
exit to mercy for man. And now the tone of derisive
ridicule rises again. For Clamence, "an empty prophet
for shabby times," seems to have found a temporary
escape at last. To be judged without law is the keenest
of human torments, but Jean-Baptiste has discovered
a stratagem to circumvent judgment—in short, he
is a judge-penitent. His explication of this wily profession he reserves for the next and final day's monologue.

Clamence's tirade of this fourth day centers
almost exclusively in the ambiguities of existence.

His analysis of the fundamental duplicity of human nature gives to these two chapters a tone of deeper seriousness than that of the previous three. Human double-dealing, wherever found, creates doubt and distrust, and eventually the charge that man and nature are Janus-faced. The *New Testament* and other great spiritual works of the past reveal, to be sure, a profound awareness of the law of the flesh and the law of the spirit, of the "new man" casting out the "old man." But the "hero of our time" no longer accepts the solution of Christ and his followers. And so for him existence itself is ambiguous; innocence is dead; all men are guilty; despair is man's destiny.

This is the attitude toward existence that Camus is satirizing in Clamence. Camus himself passionately rejected every form of despair and nihilism throughout most of his life. In his *Notebooks* are frequently found such statements as the following addressed to a friend:

> I cease to agree when you try to base your life in despair, maintain that everything is equally pointless, and withdraw behind your disgust. For despair is a feeling, not a permanent condition. You cannot stay on in despair.

At another time he wrote: ". . . . if we believe optimism is silly, we also know that pessimism about the action of man among his fellows is cowardly." [10] *The Fall* is far from expressing a belief in the universal evil of mankind. Rather, it boldly satirizes such a belief as a weapon for reducing men to the roles of master and slave—whether on a personal, national,

10. Quoted in Nicola Chiaromonte, "Albert Camus: In Memoriam," *Dissent*, VII (1960), 270.

or international level. Jean-Baptiste Clamence calls himself an "enlightened advocate of slavery," and he is. In him, both universal guilt and the degradation of mankind which it advances are devastatingly attacked by Camus.

One can understand Camus' point of view better by recalling his own statement that his work evolved around successive themes: absurdity, revolt, measure, and love.[11] The "absurdity" of life, Camus believed, can be explained only in reference to an implied standard of unity and consistency. Man himself, he asserted, "possesses value and meaning precisely because he is the one creature whose desire for these things is constantly thwarted in the world." The awareness of the absurd, Camus declared, is a form of revolt, at least in a negative sense. For such awareness implies a value judgment. Revolt against the human condition, according to Camus, has taken two main forms—religion and politics. A desirable concept of revolt is centered in the idea of limitation or measure, not in absolutism or extremism.

The fourth section of *The Fall* discussed above is related (ironically, to be sure) to "the concept of limitations," which means that an affirmation of life must be made which does not end in complete negation of the world. To admit that men are selfish and hypocritical does not imply that one renounces all values. In *The Fall* Camus faces the problem of man's imperfection, and in the character of Clamence he satirizes the disastrous results of the negation of man's relative innocence. Indirectly, Camus accepts

11. See Brée, Introduction to *Critical Essays*, p. 9.

man's limited innocence through rejection of the
denial of innocence. In this acceptance, however,
Camus' thought on the problem of good and evil in
man has not found its culmination. "At the end of
the tunnel of darkness," he wrote in *The Rebel*, "there
is inevitably a light, which we already divine and for
which we only have to fight to ensure its coming. All
of us, among the ruins, are preparing a renaissance
beyond the limits of nihilism. But few of us know
it." [12] The light of which Camus speaks is his fourth
theme of "love" which was left comparatively unde-
veloped at his sudden death. Camus was aware of the
incompleteness of his thought. "All my work lies
ahead of me," he said not long before he died. This
final theme of Camus can best be discussed with relation to the fifth and last day of Clamence's monologue on modern man. Its psychological implications
as revealed in the behavior of Jean-Baptiste are indeed more meaningful to the reader than the ab-
stract statements of Camus' more philosophical
works. The author himself knew this too. "People
can think only in images," he inscribed in his *Notebooks*. "If you want to be a philosopher, write novels."

THE BURDEN OF EXISTENTIAL FREEDOM

The final day of Clamence's monologue begins
with sardonic reference to psychosomatic symptoms
in the speaker. Since he has reached the last chapter
of his self-revelation, his narrative naturally strikes
at the bitterest core of his pride. Suffering from
fever, he begins his discussion in a cloud of ambiguous statements. "It is hard," he declares, "to disen-

12. *The Rebel*, p. 305.

tangle the true from the false in what I am saying."
But after all, lies lead to truth, and sometimes it is
easier to see clearly into the liar than into the man
who tells the truth. For truth blinds.

To reinforce his earlier position on the evil
in man, Jean-Baptiste ventures to unburden himself
of some of his political adventures. With typical
cynicism, he asserts that, just as hell is the judgment
of other people, patriotism is hostility toward the
enemy. Once when he was interned in a prison camp
near Tunisia, Clamence was elected "pope" by his
fellow prisoners. His qualification for the pontificate
was that he laid claim to a greater number of personal vices than any of his companions. The reason
for relating the episode, however, is to point out
what he discovered about human nature in executing
his office. As "pope" he found it impossible, for example, to treat all prisoners with equality. After many
humiliating disappointments in himself, he finally
sank to drinking the water of a dying comrade, con-
vincing himself that the prisoners needed his services
more than the dying man needed water. The guilty
implications of such a choice would have been unbearable for the pharisaical Jean-Baptiste, however,
except for one circumstance. The experience gave
further validity to his conviction that man can endure
intolerable guilt only by incorporating his fellow
men in his shame.

Clamence is at last close to his definition of
judge-penitent and, in order to strengthen his argu-
ment, he recalls to his listener a symbol referred to
in the first night's monologue. In the closet of his
room he has hidden a famous painting by van Eyck,

called "The Just Judges." The picture once covered the empty rectangle on the wall of the Mexico City bar, whose proprietor never knew that the thief who exchanged it for liquor had purloined a masterpiece. The symbolism of the painting becomes immediately clear. The "Just Judges" are on their way to adore the "Lamb of Innocence," but for Jean-Baptiste "there is no . . . lamb of innocence." Innocence is dead, killed by the universal guilt of all men. Of more personal importance to Clamence is the fact that he can dominate other men because he alone possesses the true painting of the "Just Judges." Everyone else believes that the copy substituted for the original picture in the Cathedral of Ghent is the unique work of art. If men cannot distinguish truth from falsehood, Jean-Baptiste argues, then they have no right to the truth and no injustice is done them in depriving them of it. Thus, secure in the knowledge that he alone possesses the truth, Clamence can practice his difficult role of judge-penitent, maintaining his superiority over all.

Because he has reached the central point of his self-revelation, Jean-Baptiste now finds it more and more difficult to breathe, recalling to the reader his earlier statement that domineering others is as natural to man as breathing. The definition of his profession is a harrowing experience for Clamence, but he carries it off admirably. His five days of talking, he declares, have had one purpose—to silence the laughter of derision and avoid personal judgment. The great thing that stands in the way of escaping judgment, Jean-Baptiste has learned, is the fact that *each man is the first to condemn himself*. Therefore, it is absolutely essential to extend condemnation to all, in order to "thin it out at the start." This Clamence has achieved by refusing innocence to all men without exception. He denies "the good intention, the respectable mistake, the indiscretion, the extenuating circumstance." Thus Camus' concept of limitation, of measure, of relative innocence, is explicitly negated by Jean-Baptiste. He denies man the freedom to do limited good. Slavery is an absolute necessity for him; it provides the only possible reprieve to his sentence of condemnation.

Clamence has not failed to consider all the possibilities of freedom. And here is the crux of the matter: freedom is too heavy a burden for him to bear. Alone at midnight, with no one to sanction or condemn—with no judge—it is unendurable for the "hero of our time" to confront the choice between good and evil. Jean-Baptiste discovered this long ago on the Pont Royal. Man demands a master; slavery is the only solution. For man, alone, dreads freedom. And so Clamence preaches slavery nightly to his patrons at the Mexico City bar.

But slavery is not immediately realizable for all. In the meantime, Jean-Baptiste has devised a provisional solution in order to make his life tolerable: the profession of judge-penitent. To practice his calling, he first indulges in public confession of his vices to each new client, but he does so in such a manner that the portrait he presents of himself is the image of all men and no man. It becomes a mirror in which his contemporaries view themselves. Thus he provokes his listeners to self-judgment. The more severe his self-accusations, the more inviolable his

right to judge his listeners. Night after night, he pro-
claims his vileness to his companions, and night after
night they in turn collapse in the horror of confessing
their own reflected baseness. Thus Clamence becomes
god, he sits enthroned among his bad angels, he pities
without absolving, he understands without forgiving.
At last he feels himself adored! Only thus can he endure the guilt and shame he is forced to accept as his
own.

     Jean-Baptiste is willing to admit that his solu-
tion is neither permanent nor ideal. But he can find
no other. He cannot become what he is not. To become another, he would have "to forget himself for
someone else," but this he cannot do. "We have lost
track of the light," says Clamence, "the holy innocence of those who forgive themselves." This is
the innocence that is lost to the "hero of our time." If
he could forgive and thus truly love himself, then he
would be capable of forgetting himself and loving
others. Judgment would no longer be unavoidable.
But the price demanded would be high indeed: Is it
possible to become another? If Jean-Baptiste were
given a second chance on the Pont Royal, would he
redeem himself? It is too late, he declares, and it will
always be too late. Fortunately, for he would never
be able to survive the trial of innocence! This very
last statement of Clamence's interminable monologue
is thus more bitter and repulsive than the first. Perhaps the greatest irony of the entire novel is that
Jean-Baptiste gradually grows so hopelessly cynical
that, when he finally admits indirectly that love is the
only absolute answer to his problem, he cancels all
the value of his vision by a categorical denial of the

possibility of its achievement. In reality, the message of the judge-penitent is one of absolute despair.

Three main psychological implications emerge from this final act of Jean-Baptiste's personal drama. The first is that the man who makes himself his own god by judging men condemns himself to psychological and spiritual anguish, symbolized by the dungeon of torture in which one can neither stand nor lie. The second is that freedom is too heavy a burden for the man who is his own god: his existential guilt is intolerable. And the third is that such a man can find his lost innocence—and therefore happiness—only by forgiving himself and freeing himself for love, thus canceling the necessity to project his own guilt to his fellow men.

In *The Rebel* Camus expresses his passionate antagonism to the "modern man," Clamence, when he speaks of "the only original rule of life today: to learn to live and to die, and, in order to be man, to refuse to be god." [13] The judgment of man by man was rejected by Camus in every one of his works, for the self-idolatry which is basic to man-as-judge negates all that is human. It is man's nature to turn toward the world and other men in openness, to be in harmony with creation, to participate in being. "Self-enjoyment," writes Camus, "is impossible." In opposing Malraux, Gide, and Sartre, Camus insists that man cannot be a superman, a pleasure-seeker, or a judge, and still be a complete man. Jean-Baptiste attempts to be all three, and he becomes the most pitiable of all Camus' character creations.

The answer to Clamence, Camus believes, is the "concept of limitations," an affirmation of life, as

13. *Ibid.*, p. 306.

already stated, which accepts the limited innocence of
man and endorses openness to being at each present
moment. Only the man who is aware of his own limitations and those of all men can bear the burden of
freedom in full responsibility. Such a man will accept
his own personal guilt squarely, without the neurotic
necessity of indicting all men. He will achieve this
acceptance, to be sure, only through love and harmony with other men. It is this final concept of love,
the last of his four main themes, that Camus did not
live to develop completely in his works.

The theme of love as the solution to Jean-
Baptiste's problem is implicit in the total development of *The Fall*. Clamence, the Sadducee, desires an
absolute law which will free him from guilt and con-
firm him in self-righteousness. He desires a master,
but not one who rules by love. All of his relationships
with his fellow men prove that the *one* experience of
which he is completely incapable is love. In his supreme egotism, he can relate to other men only in
guilt. Yet, ironically, Clamence's very name means
"mercy, forgiveness," precisely the quality he lacks,
the quality which would render him capable of love.
His entire monologue, which might have been a
bridge from pride to humility through healing remorse, thus becomes only diabolical accusation of
others. A judge-penitent is a monster of pride who
maintains his feeling of self-righteous contempt by
trapping others into self-condemnation. Camus creates in Clamence a menace to all the values that he
himself holds dear. In his *Notebooks* Camus once
wrote: "The misery and greatness of the world: it
offers no truths, but objects for love. Absurdity is
king, but love saves us from it."

LOVE AS RESPONSE TO EXISTENTIAL GUILT

To state that in *The Fall* Albert Camus found a self-satisfying solution to the problems of evil, shame, and guilt would be an exaggeration. "No man can say what he is," Camus wrote. "But it sometimes happens that he can say what he isn't. He who is still looking is then judged to have concluded. A thousand views already announce what he has found, whereas he knows it is not that." [14] It would be presumptuous to exaggerate the philosophical or theological implications of *The Fall*, for in this book Camus has said "what he is not." Therefore one cannot endorse those critics who have interpreted Camus' "light at the end of the tunnel of darkness" and "sun at the center of his work" as evidence that he implicitly accepted Christianity. Neither can one subscribe to the opposite interpretation that for Camus there is "no transcendence" at all. Camus died without *clarifying* an essential positive attitude toward human existence.

On the other hand, the existential psychological implications of *The Fall* are valid. For Camus, who declared that philosophers should write novels, *The Fall* is an ironic satire of the "hero of our time" who wears the mask of superman, pleasure-seeker, and judge of others. Existential psychological analysis reveals that the mask conceals a hell of self-condemnation. Love is the only permanent exit for "modern man," but *The Fall* draws no map for the pursuit of love.

14. Quoted in Brée, *Camus*, p. 197.

QUERRY IN GREENE'S
A BURNT-OUT CASE

A Burnt-Out Case by Graham Greene is the story of a man who discovers, in his late fifties, that the mode of existence he has pursued unquestioningly for forty years has been a shocking negation of reality. His faith has been false. His love has been egotism. His supposed genius has been mediocrity. Recognition of his long fantasy of happiness and success leads him straight to what Greene considers the characteristic psychical disease of twentieth century man: the ennui of those who awake one morning to discover that their existence is nothingness. For Greene, this situation is the core of the existential crisis. Forty years ago Freudian analysis might free a man suffering from a religious or sexual neurosis for a full life. But when man's neurosis is his very existence, indeed his very self, he faces a life-or-death choice. In such straits, some men commit suicide, preferring death to death-in-life. Others choose to remain physically alive, facing each day the pursuit of nothingness; they live out their existence in "quiet desperation." Only the daring have the "courage to be," to transcend nothingness on a new level of being. Querry, Greene's enigmatic protagonist whose name symbolizes both seeker and victim, experiences existential crisis in a universe grounded in irony and ambiguity.

Greene prefaces his novel with a line from the *Inferno:* "I did not die, yet nothing of life remained." The epigraph is fitting for Querry, whose life so nauseates him that he chooses to neither live nor die, but only to hide himself away in a dark corner of the world like a sick animal. Past all caring, beyond all desire except to be left alone to lick his wounds, he is incapable even of wishing for a cure. His last frontier of hope, as he crouches at the rock-bottom of his existence, is to cling to death-in-life. To use Dante's terminology once more, he stops short of the door of hell: "Abandon all hope, you who enter here."

The key to the symbolic meaning of the "burnt-out case" is found in a second quotation, this time from a pamphlet on leprosy, which Greene also places at the beginning of his tale:

Within the limits of normality, every individual loves himself. In cases where he has a deformity or abnormality or develops it later, his own aesthetic sense revolts and he develops a sort of disgust towards himself. Though with time he becomes reconciled to his deformities, it is only at the conscious level. His sub-conscious mind, which continues to bear the mark of the injury, brings about certain changes in his whole personality. . . .

This description of the "burnt-out case" incorporates both the physical and psychological effects of the disease. In Greene's novel, psychical mutilation is incarnated in Querry himself at the center of the action. Physical deformity is reflected in the little servant with the unbelievable name, Deo Gratias. In him, leprosy has finally run its course, but only at the expense of having eaten away fingers and toes, ears and nose. He is mutilated, but cured: his problem is to live with himself.

A Burnt-Out Case is essentially a modern exemplum, a sustained metaphor of two-hundred fifty pages, with a complexity of symbolism magnificently integrated within a totality of meaning. Structurally, the story is divided into three major sections, each preceded by briefer chapters. The latter transitional sections clarify the changes in Querry's character as he advances deeper and deeper into the jungle of his existence on his dark odyssey toward self-revelation. In each of the three central parts of the novel, Querry meets in existential encounter characters who symbolize various aspects of the demonic in his own nature. Always present are Deo Gratias, who represents Querry's better self, and Dr. Colin, who is a kind of Greek chorus to the dramatic action. Querry himself may be compared with Henry James' "central intelligence" in fiction. With a wonderfully comprehensive existential approach, Greene places Querry at the center of a circle, as it were, and lets him view himself through his relationships with his "other selves" on the periphery. Each of these characters in his own way

reflects Querry's psychical disorder, turning brilliant
or dull or refracted light upon his situation. Each is a
mirror in which Querry sees himself with pitiless
honesty, until the complex, ambiguous lights of
mirror within mirror finally clash in a kaleidoscope of
chaotic absurdity. It is a triumph of Greene's talent
that the absurdity itself in the end gives unity and a
degree of resolution to the meaning of Querry's
existence. He literally dies of irony, but the very
extremity of his situation gives meaning to its ambiguity. For the death of Querry is a powerful either/or
situation. Under the precise pen of Graham Greene,
Querry's death points to only one conclusion: his life
was either a monstrous, grotesque joke or the profoundest of mysteries.

A PSYCHOLOGICAL ODYSSEY

In the opening chapter of the novel, we meet
Querry in a small paddle-steamer on the outermost
tributary of the Congo River, his only companions a
Flemish priest who speaks no French and a few
natives who know only their own private Mongo.
The strange African atmosphere makes so physical an
assault upon our senses that we soon become aware
that the Belgian Congo is a heart of darkness into
which Querry is sinking, a jungle of the unconscious
which is completely driving out the comfortable,
everyday familiarities of his European life. An inter-
nationally famous Belgian architect, suddenly sick of
his own success, Querry has abandoned everything
that he has known, and without even taking luggage,
has compulsively boarded a plane for Africa. The

natives on the Congo, who compose their own secret
songs about newcomers to this land of paradoxical
sunlit heat and darkness, reflect Querry's vision of
himself: "Here is a man who . . . comes from a long
way away—we do not know from where—and he
tells no one to what place he is going nor why.":
Here, indeed, is a region less geographical than
psychological.

When Querry engages in brief conversation
with a priest in a seminary along the Congo where
he stops for the night, Greene reveals with his unique
economy of style a striking psychological truth about
the man. With a sudden impulse to speak, the
traveler declares to the priest that he has "come to
the end of everything" in his life. Somehow, we are
unimpressed with Querry's intimate confidence to a
stranger. Is he a mere masochistic exhibitionist? But
this judgment is suddenly checked by the harsh
honesty of Querry's self-appraisal. When the childlike laughter of the seminarians at recreation irritates
him like the unknown words of an alien tongue, he
wonders privately when he first began "to detest
laughter like a bad smell." With inadvertent comic
irony, the priest in charge innocently offers Querry a
bar of Lifebuoy soap as he retires for the night! Thus
the tone of the novel is defined: the absurdity of life
is inextricably bound up with man's deepest search
for meaning. And Querry's later conquest of laughter
is to be the ambiguous symbol of both his cure and
his defeat.

The wanderer's arrival at the leper colony,
where the priests permit him to remain with no
questions asked, is signaled by the first of three highly

symbolic dreams which precede crucial experiences in his life. The dream occurs on the road to the town of Luc, where Querry journeys to transport supplies for the mission. He dreams of a girl whom he once knew and thought he loved. She comes to him in tears because she has broken a vase which she valued, and she becomes angry with him because he does not share her suffering. She strikes him in the face, but he does not feel the blow. He says to her, "I am sorry, I am too far gone, I don't feel at all, I am a leper." The girl is a symbol of Marie Morel, later identified as a young woman who killed herself to escape the tyranny of her sexual relationship with Querry. In his dream, Querry experiences all the horror of his psychological disease, which precludes the possibility of guilt, re-morse, or even pity for his victim. The burnt-out case is thus initially defined by Querry's unconscious, and he awakens to a clear vision of his existential neurosis.

With his usual shattering juxtaposition of the tragic and comic, Greene now precipitates Querry into a sudden fantastic meeting with M. Rycker, a monster of pompous religiosity, who is destined to become the ironic instrument of Querry's grotesque death. Rycker, as a symbol of spiritual hypocrisy, provides Querry with his first existential encounter with the demonic in his own character. It is a tribute to Greene's art that the reader is simultaneously aware of Rycker on an actual and a symbolic level. This repulsive character, through a distorted projec-tion, decides at once that Querry is a saint undergoing a dark night of the soul. Rycker has discovered an "affinity," and he is mad to share his "spiritual" thoughts! He likes to talk about love—"agape, not eros"—and when Querry finally escapes him, he feels that the darkness of the night croaks with Rycker's hollow phrases.

When Querry returns to the leprosarium, he reacts violently against his encounter with Rycker by talking to Dr. Colin "as a hungry man eats." An agnostic with a tough-minded dedication to healing the lepers, Colin becomes the one man who understands Querry as the burnt-out case that he is. With a genius for penetrating the unconscious defenses of others, Colin is as clear-sighted as a prophet. If he cannot cure the subterranean ills of the psyche as he can the leprous infection, he is as deeply aware of the one as of the other. Colin is a rare twentieth-century seer on the furthest frontier of the quest for existential meaning. "Now that a cure had been found for the physical disease," says Greene, "he always had to remember that leprosy remained a psychological problem." One is reminded of Greene's reference in his Congo journal to lepers who are cured but still treated regularly by a doctor—to prevent psychological breakdown. If no natural therapy yet exists for a man like Querry, the Colins of the world will be on hand when it is discovered.

The encounter between Colin and Querry establishes, on one level, a type of client-patient relationship, and on another, a friendship. Querry confesses to Colin that he once thought both his profession and women meant much to him, but the two passions died together from the absolute egoism of his self-expression. At the same time, he began to experience nausea at the very mention of the word "prayer." Significantly, laughter and prayer were the two forms of human expression that especially sickened him. Colin blandly remarks that he cannot offer Querry death. At the same time, his disease has not sufficiently burned itself out for a cure. Meanwhile, Colin suggests that Querry might help out at the leprosarium, but the latter retorts that he hasn't enough sympathy left for human beings even to do anything for them out of pity: he will not dissimulate what he cannot perform with meaning. He begs Colin not to talk to him like a priest about his duty.

That same night Querry experiences his second highly symbolic dream. Graham Greene, in his African journal, relates that the interest he has always felt in dreams, not only his own but those of his characters, is the result of his having been psychoanalyzed at the age of sixteen. Querry's second dream, Greene states in the same journal, "is an exact reproduction of one of my own dreams which occurred while I was writing the novel at the precise moment when I needed it. I wrote it in the next morning." [1] Querry dreams that he is a priest who needs wine to offer Mass immediately. He must do so at once. Tomorrow will be too late. If he waits, he will lose his chance forever. After a long journey he finds, with a tremendous feeling of relief and security, a priest who possesses wine. Querry is about to take the wine, to surrender his terrible burden of fear and responsibility, when another priest suddenly enters and walks away with the precious decanter. Crying out in anguish, Querry awakens. His bed with its

1. Graham Greene, *In Search of a Character* (New York: The Viking Press, 1962), p. 52.

mosquito netting at once suggests a coffin to him. Quite obviously, Colin is the "priest" in Querry's dream, and the latter's rejection of the "wine" offered by Colin on the previous day is the cause of his anguish. The concrete result of this graphic message from Querry's unconscious is that he presents himself to Colin the next morning, offering to draw up plans for a new hospital for the leper colony. Dr. Colin, who knows nothing of Querry's dream, interprets the symbolism of the coffin with telling dramatic irony when he congratulates Querry on rejecting an impossible experiment. A man can't live with nothing but himself, declares Colin, for sooner or later he will kill himself! Querry's second dream, then, by identifying death as the only possible term of his static situation, launches him upon a real, if lifeless, service of other human beings.

Very soon another gratuitous experience unexpectedly catapults Querry into a brief but real excursion into human sympathy. Confronted with an actuality of human suffering that compels him to an immediate decision, Querry discovers that his indifference is forced to turn to involvement. Deo Gratias, the leprous burnt-out case who is Querry's servant, is troubled by memories of a wonderland of dreams called "Pendéleé" to which his mother once took him as a little boy. With childlike simplicity, the leper wanders off into the bush one night when the moon is full to seek his lost childhood. Like Querry, he leaves behind the familiar land of everyday and strikes out into the unknown. Each traveler is destined in his search to find the other. On a symbolic level, the encounter of the two is the self-dialogue of Querry which holds the potentiality for his cure. For Deo Gratias is a mirror reflecting Querry's better self.

When the servant fails to return from his expedition, Querry sets out alone in search of him because the other lepers are afraid of the forest and the night. The little leper has fallen into a swamp and is unable even to move his stump-like feet. Because Querry cannot carry him, and because Deo Gratias is afraid to be alone, Querry remains in the swamp with him throughout the long night. Later, Querry wittily remarks to Colin that "both of us had time to think." Moreover, for the first time in years Querry "had the odd sensation that someone needed me." To be needed, he discovers, is quite different from to need. Interest in another human being begins "to move painfully in him like a nerve that has been frozen."

Again it is the always-understanding Colin who defines Querry's experience for him. Hope, he declares, can be one of the diseases of age—the cancerous growth you find unexpectedly in the dying after a deep operation. Querry's intellectual appreciation of the doctor's diagnosis is so rich that he actually laughs for the first time. While laughter was earlier associated with a "bad smell" in Querry's mind, now the return to laughter, however grotesque, is linked with hope, a wild growth on the last frontier of life. Colin realizes with astonishment that Querry's laugh is a symptom of his return to life. Though the sufferer himself is unaware, the prognosis in Querry's existential crisis is good.

DEMONIC ENCOUNTER AND SELF-DISCOVERY

Querry's new ability to laugh is a white spot in the darkness of his existence. Significantly enough, the next stage in his psychological odyssey through the African regions of his soul finds him, like Deo Gratias, in search of his own Pendéleé—whimsically and vaguely, but nevertheless in search.

When the attractive and seemingly innocent young wife of the preposterous M. Rycker visits the leprosarium, she inspires one of the many dialogues between Querry and the religious Superior of the mission which stud the novel. The Superior, whose hallmark is an ever-present cheroot, is shy, knowing, tolerant—one of the few priests in Greene who is at once both lovable and good. Querry remarks to this man, apropos Marie Rycker, that growing up is too complicated, so that most of us grow up badly. The Superior retorts that we make our own complications. Querry contests the point, but adds that he himself actually has no interest in anything, he has come through to the "other side," to nothing. When the Superior associates Querry's "nothingness" with the "no-thingness" which is God, Querry objects to his drawing everything into the net of his faith. The Superior disturbs him, all the same: Querry strikes his hand furiously on the table, displaying anger for the first time since coming to Africa. Immediately he calls for Deo Gratias and asks him, with apparent irrelevance, whether the little leper will take him along the next time he seeks for Pendéleé. Deo Gratias does not answer. When Querry questions him about the beautiful waters of Pendéleé, all that the leper will say is that "it fell from the sky."

The symbolism of the incident is clear enough. For all his protestations of indifference, the once-Christian Querry cannot conceal his defenses against the lost faith of his childhood. With irrational fury he struck the table, he declares obscurely, because it seemed to him that the Superior had used "a phrase applicable only to the stigmata." To be sure, the offensive phrase, "bloody tears," would be innocent of all religious meaning to hundreds of men. Nor does Querry consciously realize that he immediately seeks out Deo Gratias because his unconscious is stirred with recollections of the lost Pendéleé of his own childhood. The supernatural symbolism of the sacrament of baptism in the beautiful water that "fell from the sky" is dramatic. With nostalgia for the faith of his boyhood, Querry can say with Deo Gratias, "Back there, nous étions heureux." Nor does the episode on faith end here. Soon after, as Colin and Querry listen together to one of the Superior's sermons on Christian virtue, Querry becomes so emotionally involved in challenging the speaker that the shrewd doctor observes that his friend "talks as if he'd lost something he loved." Querry protests that he is cured of Christian love. But, Greene adds, he protests "without conviction."

Querry's uncomfortable stirrings of lost faith are transitional to the second major section of the novel in which he meets in existential encounter two more striking characters who, like Rycker, reflect the demonic in his own nature. Father Thomas, a ludicrous misfit among the missionaries, is superficially devout, absurdly vain, and entirely uncomprehending of either Querry's character or the religious vocation he himself seeks to follow. He is the type of man who upsets the order of the refectory because he "happens to be fasting for a private intention." Like Rycker, he too believes that Querry is a saint undergoing a

dark night of the soul. And like Rycker, he insists on
having soul-to-soul talks with him. The simple and
wise Superior throws a sharp new light on Querry's
character when he remarks casually that he can understand why Father Thomas is attracted to him: they
are "both men of extremes." The comic irony of the
situation is highlighted by the Superior's innocent
observation which suddenly places Querry in spiritual
kinship with the two men whose presence he cannot
tolerate. The psychological implications of the conceited projections of Rycker and Thomas become
more pregnant with mockery when Thomas asks
Querry why he imbibes more "sense of faith" from
him than from anyone else even though Querry denies
all faith. Both Rycker and Thomas, unconsciously
aware of their own spiritual inadequacies, instinctively know that Querry is still fingering the wound
of his own loss of faith. Just as the Superior naively
compares Thomas with Querry, later in the novel
Marie Rycker compares her husband with him, and
on precisely the same grounds: the quality of his
faith.

The worst is yet to come, however, in the
paradoxical encounters of Querry with men who,
mirror-like, reflect the symptoms of his own disease.
Probably the most unpleasant of the lot is the incomparable Montagu Parkinson, venal, greedy, unprin-
cipled journalist of the *London Times*, who symbolizes
the intrusion of the total corruption of the "outside
world" on the little leper colony. Characteristically,
he arrives at the most inopportune moment, just
when Querry, temporarily captivated by the quiet
loveliness of a Congo twilight, at last admits to Colin

that he is happy in his African retreat. Having heard from Rycker that Querry is a combination saint and Albert Schweitzer, Parkinson immediately smells out a sensational feature story for the *Times*. The "reformed saint of the jungle" is naturally nauseated with all that Parkinson stands for. But the cheap journalist has dug up the juicy scandal of Marie Morel's suicide over Querry, and he will not be curbed. When Querry challenges his veracity, he glibly quotes "Parkinson's Law" by which he operates: "A truth is a truth insofar as it is believed." Sensing the danger to his friend, Colin warns Parkinson that Querry is a burnt-out case: limelight is bad for the mutilated. Where will Querry find peace if Parkinson exposes him? But the contemptible journalist is not a man to be sidetracked by sympathy for his victim.

The dialogue which emerges between Querry and Parkinson is one of the most hard-hitting, violently honest in the whole of Greene. Therapeutically, it is probably the most powerful encounter that Querry experiences. For, as Querry bluntly declares with a kind of masochistic pleasure, he and Parkinson are "two of a kind." Both are burnt-out cases, washed up together in the regions of darkness. Both are different from common men: they are "men with vocations," "spoiled priests." The architect has become the common builder; the writer, the hack journalist. Both have been greedy and sensual, but they have become bored with all that too. Relentlessly, Querry forces the uneasy Parkinson to admit their common guilt. The journalist's last feeble challenge is to declare that "none of us really know ourselves." But

Querry counters without pity: "We have to if we are to be cured. When we reach the furthest point, there's no mistaking it. When the fingers are gone and the toes too and the smear-reactions are all negative, we can do no more harm. . . ."

It requires only the human encounter with the sickening Parkinson to bring Querry to a head-on, face-to-face clash with his own worst demon. Now that he meets squarely the threat of his darkest self, he almost experiences fear again. The reader recalls an earlier statement of the Superior that he "was disturbed by a man without fear as he would be by a man without heart." Fear saves man from many things. Now Querry's fear is that his deepest self is so monstrous that *even Parkinson* may not understand him. But he breaks through, nevertheless, to the core of his own revolting infection. Sick for hope after his night-long encounter with Deo Gratias in the swamp; sick for faith after his soul-searing dialogue with the Superior; now his violent encounter with Parkinson stirs up in his burnt-out existence the sickness for love. Just as Rycker and Thomas opened themselves to him, Querry now reveals himself to Parkinson, with this difference: Querry knows himself, the other two did not. He forges ahead, confessing to Parkinson his ruthless subjection of women, his prostitution of his art and, worst of all, his utter weariness with life itself, his absolute existential boredom. Then he dares to make his final confession—his desperate hope that in the Congo he may find enough fear and enough pain to bring him back to life. Life is possible only with love. And perhaps it is true, he adds sadly, that it is impossible to believe in a god without loving a

human being, or to love a human being without believing in a god. As the unique dialogue closes with
sharp dramatic resonance, Querry bluntly admits his
hatred for Parkinson, equal only to his hatred for
himself. With sudden insight, he declares that he has
been unconsciously waiting for Parkinson: "You are
my looking-glass. I can talk to a looking-glass, but
one can be a little afraid of one too. It returns such a
straight image."

Querry has now reached the core of his self-
revelation, the rock bottom of his hope for a cure.
And the novel seems, at last, to have reached its climax. Alone in his room after the complete catharsis
of his cruel encounter with Parkinson, Querry addresses all the men and women in his past whom he
has hurt through his own non-existence: " 'I can
promise you, all of you, never again from boredom or
vanity to involve another human being in my lack of
love.' I shall do no more harm, he thought, with the
kind of happiness a leper must feel when he is free at
last by his seclusion from the fear of passing on
contagion to another."

Had the novel ended here, the reader might
close the book with a feeling of happy release, of full
identification with a psychological burnt-out case who
has found his way back to meaningful existence after
the most excruciating interior dialogue. But such an
ending to Greene's story would lack inevitability, for
the tone of the novel from beginning to end is a concentration of the irony, the ambiguity, the mystery of
existence. Querry has yet to endure one more encounter with a character reflecting back his own
demon, an encounter more shockingly equivocal than

any he has yet experienced, which will bring the mystery of his immediate existence to a climax commensurate with the violent irony of his whole life.

EXISTENTIAL CRISIS AND REBIRTH

After his outbreak to Parkinson, Querry feels as if some persistent poison has been drained from his system. He experiences a completely satisfying peace which he expresses as "consummatum est": pain over and peace falling round him like a little death. In a symbolic language which Colin understands perfectly, Querry asks the doctor whether a negative smear test always remains permanent. Colin responds that it is too early to loose the patient on the world until the tests have been negative for six months. Relapses do happen. Moreover, for burnt-out cases, life "outside" is not easy. The reader becomes more and more conscious, as the conversation progresses, of the deeply symbolic therapist-patient relationship between Colin and Querry, analogous to the latter's doctor-leper involvement in the leprosarium. When Querry abruptly asks Colin whether the Christian myth—not the Christian faith—is enough for him, the doctor replies that he sees the Christian myth as part of a wave of evolution. Suppose love were to evolve in man's brain as rapidly as technical skill has done? Then what? Colin, for one, wishes to be on the side of hope. But, Querry asks, what if man is incapable of love? No such man exists, declares the Doctor promptly. When Querry insists that he has found no trace of love in himself, Colin responds that Querry may be looking for something "too big, too important, too active." As the discussion closes, the reader feels that the end of the therapy hour has come, but not the end of the therapy.

Following this incisive conversation, Querry experiences the last of his three unusual dreams. This one points backward to his talk with Colin and forward to perhaps the most significant experience of his life, soon to occur. Querry imagines himself in a boat traveling down a narrowing tributary of the Congo into denser and denser forest. A corpse lies in the cabin of the little steamer. Querry and the Bishop of Luc are taking it to Pendéleé for burial. Querry is surprised that he once considered the leprosarium the furthest point of his journey into the interior of Africa. For now he is once again in motion, going deeper and deeper into the jungle. At this point he wakens suddenly to an immediate series of situations which precipitate his own death.

Just as Querry's two earlier dreams revealed, first, his existential neurosis as a burnt-out case, and second, his possible cure through acceptance of the "wine" of service to others, so now the final message from his unconscious is prophetic too, but in a much more ambiguous sense. On a literal level, it predicts that he will never leave Africa. On a psychological plane, the dream implies a deeper interior dialogue for Querry, pointing to self-knowledge on a more transcendent level. From a spiritual aspect, it suggests a return to the lost faith or Pendéleé of his childhood, to be achieved only through death.

Querry awakens to find Father Thomas at his side, excitedly announcing the publication of Parkinson's article on "An Architect of Souls: The Hermit of the Jungle" in an international periodical. Rycker,

Thomas, and Parkinson have all together succeeded in violating the small area of peace which Querry has found in the jungle. He recognizes with pain that he has come a long way in a few months, and now he must fight to maintain his ground. Even a selfish man has some right to privacy!

Querry's effort to defend his little acre of contentment leads straight to his encounter with the fourth and last person in whom he sees reflected the demonic in himself. In this final encounter the mirror becomes more fragile and delicate so that even Querry, with all his subtle insight refined in previous involvements with men like Rycker and Parkinson, remains unaware of its disclosure until he is duped.

As soon as Querry learns of Parkinson's nauseating article and of a second, to be called "A Saint's Past: Redemption by Suffering," he determines that at all costs he must muzzle Rycker, the source of Parkinson's lies. With the intention of attacking him physically, Querry seeks Rycker out, but finding him sick with fever, he merely appeals to him to be left in peace. Through a series of accidents, Querry finds himself accompanying Marie Rycker, the childlike wife of Rycker, into the town of Luc. The unhappy, frightened girl, who hates both Africa and her husband, wishes to consult a doctor to determine for certain whether she is to have a child. The architect and the young woman spend an innocent night together in Marie's hotel room. Querry is reminded of the night he spent in the swamp with the little leper, Deo Gratias, who was also afraid.

To distract Marie from her fear, Querry tells her the story of his life in a parable which is a long

THE DEMON AND THE DOVE   278

self-sentence. Since the entire novel is an exemplum,
Querry's tale is really a parable within a parable. Beginning with "once upon a time," it is doubtless one
of the wisest and most sophisticated fairy tales ever
written. The convent-bred Marie responds with
spontaneous naïveté to all that Querry relates to her,
falling asleep over his bedtime story even before he
has finished speaking. Querry's story is the life of a
boy who believes the tale his parents tell of the great
King who lives as far away as the farthest star. The
boy grows up to be a famous jewel-smith who loves
many, many women. Nobody refuses him anything.
But as he grows older he becomes more and more
bored with his precious jewels and his beautiful
women. And then he makes four amazing discoveries
about himself. First, he unveils the startling truth
that he has never really loved anyone at all. What he
thought was love is only pleasure, and he has come to
the end of it. Second, he discovers that he is not an
artistic genius at all, but merely a clever craftsman.
Success has become for him a mutilation of the natural
man: he has reached the end of work as well as of
pleasure. Third, he realizes that he no longer believes
in the great King whom his parents accepted with
simple faith. The jewel-smith concludes that, since no
King like the one he believed in has ever existed, all
that he has ever done has been for himself alone. But
if this is true, his whole life is an absurdity—a total
vacancy of nothingness. Perhaps, he considers, that
is what people mean by "pain." Perhaps he can discover life, but if so he will have to "cross acres and
acres of daylight . . . and acres of darkness as
well. . . ."

As he finishes his story, Querry ruminates inwardly: the King is dead, long live the King. Indeed he feels, with a strange elation very like hope, that he may have found a new country and a new life. His little moral drama is a quaint miniature of the theme of the novel: a man whose whole life has been a fantasy discovers in his middle years the shocking emptiness of his existence and starts his solitary journey to reality over acres and acres of darkness. At precisely this happy moment, the bitterest irony of the entire novel suddenly occurs. For before the childlike Marie falls asleep listening to Querry's story, she giggles under the sheet and wonders slyly whether she can compromise the story teller by confessing to her husband that she has spent the night with Querry. Then the pious fool Rycker will send her home from hated Africa!

Querry's symbolic outpouring to Marie affects him even more strongly than his earlier confession to Parkinson. He feels "a sense of freedom and release, like that of a prisoner who at last comes clean, admitting everything to his inquisitor." It is as though he were on the verge of acceptance to a new country. "Like a refugee he watches the consul lift his pen to fill in the final details of his visa." But he remains apprehensive all the same. Hasn't Colin told him that a burnt-out case requires six months of testing before he can be declared finally cured? Yet the evidences of his cure are now frequent. For example, he is capable of voluntary movement toward companionship. More significantly, he discovers that he can laugh with the priests of the mission in their simple pleasures. Months ago, he recalls, he found their laughter and

their infantility intolerable. Finally, he finds deep
peace in sitting quietly with his leper counterpart,
Deo Gratias. He tells Deo Gratias wistfully that he
wishes they could go together to Pendéleé. And the
reader knows that Querry is symbolically carrying
on a happy interior dialogue with the self he has long
been seeking, reflected in the contemplative little
leper. For while Querry speaks, Deo Gratias sits
"with his head down, saying nothing."

A day or two after Querry's return from the
town of Luc and Marie Rycker, Deo Gratias asks
him if he will now go back to the life he left before
coming to the Congo. The symbolism of the scene is
quite lucid as Querry responds, "I can't go back
where I came from, Deo Gratias. I don't belong there
any more." He can't go back simply because he has
"killed everything" there. Deo Gratias *seems* not to
understand, protesting that he will go with Querry.
To be sure, the leper does understand far better than
his master, for he knows instinctively that the end of
Querry's long odyssey is close at hand.

Even as the two speak, the message of the
impossible has arrived. Marie Rycker, seizing upon
her fantastic scheme to escape Africa and her husband, has accused Querry of fathering her child. The
seeming personification of childlike innocence has revealed herself as a "pocket of dynamite" in disguise.
"God preserve us from all innocence," declares
Querry helplessly. "At least the guilty know what
they are about." Precisely here is revealed the final
crisis in Querry's successive encounters with human
beings who reflect his own demonic modes of existence. The mirror which Marie holds up to Querry is

so delicately subtle that he does not see his own image until it is too late. Indeed, the tables are turned ironically and completely: Querry becomes the "innocent" victim of the monstrous child Marie who abjures all moral values to obtain her selfish desire. "For the first time," Graham Greene writes succinctly, "Querry was confronted by an egoism as absolute as his own." Marie is deliberately false innocence, more deadly than the vain religiosity of Father Thomas, the spiritual hypocrisy of Rycker, or the downright corruption of Parkinson. Against the Maries of this world there is no defense. So Querry has no choice: he must leave the leprosarium on the Congo, the only home where he has found peace. When Querry confesses to Colin the pain he feels at this exigency, the doctor at once declares him completely cured: "No further tests are required in your case." The existential neurosis is cured: Querry is alive through suffering.

The central crisis of Querry's life is now past. Greene might send him back to Europe, suffering but cured. The life "outside" would not be easy for the burnt-out case, as Colin has declared; yet it would be comparatively peaceful. But no such end awaits Querry. "I feel," wrote Greene in his *Congo Journal*, "that Querry must die because an element of insoluble mystery in his character has to remain. Of course he could simply walk off like an early Chaplin."[2] The catastrophe that Greene plans for Querry is entirely in keeping with the tragic-comic situations that have complicated all the crises of his life.

2. *Ibid.*, p. 38.

Just as Querry, cured but sorrowful, resigns himself to leave the leper colony, the fantastic Rycker arrives, melodramatically brandishing a gun. Nobody believes he will shoot, for the man is a coward as well as a fool. But Querry, contemplating the comic irony of his situation, cannot help but laugh: he, who has survived numberless adulteries and treasons unscathed, only to penetrate at last the core of reality, is threatened by a half-wit for a crime he never committed! The ultimate irony, to be sure, lies in Rycker's vanity: the man can endure anything but ridicule. So Querry is shot to death in a situation which would be a master stroke of tragic waste if it were not at the same time a triumph of grotesque comedy. Querry lives long enough to set the record straight, to establish the fact that he was laughing at *himself*. And then comes the maddeningly ambiguous ending so characteristic of Greene and yet demanded by the theme, the tone, and the unity of the novel. "Absurd," declares Querry as he dies, "this is absurd or else. . . ." The alternative he has in mind his listeners never know.

There is, however, a passage on absurdity in Greene's African journal, written while he was working on the novel, which throws some light on Querry's final ambiguous statement. Greene wrote:

> How often people speak of the absurdity of believing that life should exist by God's will on one minute part of the immense universe. There is a parallel absurdity which we are asked to believe, that God chose a tiny colony of a Roman empire in which to be born. Strangely enough two absurdities seem easier to believe than one.[3]

3. *Ibid.*, p. 26.

In the case of Querry, perhaps two absurdities are also easier to believe than one. For him to accept the first absurdity that his death depended on a fool's misinterpretation of a laugh is to ask too much. For him to believe that a personal Divine Providence governed the circumstances of his death is also to ask too much. But both absurdities together may be easier to believe than either alone. Together, they may cancel out the absurdity, so that only mystery remains.

Before the novel closes, Greene allows Colin and the Superior, the only two men in the book except Deo Gratias who merit Querry's respect, to comment on his life. Colin declares that Querry was truly a burnt-out case, cured of everything but one sore which he rubbed all the time—his loss of faith. The doctor adds that Querry, whose very name symbolized the questioner, was not content to question: he had to believe or disbelieve. Colin defines Querry's cure in his ability to laugh, to suffer, and to serve others. The Superior, however, interprets these same changes as "finding faith again." Pascal, he reminds Colin, said that a man who starts to look for God has already found him. The same may be true of love, he suggests: when we look for it, we have already found it. Moreover, Colin sees Querry's death as a tragedy, while the Superior sees it as a happy transcendence— as "going a bit further." The reader recalls Querry's dream of going further into the interior of Africa, into his long-lost Pendélee, and the insistence of Deo Gratias, his better self, that he will "go with him." Is Deo Gratias like Good Deeds, the only character willing to accompany Everyman to death? In the symbolism of the exemplum, the weight of the parabolic conclusion favors the Superior's interpretation over Colin's. But then, the believers of the world are always apt to see more meaning in symbols than the Colins of the world! And on two different levels, both men speak the truth.

EXISTENTIAL NEUROSIS AND FAITH

A Burnt-Out Case is one of the finest modern novels offering a detailed psychological analysis of the existential neurosis which is the long disease of contemporary man. The anguish of its creator would seem to be the measure of its artistic success. For Graham Greene, who survived the whisky priest and Scobie with apparently undiminished vigor, had this to say after the burial of Querry:

> . . . .Never had a novel proved more recalcitrant or more depressing. The reader had only to endure the company of the character called Querry for a few hours' reading, but the author had to live with him for eighteen months . . . It seemed to me when I wrote the last words that . . . another full-length novel was probably beyond my powers.[4]

That the personal price Greene paid was proportionate with his creation may be gauged by his complete victory in making the reader care for a character who is himself beyond caring.

There is no question that the central theme of the novel is the life-crisis of the major character. It is interesting to note, therefore, that critics of Greene have accused him of writing with tongue in cheek when he declared, in the dedication to *A Burnt-Out Case*, that the novel was "an attempt to give dramatic

4. *Ibid.*, p. xiii.

expression to various types of belief, half-belief, and non-belief. . . ." Psychological analysis reveals the close relationship between loss of belief and existential neurosis in the character of Querry. Moreover, the other *dramatis personae* of the novel, reflecting as in a mirror various aspects of Querry's personality, reveal the "belief, half-belief, and non-belief" characteristic of him at various stages of his life. And the unique attitude of Querry toward faith during the central crisis of his life is crucial to the novel.

Now, Querry's disease is a complete ennui of existence. It is encounter with nothingness. Incipient return to life is evident in hope, the cancerous hope found in the dying. Cure is achieved through suffering. The outward signs of inward cure are laughter, companionability, and service to others. Significantly, however, Querry never positively attains faith or love. Querry himself provides the only clue to his ambiguously successful spiritual search when he declares to Parkinson that, "Perhaps it's true that you can't believe in a god without loving a human being or love a human being without believing in a god." Precisely here is the fundamental relationship between Querry's existential crisis and his faith, and the justification for Greene's statement that the novel is an attempt to give dramatic expression to types of belief. Perhaps we may conclude that, for Greene at least, loss of faith is at the core of the existential crisis of contemporary man. In the very last sentence of the novel, the always-restrained Dr. Colin explodes in "suppressed rage" at a twentieth century universe in which man can at last cure his physical diseases without disfiguration but remains helplessly trapped by spiritual mutilations.

CONCLUSION

THE early chapters of our study have analyzed the close partnership of literature and psychology in unveiling the depths of human experience. The crucial importance of man's confrontation of the darkness and the light, the evil and the good, the demon and the dove within his own nature was clarified. Personality development was seen to be possible only through continual death to a self that is outgrown, existential decision to rise above and beyond one's immediate experience, and rebirth to a new life on richer and deeper levels of existence. Real personality growth is no passive or static experience. It is only for the daring who are willing to risk the sometimes frightening odyssey through both the negative and positive phases of existential crises faced by all men who are not afraid to live.

The great masterpieces of literature offer us, in their universal truth, our richest examples of the anguish and the joy of man's continual journey over ever-changing thresholds of his existence. Literary genius is uniquely qualified to reveal man to himself in poetry, drama, and fiction. The mirror of literature is always present to him, provided he is not afraid to look and to discover his own identity in the common experience of universal man.

In the second half of our book we have illus-

trated through existential psychological analyses of
five great literary characters the conflict between the
demon and the dove which is common to all creative
interpretations of the human situation. On a larger
canvas, and with more intense strokes, we view ourselves and our own human strife acted out by characters larger than life. With J. Alfred Prufrock, we
can say "I am no Hamlet," conscious of our personal
limitations before the magnitude of the character
created by genius. But deep within us, on a humbler
level of response, we know that despite all our inadequacies we *are* Hamlet. We are not cursed with
the burden of setting all things right in the rotten
state of Denmark, but we know Hamlet's confrontation with evil, his disillusionment, his anguish of
decision, his helplessness in the face of the human
predicament—all these we know in the measure of
our own insights and limitations. Hamlet tells us
who we are. In creating Hamlet, Shakespeare found
himself, and in giving us Hamlet he gave us, in a
sense, ourselves.

The literary characters we have interpreted
also tell us who we are in various aspects of our personalities. They do not tell each of us precisely the
same thing; they speak to each of us on the level of
our own understanding. We do not all have the same
eyes to see and ears to hear. But we can help to open
one another's eyes and ears through communication
of our personal insights. We can penetrate to the
core of meaning of literary masterpieces and find our
common humanity. And we can continually transcend
our human situation and become the persons we

potentially are by learning the truth about ourselves from the lips of genius.

Angelo in *Measure for Measure* tells me that it is possible for me to be an unauthentic person without knowing it. Perhaps he shows me how to discover, step by step, my unauthenticity, for none of us is completely authentic. Angelo reveals to me the radical difference between conformity to a collectivity and real existential decision. If my self-identity is weak, Angelo can tell me much about the discovery of identity through acceptance of reality.

The tragic Anna Karenina is the prototype of all those who attempt to live two incompatible projects of existence. In her, the conflict between the demon and the dove finds its term in terrible destruction. When I read *Anna Karenina*, I find an aspect of myself in her. I know what it means to be torn by conflicting passions, by the violence of a "love" that is essentially hate. Anna is not alien to me. Through her agony, she tells me how to love.

John Marcher, in *The Beast in the Jungle*, is the perfect exemplar of existential transference to one's own ego. His deepest communication to me is his life-long failure to be aware of his own egotism. And concomitant with this failure is his profound inability to love because of his self-centeredness. Marcher tells me that my power to love—the deepest and most significant need and desire of my life—may be dependent on my confrontation with my own demon of egotism. Here is meat for contemplation.

In Camus' *The Fall*, Jean-Baptiste Clamence reminds me with intense subtlety that my motives frequently are not what I think they are. He asks me if I am capable of confronting my own motives in their naked reality. He leads me down sheer chasms of the mind where I may not care to go. But if I risk the journey, I may find my real self in the darkness.

Graham Greene's Querry leads me to the core of existential neurosis—the characteristic disease of contemporary man. Querry tells me why my life may seem empty and boring and meaningless. And before I realize it, I find myself face to face with existential decision—the decision to love which alone gives meaning to life. Querry is uncompromising: there is no other decision to be made, no other answer to be given.

We have named here only a few of the approaches through which the literary works discussed in this study tell us the truth about ourselves. This is not to say that literature is didactic or that we prostitute literature for personal development. Not at all. Personality growth through literature—through learning who we are—is a free gift given to us with aesthetic experience and not to be separated from aesthetic experience. The two are one. The genius discovers who he is through his own creation. I can discover who I am through his creation. And I can learn to become who I potentially am by viewing myself in the characters of the masterpieces of poetry, fiction, and drama. Because they are universally true, they mirror even me.

SELECTED BIBLIOGRAPHY

Allport, Gordon W. "The Psychology of Participation," *Psychological Review*, LIII (1945), 117-132.
    Becoming. New Haven: Yale University Press, 1955.
    Personality and Social Encounter. Boston: Beacon Press, 1960.
    Pattern and Growth in Personality. New York: Holt, Rinehart and Winston, 1961.
Askew, M. W. "Literature and the Psychotherapist," *Psychoanalysis and the Psychoanalytic Review*, XLV (1958), 102-12.
    "Catharsis and Modern Tragedy," *Psychoanalysis and the Psychoanalytic Review*, XLVIII (1961), 81-88.
Barral, Mary Rose. *Merleau-Ponty: The Role of the Body Subject in Interpersonal Relations*. Pittsburgh: Duquesne University Press, 1965.
Basler, R. P. *Sex, Symbolism, and Psychology in*

Literature. New Brunswick: Rutgers University Press, 1948.

Bergson, Henri. *The Creative Mind*, trans. Mabelle L. Anderson. New York: The Philosophical Library, Inc., 1946.

Binswanger, L. *Grundformen und Erkenntnis menschlichen Daseins*. Zurich: Max Niehans, 1942.
Being-in-the-World, trans. Jacob Needleman. New York: Basic Books, Inc., 1963.

Bodkin, Maud. *Archetypal Patterns in Poetry*. New York: Oxford University Press, 1934.

Buytendijk, F. J. J. "The Phenomenological Approach to the Problem of Feelings and Emotions," *Feeling and Emotions*. The Mooseheart Symposium in cooperation with the University of Chicago. New York, Toronto, London: McGraw-Hill Book Co., 1950.
Phénoménologie de la rencontre. Paris: Desclée de Brouwer, 1952.
La Femme. Bruges: Editions Desclée de Brouwer, 1954.

Deutsch, H. "Don Quixote and Don Quixotism," *Psychoanalytic Quarterly*, VI (1937), 215-22.

Edel, Leon. "Notes on the Use of Psychological Tools in Literary Scholarship," *Literature and Psychology*, I (1951), 1-3.

Farber, Leslie H. "Despair and the Life of Suicide," *Review of Existential Psychology and Psychiatry*, II (1962), 125.

Feldman, A. B. "Fifty Years of the Psychoanalysis of Literature," *Literature and Psychology*, V (1955), 40-42; 54-64.

Fiedler, L. A. *Love and Death in the American Novel*. New York: Criterion Press, 1960.

Fingarette, H. *The Self in Transformation*. New York: Harper and Brothers, 1965.

Fraiberg, L. *Psychoanalysis and American Literary Criticism*. Detroit: Wayne State University Press, 1960.

Freud, Sigmund. *On Creativity and the Unconscious*. New York: Harper and Brothers, 1958.

Hallman, R. *Psychology of Literature: A Study of Alienation and Tragedy*. New York: Philosophical Library, 1961.

Heidegger, Martin. *Existence and Being*. Introduction by Werner Brock. Chicago: Henry Regnery Company, 1949.

Hoffman, F. J. *Freudianism and the Literary Mind*. Baton Rouge: Louisiana State University Press, 1945.

Jaspers, Karl. *Existenzerhellung*. Berlin: J. Springer, 1932.
Man in the Modern Age, trans. Eden and Cedar Paul. New York: Doubleday & Company, Inc., 1957.

Jones, Ernest. *Hamlet and Oedipus*. New York: Doubleday Anchor, 1954.

Kaplan, Bernard. "Radical Metaphor, Aesthetic and the Origin of Language," *Review of Existential Psychology and Psychiatry*, II (1962), 75-84.

Kohlberg, L. "Psychological Analysis and Literary Forms," *Daedalus*, XCII (1963), 345-62.

Kubie, L. S. *Neurotic Distortion of the Creative Process*. New York: Noonday Press, 1961.

Kwant, Remy C. *Encounter*, trans. Robert C. Adolfs. Pittsburgh: Duquesne University Press, 1960.
Phenomenology of Language. Pittsburgh: Duquesne University Press, 1965.

Laing, R. D. *The Divided Self.* Chicago: Quadrangle Books, Inc., 1960.

Lanteri-Laura, Georges. *La Psychiatrie Phéno-ménologique.* Paris: Presses Universitaires de France, 1963.

Lesser, S. O. *Fiction and the Unconscious.* Boston: Beacon Press, 1957.
"Tragedy, Comedy and the Esthetic Experience," *Literature and Psychology*, VI (1956), 131-39.

Lowenthal, L. *Literature and the Image of Man.* Boston: Beacon Press, 1957.

Luijpen, William A. *Existential Phenomenology*, trans. Henry J. Koren. Pittsburgh: Duquesne University Press, 1960.

McCurdy, H. G. "Literature as a Resource in Personality Study," *Journal of Aesthetics and Art Criticism*, VIII (1949), 42-46.

Malin, I. *Psychoanalysis and American Fiction.* New York: Dutton, 1965.

Marcel, Gabriel. *Being and Having.* London: Dacre Press, 1949.
The Mystery of Being, trans. René Hague. Chicago: Henry Regnery Company, 1950.
Man Against Mass Society, trans. G. S. Fraser. Chicago: Henry Regnery Company, 1950.
The Philosophy of Existence. London: Harvill Press, 1954.

May, Rollo and others, eds. *Existence: A New Dimension in Psychiatry and Psychology.* New York: Basic Books, Inc., 1958.
Existential Psychology. New York: Random House, 1961.

Morris, R. "The Novel as Catharsis," *Psychoanalytic Review*, XXXI (1944), 88-104.

Moustakas, Clark E., ed. *The Self. Explorations in Personal Growth*. New York: Harper and Brothers, 1956.

Nédoncelle, Maurice. *La réciprocité des consciences. Essai sur la nature de la personne*. Aubiers: Editions Montaigne, 1942.

Phillips, W., ed. *Art and Psychoanalysis*. New York: Criterion, 1957.

Pieper, Josef. *Leisure, The Basis of Culture*, trans. Alexander Dru. New York: Pantheon Books, Inc., 1952.

Pratt, Carroll C. *The Meaning of Music*. New York: McGraw-Hill Book Company, 1931.

Praz, Mario. *The Romantic Agony*. New York: Oxford University Press, 1951.

Rabkin, Leslie Y., ed. *Psychopathology and Literature*. San Francisco: Chandler Publishing Company, 1966.

Rather, L. J. "Existential Experience in Whitehead and Heidegger," *Review of Existential Psychology and Psychiatry*, I (1961), 113-19.

Reik, T. *The Secret Self*. New York: Farrar, Straus and Young, 1952.

Reymert, Martin L., ed. *Feeling and Emotions*. The Mooseheart Symposium in cooperation with the University of Chicago. New York, Toronto, London: McGraw-Hill Book Company, Inc., 1950.

Riviere, J. "The Unconscious Phantasy of an Inner World Reflected in Examples from English Literature," *International Journal of Psychoanalysis*, XXXIII (1952), 160-72.

Rogers, Carl. *Counseling and Psychotherapy*. New York: Houghton-Mifflin Company, 1942.

"The Loneliness of Contemporary Man," *Review of Existential Psychology and Psychiatry*, I (1961), 94–101.

Rogers, R. "The Beast in Henry James," *American Imago*, XIII (1956), 427–54.

Rosenfield, C. "The Shadow Within: The Conscious and Unconscious Use of the 'Double'," *Daedalus*, XCII (1963), 326–44.

Scheler, M. *Man's Place in Nature*. Boston: Beacon Press, 1961.
Wesen und Formen der Sympathie Phänomenologie und Theorie der Sympathiegefühle. Frankfurt-Main: G. Schulte-Bulmke, 1948.

Shoben, E. J., Jr. "A Clinical View of the Tragic," *Literature and Psychology*, XIV (1964), 23–24.

Shumaker, W. *Literature and the Irrational: A Study In Anthropological Backgrounds*. Englewood Cliffs, N.J.: Prentice-Hall, 1960.

Spiegelberg, H. *The Phenomenological Movement*. 2 vols. The Hague, Netherlands: Martinus Nijhoff, 1960.

Stafford, J. "The Psychological Novel," *Kenyon Review*, X (1948), 214–27.

Stone, Alan A. and Stone, Sue Smart, eds. *The Abnormal Personality Through Literature*. Englewood Cliffs, N.J.: Prentice-Hall, 1966.

Strasser, S. *Das Gemüt. Grundgedanken zu einer Phanomenologischen Philosophie und Theorie des Menslichen Gefühlslebens*. Utrecht: Het Spectrum, Freiburg: Verlag Herder, 1956.

Talbert, E. L. "The Modern Novel and the Response of the Reader," *Journal of Abnormal and Social Psychology*, XXVI (1932), 409–14.

Thayer, L. D. and Pronko, N. H. "Some Psychological Factors in the Reading of Fiction," *Journal
of Genetic Psychology*, XCIII (1958), 113-17.

van der Berg, J. H. *The Phenomenological Approach to
Psychiatry. An Introduction to Recent Phenom-
enological Psychopathology*. Springfield, Illinois:
Charles C Thomas, 1955.

van Croonenburg, E. J. *Gateway to Reality* (An Introduction to Philosophy). Pittsburgh: Duquesne
University Press, 1964.

van Kaam, Adrian. "The Addictive Personality,"
Humanitas, I (1965), 183-93.
The Art of Existential Counseling. Denville, New
Jersey: Dimension Books, Inc., 1966.
"Assumptions in Psychology," *Journal of Individ-
ual Psychology*, XIV (1958), 22-28.
"Clinical Implications of Heidegger's Concepts
of Will, Decision, and Responsibility," *Review of
Existential Psychology and Psychiatry*, I (1961),
205-17.
"Commentary on 'Freedom and Responsibility
Examined'," *Behavioral Science and Guidance,
Proposals, and Perspectives*, eds. Lloyd-Jones and
E. M. Westervelt. New York: Teachers College,
Columbia University Press, 1963.
"Counseling and Existential Psychology," *Har-
vard Educational Review* (1962). This article was
later published in *Guidance—An Examination*,
New York: Harcourt, Brace & World, 1965.
"The Existential Approach to Human Poten-
tialities," *Explorations in Human Potentialities*,
ed. Herbert A. Otto. Springfield, Illinois: Charles
C Thomas, 1966.

"Existential and Humanistic Psychology," *Review of Existential Psychology and Psychiatry*, V (1965), 291-96.

"Existential Psychology as a Theory of Personality," *Review of Existential Psychology and Psychiatry*, III (1963), 11-26.

"Die existentielle Psychologie als eine Theorie der Gesamtpersönlichkeit," *Jahrbuch für Psychologie und medizinische Anthropologie*, 12. Jahrgang Heft 4.

"The Fantasy of Romantic Love," *Modern Myths and Popular Fancies*. Pittsburgh: Duquesne University Press, 1961.

"The Field of Religion and Personality or Theoretical Religious Anthropology," *Insight*, IV (1965), 1-7.

"Freud and Anthropological Psychology," *The Justice*. Brandeis University, 1959.

"The Goals of Psychotherapy from the Existential Point of View," *The Goals of Psychotherapy*, ed. Alvin R. Mahrer. New York: Appleton-Century-Crofts, 1966.

"Humanistic Psychology and Culture," *Journal of Humanistic Psychology*, I (1961), 94-100.

"The Impact of Existential Phenomenology on the Psychological Literature of Western Europe," *Review of Existential Psychology and Psychiatry*, I (1961), 63-92.

A Light to the Gentiles. Milwaukee: Bruce Publishing Company, 1962.

"Motivation and Contemporary Anxiety," *Humanitas*, I (1965), 59-75.

"The Nurse in the Patient's World," *The Ameri-*

can Journal of Nursing, LIX (1959), 1708-1710.
Personality Fulfillment in the Spiritual Life.
Denville, New Jersey: Dimension Books, Inc.,
1966.

"Phenomenal Analysis: Exemplified by a Study
of the Experience of 'Really Feeling Understood'," *Journal of Individual Psychology*, XV
(1959), 66-72.

"A Psychology of the Catholic Intellectual," *The
Christian Intellectual* (Samuel Hazo, ed.). Pittsburgh, Pennsylvania: Duquesne University Press,
1963.

"A Psychology of Falling-Away-From-The
Faith," *Insight*, II (1963), 3-17.

"Religion and Existential Will," *Insight*, I
(1962), 2-9.

"Religious Counseling of Seminarians," *Semi-
nary Education in a Time of Change*, eds. James
Michael Lee and Louis J. Putz. Notre Dame,
Indiana: Fides Publishers, Inc., 1965.

"Review of *The Divided Self* by R. D. Laing,"
Review of Existential Psychology and Psychiatry,
II (1962), 85-88.

Religion and Personality. New Jersey: Prentice-
Hall, Inc., 1965.

"Sex and Existence," *Review of Existential Psychology and Psychiatry*, III (1963).

"Sex and Personality," *The Lamp*, LXIII (1965),
5-7; 20-22.

The Third Force in European Psychology. Green-
ville, Delaware: Psychosynthesis Research Foun-
dation, 1960. (Greek translation, Athens, Greece,
1962.)

The Vocational Director and Counseling. Derby, New York: St. Paul Publications, 1962.

Weissman, P. "Conscious and Unconscious Autobiographical Dramas of Eugene O'Neill," *Journal of the American Psychoanalytic Association*, V (1957), 432-60.

Creativity in the Theater. New York: Basic Books, 1965.

Wilson, R. N. "Literature, Society, and Personality," *Journal of Aesthetics and Art Criticism*, X (1952), 297-309.

"Literary Experience and Personality," *Journal of Aesthetics and Art Criticism*, XV (1956), 45-57.

INDEX

ACKNOWLEDGEMENTS

Little, Brown and Company, *Poems*, by Emily Dickinson.

"He ate and drank the precious words" and "There is no frigate like a book." 1948.

Random House, Inc., *Anna Karenina*, by L. Tolstoy.

Edited by Leonard J. Kent and Gina Berberova, Copyright 1965.

DATE DUE
